A FOOLISH ESCAPE

THE DREAM MADE REAL

NEIL HAWKESFORD

Published by

Copyright © 2020 Neil F.Hawkesford

All rights reserved.

No part of this book may be reproduced in any form or by any electronic or mechanical means, including information storage and retrieval systems, without written permission from the author, except for the use of brief quotations in a book review.

Copyright enquiries should be directed by e-mail to neil@neilhawkesford.com

ISBN-13: 979-8679138933

ISBN-10: 8679138933

DEDICATION

Sailing Friends

- Jake Woodnutt - S/V A Roamer
- June & Garry - S/V Friendship
- Jackie & Ian - S/V Rivalady
- Pat & Duncan - S/V Samji
- Pam & Roger - S/V Déjà vu
- Andrea & Andrew - S/V Chin Chin
- Jane & Phil - S/V Barracuda III
- David - S/V Golden Hours

Yacht Port Cartagena Friends

- The 'marineros' - Andreas, Christian, Jose & Jamie
- The office - Mar and Julia

*And especially
Michael & Andrea*

*The world is waiting for you
Sail her there!*

CONTENTS

Preface	ix
Introduction	xiii
1. Messack	1
2. The Marina	11
3. The Sea At Last	22
4. Alderney	40
5. France	50
6. Biscay	65
7. Galicia	76
8. Northern Portugal	96
9. Central Portugal	108
10. The Algarve	126
11. Winter In Lagos	138
12. East To Eden	154
13. River Life	166
14. Off The Hook	180
15. Rota & Gibraltar	196
16. The Mediterranean	212
17. The Ancient City	230
18. Merchants & Slaves	246
19. Challenges	258
20. Back To The Sea	270
21. Everything Changes	278
Epilogue	291
Postscript	295
A Gift For You	297
About the Author	299

PREFACE

Writing is a journey; where you start is rarely where you end up. This is my third book and while not originally intended to be a trilogy, things seem to have panned out that way.

Book 1 - A Foolish Voyage
Book 2 - A Foolish Odyssey
Book 3 - A Foolish Escape

ALL AVAILABLE ON AMAZON

Maybe reading the first two before this one would help put the story of *Foolish Escape* in context and increase your enjoyment.

But don't worry, this story stands alone.

INTRODUCTION

It's late September 2014.

My self-built Wharram Tiki 38 catamaran 'Gleda' is moored in Messack Creek, an idyllic spot on the Roseland peninsula of Cornwall, in the UK.

The boat had been launched in early June. We'd worked solidly in the weeks that followed getting her ready to sailing properly, preparing her for our first proper voyage.

The plan?

To sail her south.

We had a winter berth booked in Lagos Marina on the Portuguese Algarve.

All we had to do was get there.

Years of blood, sweat and tears had brought us to the start line.

We'd made it. We were ready for our foolish escape.

Truro

MAGGOTY BANK →

Perranwell

Great Western Railway

MESSACK CREEK ↘

← SAINT JUST POOL

MARINA ↓

Penryn

St Mawes

Falmouth Docks

1

MESSACK

I eased myself down to a sitting position on the deck, and slowly leant my stiff aching body against the deckpod. My legs and arms ached only slightly less than my back, I felt utterly washed out.

As I sipped from a mug of steaming coffee, my head span.

Gail thought I was suffering from cumulative fatigue. Perhaps she was right. It had been a full-on year right from the start.

For the first four months I'd been working flat out to get 'Gleda' finished and ready for transport to the coast.

Gail and I had moved out of our rental cottage and made the boat home.

Seeing thousands of hours of labour, and everything I owned in the world hanging precariously from various cranes had added to my stress levels.

We'd arrived at Weir Quay boatyard in late May and then spent June, July and most of August getting 'Gleda' rigged and prepared to sail.

We'd cruised between Plymouth and Falmouth visiting Fowey for the regatta and Falmouth for the Tall Ships Race.

I'd sailed back to Falmouth single-handed and now we'd been in Messack Creek for two weeks, working hard to get prepped for our voyage south.

We'd done so much, come so far, but there was a lot still to do.

Ever since we'd got on the water I'd had one overriding aim; to cross the Bay of Biscay and get to Southern Portugal for the winter.

'Gleda' was everything I'd hoped for in the way she sailed. But Wharram catamarans are not the most comfortable of liveaboard boats when the weather is bad. I'd known that from the start. James Wharram designs his boats for the sea first and people second. It was one of the many reasons I built one. A bit of discomfort seemed a minor price to pay for safety.

Three days of torrential rain had kept Gail and I cooped up in the cabins a few weeks before. Even that had made life difficult. I knew from experience what it was like living on a basic boat through a Cornish winter. I wasn't sure I could do it again; I was certain Gail couldn't. Life wouldn't be difficult, it'd be impossible.

To survive the winter we'd need heat, and there was only one heating system I could see working for 'Gleda'; the latitude system. We had to sail south until the temperature was just right.

September in Messack Creek had been magical. It turned out to be the driest September in Cornwall since records began in 1910, and the fourth warmest. The sun shone; the winds had been light. Now it was almost the 1st of October. The weather would not last.

The sea-gypsy life had been calling me for decades. The freedom of the open ocean, the freedom to follow the sun. That's what was driving me now. It'd been a year of transition from land to water. Now it was time to make that change permanent.

I'd bought a box of paperwork onto the boat. Old utility bills, bank statements, random writings and documents from what was now my old life. I dug a hole in the foreshore and made a fire. I burnt it all. Watching as the sparks and smoke spiralled up into the clear blue sky. It felt like an offering to the Universe. A kind of alchemy, turning negative energy into positive. It felt good.

I'd been watching the weather. Looking for a 'window' in which we could leave.

We had no internet connection on the boat. Messack was remote. Pubs and cafés were our only choice, and they weren't easy to get to.

St Mawes was the nearest town. To get there meant walking a mile through the fields, around the head of the creek and up the hill to St Just in Roseland. From there it was a 15-minute bus ride. Beautiful though it is, there's not a lot to St Mawes. For proper shopping it had to be Falmouth. That meant adding a 20-minute ferry trip across the Carrick Roads to the journey. It was no hardship. The entire area is stunningly beautiful. As Gail said, it all felt a bit Swallows and Amazons living in Messack Creek.

The most recent weather forecasts showed a strong possibility of a decent window opening within the next few days.

I'd made the call to Jake on Alderney. He was on a plane heading for Exeter Airport.

If you've read 'A Foolish Odyssey' you may remember Jake. He's the young lad who'd sailed his little Wharram Tiki 26 'A Roamer' to Weir Quay, especially to help me get 'Gleda' on the water.

We didn't know each other before that, we'd never met. He just took it on himself to jump on his boat, sail single-handed across the English Channel and spend a week working on a boat he didn't own.

I'd defy anyone not to like Jake. Young, fit, tanned, polite, full of energy. Ladies of all ages swooned. Gentleman of later years envied.

We'd become excellent friends and his enthusiasm for Wharram's and sailing made it easy to invite him to crew for us down to Spain. He'd waited patiently, now it was time.

We got back from the airport just after midnight the next day. I'd taken the opportunity of our visit to civilisation to check the weather again. The window had closed. It now looked as if we'd have to wait at least 48 hours. That was OK. Jake hadn't yet seen the boat rigged. It'd give me time to show him the ropes, literally.

The following day we headed into Falmouth. Jake had never been there, and apart from anything else I wanted to sit down with him and look at the weather again. Gail and I now had a favourite venue in town, a combined pub and bookshop called Beerwolf. We convened there and fired up the laptop. The maps didn't make good viewing. There was the possibility of some northerlies going into the weekend, but after that strong and consistent southwesterlies dominated. Southwest was the direction we wanted to go. That beckoning open window had slammed firmly shut.

Jake suggested using the northerlies for a dash across the Channel to Brittany in France. We could wait it out there.

I wasn't keen for two reasons. I didn't have any charts for that area, and we'd probably have to pay marina fees. With money so tight it was an expense I could do without. Messack might have been remote, but it was safe and free.

There was another reason. When we left, I wanted it to be for Spain; I needed it.

The change in weather meant deciding. Gail was planning to drive back up country the next day. If Jake stayed on with me, he'd have a tough journey to get back to an airport. Cornwall is a long way from the rest of the country.

All the forecasts agreed that any major change in the winds was at least a week away. Jake's girlfriend was working in Dublin, he wanted to go visit. I told him to go. He could get a lift back to Exeter with Gail. In a show of faith I appreciated, he left all his sailing kit aboard 'Gleda'. "I'll be back soon anyway" he said.

It was tough seeing them drive away. As I walked back down the sheep field towards the creek, my emotions got the better of me. Gail had made her decision a few weeks before. She didn't feel ready to sail across Biscay. It was the right call. But now I was alone, and it felt horrible. I didn't know when and where we'd be together again. I also felt guilty about Jake. He'd wasted a chunk of money and time because I'd made the wrong call.

Messack felt different that night. Quiet turned into silence. The night seemed darker. Sleep came hard, as my head span with thoughts. What was I doing? Why was I making life so difficult? Fear and doubt crowded in. Maybe I should make the simple choice. Stay put for the winter. Enjoy Falmouth, relax, take the pressure off. But I knew why. I'd built a boat for warmth and sunshine. Living aboard over the winter would be hell. I'd been over this so many times. Going was hard, staying would be harder.

I woke late the next morning, rolled over, and smiled when I saw Gail's side of the bed empty. She must have gone to make us a cup of tea in the galley. A few seconds later my heart sank as memory returned.

The weather forecast had been right. Over the following days the powerful winds arrived and brought the rain with them.

The creek may have been sheltered, but the wind still funnelled up from the Carrick Roads. I'd moored 'Gleda' bows to the shore with an anchor buried in the mud to hold her stern off. Then I'd run some extra stern lines right across the creek, tied to trees on the other side. I had cause to be thankful for that. During the night one hefty gust pulled the stern anchor out. It also brought down a sizeable tree branch too close to the boat for comfort.

 The rain kept me confined to the cabin, in the evenings I used the paraffin hurricane lamp to give me light and a little heat. Despite the gusts, the wind in the creek wasn't consistent enough for the wind generator to do any charging. With no sun the solar panel was redundant. The batteries were low as a result, so I conserved them as much as possible. I could have charged them by running the engines at high tide, but it seemed pointless.

 A week had passed since Gail and Jake had left. If I walked up the field a way I could get a signal on my mobile, so I'd rung Gail when I could. I'd spoken to her a few times, but the wind and rain made it impossible some nights. Apart from those short conversations I'd spoken to no one since they'd left. Actually, I hadn't even seen another human for days.

 I'd thought to go into Falmouth, but the winds were so strong they'd put the ferry out of action, so I took the bus to Truro instead. Sitting in Waterstones coffee shop I got the weather up on the laptop screen and started making notes. It was now Thursday and the weekend forecast was looking good again. The systems seemed to have settled down; the winds were turning to the north. The window was opening again. I texted Jake, told him to check flights and to call me later. I enjoyed the bus ride back to St Just. My week of limbo looked to be ending. This was it, I was sure.

 Looking back on those weeks of indecision now, I can take a fresh perspective.

 Decades before, I'd been in a similar situation. Sitting in Falmouth, desperate to leave. Watching the weather almost hourly. Trying to work out what would happen over the coming days. Knowing that getting it wrong would mean trouble.

 Those of you who've read my first book 'A Foolish Voyage'

will know that I got it very wrong. Trouble is a mild description for the consequences of that decision.

So yes, fear was overshadowing my thoughts this time round. But many things were different. I was far better prepared; The boat was right for the job and as ready as it could be. Weather forecasting had improved a lot. Satellite navigation meant I'd always know exactly where we were.

But the sea is the sea; always has been, always will be. Biscay had nearly killed me last time out. Once bitten, twice shy as they say. I was shying all right.

And this time I wasn't just taking responsibility for myself, I was taking responsibility for Jake. He was old enough to look after himself for sure, but I was the skipper, I called the shots. I would not be reckless.

I'd thought Jake would respond to my text immediately. But by late afternoon I'd still heard nothing. I'd sent another text and left a message on voicemail. Later that evening I walked up the field to try again.

He picked up. I knew immediately something was wrong. I'd expected to hear the usual cheerful Jake, but he sounded down.

His girlfriend's mother was in hospital. A previously undiagnosed cancer had appeared. It was aggressive; the prognosis wasn't good.

I knew now why he hadn't called. He was torn. He didn't want to let me down. But he wanted to be there for his girl. I made it easy for him. I told him to stay, said I didn't want him on the boat if his head was somewhere else. Biscay could wait, I could wait. I said to call me when things settled down.

I hung up and looked across the creek. The silhouette of St Just in Roseland church stood black against the moonlit sky. A heron's ugly croak came from the tide line.

A gust of rain-laden wind rippled the muddy water and blew the hood of my jacket down. I hardly noticed.

I stood there for a while staring towards the sea, feeling numb and empty.

Sleep came slowly that night as I lay there trying to process it all. There was only one thing I knew for sure; I had no clue what to do next.

THE DECISION

It was 4 °C in the cabin when I woke the next morning. I had a muggy headache. The psoriasis on my knees itched constantly. Despite sleeping through the night, I felt tired. This was crazy.

I hadn't felt this stressed in an age.

With nothing constructive to do, I went for a lengthy walk around Messack Point. Despite a few spits of rain the sky had cleared, and the views across the Carrick Roads and up the Fal were as always, stunning.

As I walked I tried to clear my head. All this stress and pressure was entirely of my making. Building 'Gleda' had always been about creating freedom. Yet here I was, feeling trapped.

A change of perspective was needed. I had to take some action. Make a decision, and stick to it.

It was now well into October. It might be weeks before Jake was free to return. I'd crossed Biscay in December once before. I already knew I would not repeat that experience.

It was obvious to me that the only way Gail would spend a winter aboard the boat was if we had electricity and could walk ashore. That meant a marina berth. I didn't know if there were any available, and I didn't know whether we could afford one. I resolved to find out next day.

At four the next morning torrential rain lashing the cabin top woke me. It would have been easy to stay in bed and mope. But I had breakfast, kitted up in boots and waterproofs and set off for St Mawes and the ferry to Falmouth.

First call was the harbour office. I knew that boats stayed on the pontoons in the Yacht Haven over the winter. That was a nonstarter. They had no space for a catamaran. The only option available was a mooring buoy in the harbour. £700 from November to March. It was an option, but a poor one. There are more than a few easterly gales over a Cornish winter. When the winds blow from that direction it exposes Falmouth Harbour to the wind and waves coming directly across from the Roseland Peninsula. There'd be days when using the dinghy to get ashore wouldn't be possible. Not only that, but without electricity there'd be no way to heat the boat. No, we'd be better off in Messack.

Next stop was the big marina up the Penryn river. By the time I'd walked there, I was soaked. The manager behind the reception desk looked less than impressed as I stood there creating a puddle on his nice shiny floor. His response to my question about a winter berth met with an equally chilly response. He screwed up his face and shook his head. I figured that was that. But despite his lack of enthusiasm, he strolled over to the big wall planner showing the berths and pondered a while.

"Actually," he said. "I might have a berth free, what size is your boat again?"

It turned out they'd just hauled out a big motorboat that was spending winter ashore. Its berth was empty. He offered a six-month deal for £1490, not including electricity.

I thanked him, asked him to hold it for us, and that I'd let him know by the following day.

I needed to look at the money and talk to Gail. But as I squelched back towards Falmouth town, I couldn't help wondering. Jake's unexpected problem. A rare marina berth suddenly becoming available. Was the Universe trying to tell me something?

As I sat in Beerwolf with a much-needed coffee, I had another look at the weather. It was blowing a gale down in

Biscay. The long-range forecast talked of continued unsettled conditions.

Constant sailing into a headwind is tough. The wind seems stronger than it is. The boat slams and bangs around, progress is slow and uncomfortable. It breaks things.

But turn around 180° and all that changes. The wind eases, the motion dies down; you glide along serenely with not a care in the world.

In my heart I knew the decision was made. It was time to stop fighting the headwinds and take it easy.

2

THE MARINA

MOVING HOUSE

Here's my logbook entry from Tuesday 14th October 2014

If all goes to plan this will be my last night in Messack Creek.
Tomorrow morning I'm taking 'Gleda' to Falmouth Marina and her winter berth.
I've realised today that I'm tired, bone tired. And I'm stressed about tomorrows manoeuvres, about wether the berth will be OK. How I'll handle the boat on my own in such a confined space etc. No reason, no logic, but now I just want to be safely tied up over there.
I want to fully relax, to regroup and take stock. The Universe has shown me that this is the right thing to do, I'm sure all will be well.
It's going to be a contrast to The Creek that's for sure.
I was up early this morning to do some prep for leaving. The kedge anchor was fouled around an old tree trunk, so I had to squelch out into the mud to dig it out. When the tide came back in I rowed across

the other side of the creek and climbed branches to untie my extra mooring lines. Messack has been home for nearly a month and a new chapter starts tomorrow.

I was awake at 2am the next morning listening to the wind and rain. It didn't help my nervousness about leaving.

By 7 the tide was already coming in. I clambered ashore and retrieved the last mooring lines then waited for the boat to float.

From the way that the trees up on the hill were moving I could tell that a decent breeze was blowing, but down in the creek we were sheltered. It was easy to motor gently astern and head down towards the Roads. As I approached Pascoe's Yard things got a bit livelier. There was a good Force 5/6 blowing from the south east. The mooring buoys are tightly packed at the creek entrance and the wind had boats veering all over the place. There were a couple of times when I had my heart in my mouth as we headed through a rapidly closing gap.

The rain was torrential and there was a decent swell rolling into the Roads. Motoring directly across it we moved around a bit. A monohull would have been on her beam ends!

Once in the lee of Falmouth docks though we were out of the swell and the worst of the wind. As I motored slowly up the Penryn river towards the marina it dawned on me that the last time I'd done this I'd been on 'Mor Gwas'. The water in my eyes wasn't just rain.

After a slow 'fly by' to confirm where I was going, I threaded into the marina and up the right cul-de-sac. Just as the berthing spot opened up I spotted an inflatable dingy tied to the pontoons blocking my entry. There wasn't a soul around, so I had to come alongside, tie up, move the offending item, then motor in. By the time I'd got sorted I was soaked to the skin, literally. I got below, put the kettle on, stripped and dried off, then had a cuppa and a sausage sandwich.

A warm fug of satisfaction and relief enveloped me. A few

hours later the sun came out. I walked up to the marina office and booked in. Security passes, showers, laundry, Sainsbury's supermarket just over the road. Yep, a different world to Messack Creek just a few miles over the water.

That night I had a hot shower and cooked steak for dinner washing it down with a glass or two of red.

I'd spoken to Gail, she said she was getting ready to head back home. After nearly five months it was only now beginning to dawn on me. 'Gleda' really was our home. Weir Quay, Fowey, Messack Creek. It didn't matter. Home really was where the boat was. And for now, it was Falmouth. It felt good to be home.

SETTLING IN

The weather during the rest of October removed any doubts I may have had about whether we could have got away. Gale force winds and heavy rain dominated. Even in the marina it was rough. There were more than a few disturbed nights when I was up adjusting fenders and mooring lines.

Gail had returned with her car, so we could get around. I'd spoken to Jake. His family health issues had eased, and it disappointed him I had postponed the trip. I told him to look forward to the spring, that we'd sail over to Alderney and pick him up. I shipped his sailing kit back to him.

Thoughts turned to money. Gail signed on as unemployed and started looking for some part-time admin work. I looked into doing some taxi driving work but discovered I'd have to pay £350 up front for documentation, and then pay for the fuel. After that fares got split 50:50. That was a non-starter. I even applied for a sales assistant job in the carpet department at Trago Mills. I never even got an interview. I put it down to being over-qualified.

The weather meant I couldn't do much work on the boat. Lack of funds meant we couldn't do much out and about.

We spent a lot of time in the National Maritime Museum in town though. The café had excellent coffee, a grand view across the harbour and fast Wi-Fi. I joined the museum library and used the space to write and peruse their wonderful collection of maritime books.

Being back around my old 'Mor Gwas' haunts had prompted me to write a book about my time there when I was a youngster. Another favourite writing spot was Miss Peapods café up on Penryn Quay. From there I could look directly across the creek to where 'Mor Gwas' had been. It seemed life had come full circle.

In November, the gales and rain continued, and to add to the fun temperatures started falling. I'd fitted two greenhouse tube heaters in the hulls hoping they'd give some background heat, but they didn't seem to make much difference. We added two fan heaters; they raised the cabin temperatures OK, but at a cost. Electricity in the marina was extra to berthing, so we got a bill at the end of each month. We could deal with that, just. Condensation was a bigger problem. It was what I'd feared most. Gail had never lived on a boat through a UK winter, I had. I knew life would get uncomfortable.

It was worst in our sleeping cabin. The hatch above our heads would drip, the sides of the hulls next to the bed got damp. I lifted the mattress one day and discovered it was soaking wet underneath. This despite having installed some expensive mesh underlay that claimed to allow air to circulate. I bought a pack of timber from Trago and made a slatted frame to go under the mattress. It improved things slightly but by the end of the winter our costly, custom-made, pocket sprung mattress looked like something you'd find in a skip.

We bought storage boxes and vacuum bags for clothes and shoes. Anything left too long in the stale cabin air got mildew on it. Someone once said you can always tell if someone is a liveaboard in the UK because the smell of mildew follows them around. It's true.

I bought some foam camping mats, cut them up and glued them to the hullsides next to the bed. I tried sticking foil-backed radiator insulation to the tumblehomes. I stuck cork tiles up above the galley worktops. Nothing worked.

Ultimately, it was an unsolvable problem. To keep warm, we had to keep the boat closed down. Open the hatches and out went all the heat. Even on 'dry' days the humidity stayed high. On the rare properly dry days we'd open everything up, get the mattress and bedding out on deck and dry out as best we could.

Ironically, Gail was coping better than me. At the end of November though, she drove back up country to see her mom. Secretly I was glad. At least she'd escape the damp for a while.

The day after she left I slid back the hatch first thing to find the decks covered in frost and the pontoons white over. I'd told her it rarely froze in Cornwall. It was to be the first of several icy mornings, and winter proper hadn't even started.

WORKING WINTER

Living on a boat is easy when the weather is good. Now we were finding out how hard life can be when it's bad.

We were safe in the marina. We had electricity for the fan heaters, but condensation continued to plague us and the long hours of darkness brought me down.

The cabins on a Tiki 38 are small, and although cosy I found that spending too much time below made me feel claustrophobic. While we'd been in Messack, we'd realised that the deckpod was an important part of our living space. When I'd built the pod I'd only thought of it as a place to drive the boat from. Now though, we knew it could be far more. Over the autumn Gail had made some canvas enclosures to make it more weatherproof. They'd worked well up to a point. But the strong winds and frequent heavy rain we had now demanded more. We did the rounds of local sailmaker's, getting quotes for better ones. We figured they'd be a worthwhile investment. Gail bought a small TV set for the saloon and I bought an aerial from Trago and bolted it on the stern, so she could watch her favourite shows. It wasn't much, but I knew I needed to do as much as possible to make life comfortable for her. I also got hold of a Wi-Fi antenna to boost the signal in the marina. They'd berthed us on the outer pontoons, which meant the signal from the office was weak. The antenna made it usable.

The constant condensation had made many of the painted surfaces in the cabin mouldy. I re-painted as much as I could with anti-mould bathroom paint. It didn't stop it completely but at least it took longer to come back after cleaning.

The lead up to Christmas wasn't great. I came down with a cough and cold. Gail had a migraine for days and felt ill on Christmas Eve. The weather was typical. Wet, cold and windy. It rained heavily during the night, and because I'd left the Wi-Fi antenna cable running through the portlight, rain leaked down onto my camera and laptop on the nav station desk. Some careful drying out left everything working OK, but once again I was cursing.

It brightened on Christmas Day. Gail made a superb effort, and we had our usual smoked salmon and bucks fizz breakfast, then a full turkey Christmas dinner. We both had some nice simple gifts to open and the new TV meant Gail could watch her favourite Downton Abbey show on Christmas night.

We'd got to know a few people in the marina and on Boxing Day we spent a pleasant couple of hours aboard 'Cape Cornwall'. Owned by Tony and Mary, she was once a St Ives fishing boat originally built in 1929. Tony had heavily modified her with high topsides to make her a comfortable liveaboard boat. She wasn't pretty. But sitting down below with his wood-burning stove roaring away, it was hard not to be envious.

Another couple, Paul and Janette, joined us. They'd lived aboard in Falmouth for years. Although I hadn't got to meet them back then, they'd been around when I was on 'Mor Gwas'. They remembered 'Abraxis' the boat Clive and I had delivered to Tenerife, and they knew Chris the one-legged guy on 'Licorne' I'd crewed for when he did his Yachtmaster exam.

The year ended with Gail full of cold and temperatures below freezing. We had to leave the fan heaters running in both hulls all night to prevent everything freezing. In the unheated toilet compartment the hatch had ice on it, inside and out. The toothpaste had all but frozen in its tube. I bought more foam camping mattresses as insulation and stuck them up where I could.

We stayed aboard on New Year Eve and had an enjoyable meal and a bottle of Rioja. Two thousand and fourteen had been a momentous year. We knew that the next one would be even better.

January is my least favourite month. I'd attempted to start a few boat jobs and one project in particular. I'd decided we needed self-steering, and I'd chosen to build a wind vane. The one I'd selected was called the 'Hebridean'. Marketed by a guy in Scotland, it came as a set of plans along with all the necessary raw stainless-steel stock, screws and bolts. All I needed to buy extra was the timber. I figured it'd be an excellent project to keep me occupied until we left, and a worthwhile addition to the boat.

I'd taken a bit of money from my pension pot, so I could add a few extra essentials to our inventory. A proper fixed GPS unit and a fixed DSC VHF radio. We'd managed up till then with handheld units but my mind was turning to making 'Gleda' as safe as possible for our onward passages.

The weather still wasn't helping me any.

January 30th: An absolutely shitty day. Worn full waterproofs all day. There's a bitter wind, heavy rain and hail so hard that the noise in the cabins made conversation impossible. I have so much to do, but I can't get on with anything. There are severe weather warnings in place up to, and including Monday. It's shit. Oh, and it's going to get colder. Everything is wet inside the boat and out, and the electric bill for the heaters is going to be huge.

February 2nd: Very icy on deck this morning. I had to chip and wire brush the ice away to make it safe to move about on deck. It's near freezing again now and it's sleeting. This is undoubtedly the worst weather we've experienced so far. Hard going.

Mood and productivity swung back and forth throughout the rest of the month, mainly with the weather.

We got a few dry days with some warm sunshine and what a difference it made. The sailmaker had fitted the new deck pod enclosures, and I had made progress building the wind vane. Other days didn't go so well. The January electric bill came in at £64, and then I float-tested my iPhone. It was in the chest pocket of my fleece. I hadn't realised I'd unzipped it. I bent down to open the forward deck hatch, and it fell out, bounced once on the deck, then slipped perfectly between the hull and deck slats straight into the water. Gone forever.

Gail was back up country. We'd texted regularly and chatted each evening. It was horrible being out of touch. The next day I walked into town and bought the most basic Nokia mobile I could find, along with a pay-as-you-go SIM card. I'd had that iPhone for years. It was one of the few things I'd bought with me from my old life. At the time it gutted me to have lost it. But before long I realised I didn't miss having a smartphone with me 24/7. I haven't had one since.

With Gail away, my mood once again slipped backwards.

Sunday 22nd February: A truly miserable day. The rain never let up and it was dull dull dull. The psoriasis on my knees is as bad as it's ever been. Sore and bleeding. I worked on the self-steering all day, but it was tough going. I broke drill bits and my 6 mm die. Nothing came easy. It's been cold and I feel low on energy. I need sun; I need warmth. I need wind in my sails. It seems like I've been working on this boat forever and yet the reward keeps moving away from me. Will I ever feel like I've succeeded?

In March, we got another example of how the Wharram bug gets under the skin and leads folks to do some crazy things.

We had a visit from a lovely Belgian couple called Tristan and Valerie. They'd emailed a few weeks previously to ask if they could come and see 'Gleda' as they were planning to build their own Tiki 38 in a few years.

What I hadn't realised at the time was that they were driving over from Belgium especially. They'd told us to expect them about lunchtime, so when the phone rang at 1:15 I thought it was them saying they'd arrived, and so it was. I started giving them directions to our pontoon, but none of my descriptions seemed to match what they were seeing. It transpired they were in the wrong marina. They were in Sutton Harbour, two-and-a-half hours up the road in Plymouth!

They made it eventually though, and we spent a great couple of hours showing them the boat and talking Wharram's. I hoped they thought the trip worthwhile.

MARCH OF CHANGE

By the middle of March I was feeling pressured again. Our deal at the marina ran out on 1st April. After that, the cost would be £22.50 per night. It wasn't an option, even if we'd wanted it.

The winter showed no signs of loosening its grip. There was still ice on deck on the 20th March.

I fought to keep my mood positive. As things turned out we stayed in the marina for the first week in April anyway. Gail's Mom came down for a visit, and we had no option. She was staying in Falmouth, and we needed to be close by with easy access to the boat.

We treated it as a holiday, although my mind was preoccupied with thoughts of moving the boat back over to Messack. I'd be doing it alone again as Gail intended driving her Mom back home and staying on for a bit.

The weather remained frosty and there was still ice about first thing in the mornings, but for the main the days were sunny and dry.

We even took Gail's mom out for a sail. We motored out into the Bay in light winds and then hauled the sails up. Although we never went faster than 3 knots, it was nice to be out. Despite the lack of wind, I thought I'd have a play with the new wind vane steering. Unsurprisingly, I didn't achieve much. Even though the wind was light, there was still a surprising amount of residual swell and chop on the water. There I was, bouncing on the stern concentrating on the job in hand when I suddenly realised I felt seasick. To be honest, I'd had a headache and felt rough even before we left the marina, but nonetheless it disappointed me. It turned out to be the one and only time I've been seasick on 'Gleda'. Bizarre.

A few days later Gail and her Mom left, and it was time for me to go.

Thursday 9th April: Well, here I am, 176 days after leaving, I'm back in Messack Creek. It's been a tiring day, but everything went fine. Gail left just after half nine. It was hard watching her drive away. But we both know it's the start of another exciting chapter for us. After waving her off I walked up to Sainsbury's for some last-minute shopping, settled the marina bill and got ready to leave.

It was sunny and calm and I got 'Gleda' manoeuvred out fairly easily, then motored over the Roads to St Just Pool and dropped the hook. After lunch, I rowed ashore and walked round to recce the creek while it was low water. It was sunny and warm out of the wind, and the walk through the churchyard and creek-side was beautiful. Wild garlic and primrose smells, warmth and light. A real tonic. I drifted 'Gleda' up the creek with the rising tide just after 19:30 and by 21:00 I had her secured in the same spot as last year. I'm tired but satisfied.

Our berth in Falmouth marina could be compared to living in a row of terraced houses. Folks walking past the front door all the time. Neighbours stopping to chat, there was always something going on. Messack was like living in a country estate with private grounds all around. For the first 48 hours I didn't see another human. It was just me, the sheep in the fields and the birds in the creek. Apart from my evening telephone conversations with Gail, I didn't speak. Some folks might find that scary. I enjoy it. For a little while at least. There was plenty to keep me occupied. Not least scrubbing off winters accumulated marina muck from the hulls at low tide.

3

THE SEA AT LAST

ALONE AGAIN

With Gail away upcountry for a couple of weeks, I was back on my own again, just me, 'Gleda' and the peace of Messack.

As if by magic, the weather turned warm and sunny. It boosted my mood and my productivity. I threw myself into all the jobs that had been impossible over the winter, mainly painting.

Anti-slip paint on the decks. Anti-foul paint on the hulls.

Despite the pleasant days, the nights reminded me it was still early spring in the UK.

> *20th April 2015: Woke early this morning feeling cold. It was below zero outside and just a few degrees above in the cabin. I've been sleeping in the foetal position, trying to keep warm despite wearing tracksuit bottoms and socks.*

One of the enormous advantages of a Wharram catamaran is that it can happily take the ground when the tide goes out. The bottom at Messack was mainly firm, with just a few inches of soft mud on top. This meant I could do all the jobs beneath the boat that would otherwise have meant using a crane to lift the boat onto dry land. It also meant a chunk of money saved.

    I serviced the twin outboards, changing the gearbox oils, lubricating the controls, etc. All fairly straightforward, if a little mucky.

    Not everything went as well. One of my two solar panels had stopped charging. I eventually tracked it down to corroded connections on the panel itself. It was my own fault. The panels were Chinese built and bought cheap on eBay. Not such a bargain after all.

    Because the port battery bank wasn't being charged, I had to start the engines manually to test them. On the third pull of the starboard side starter cord, it broke. Replacing it was a pig. I got the cover off to access the end of the rope and somehow the big steel recoil spring popped out. Imagine a giant watch spring, about a hand's width across, covered in grease, with sharp edges. Imagine trying to coil that back into a shallow tray when all it wants to do is pop out. An hour later, I succeeded. Black oily hands and fingers covered with grease filled cuts my reward. I wasn't a happy bunny.

    Later in the day I had a fresh challenge. I needed to take some more money from my pension pot. I'd spoken to my old IFA friend upcountry for some guidance. He said I should leave it be.

    It was undoubtably sound advice. He told me that the few thousand pounds I was thinking about could, if left invested, be worth tens of thousands in another 30 years or so. I didn't care.

    The whole concept of retirement and pensions seemed flawed to me.

    Maybe there was a time when it made sense. But even that's debatable.

    Let's start with the basics.

First, its fundamental premise is that we spend what are most likely to be the healthiest years of our lives working full time. We're expected to exchange our precious time for money and, if we're lucky, get two or three weeks a year to spend as we wish in the meanwhile.

I'm of a generation that was told our reward would come at the age of 60. But over the decades the rules changed, and they keep changing. Some folks are now being told they may have to wait until they are 70 or 80.

Back in the day at least the final financial reward was valuable. Invested wisely, you could potentially retire as a millionaire. Live out your days in security and comfort. Not any more.

All of this assumes of course that health issues don't overtake you before that magical date arrives.

I'm betting you know more than a few folks who never made it. Either that or they got just a few years of freedom before the final curtain came down.

However you look at it, the deal was always a lousy one. Now it's a non-starter.

Watch this space and, if I'm still around in twenty years, I'll let you know the repercussions of my decision.

But for now, I'd recommend grabbing what you can, when you can, and using it to live life today. Yes, tomorrow might be rainy, but then again it might not come at all.

Anyway, back to the challenge.

I guess this is just another example of how living on a boat differs from living ashore. Living a bricks and mortar existence, it's easy to take things for granted. Things like picking up the telephone and making a call.

I've mentioned more than a few times that Messack was remote. The creek where 'Gleda' lay sat in a deep cleft in the hillside. On all sides the water was edged by steep grassy slopes. The only way I could get a mobile signal was to walk up the sheep field until I was high enough to see out across the Carrick Roads to Falmouth.

So, grabbing the paperwork, a notebook, pen and phone, I climbed down into the dinghy and pulled myself ashore. After tying the dinghy up, I walked through the gate and up the field to my 'reception spot'. Dialling the number, I got through to the inevitable automated menu. I made my selection and, after being informed that my call was important to them, waited for an advisor to come free. Ten minutes later a cheery voice cut across the hold muzak, introduced itself as Daniel and asked how it could help. I told him I wanted to draw some cash from my pension, gave a few necessary details and was put on hold again. Five minutes after that the hold muzak changed to a beep, followed immediately by a text message notification. My pay-as you-go mobile had run out of credit. They had cut me off.

To top up my credit, I had to go online. This meant a trip back to the boat for laptop and mobile data MiFi. 10 minutes later I was back at my spot, trying to balance the laptop in one hand whilst typing with the other. Ten minutes after that I had credit on my phone again. Then it started raining.

I ran back to the boat with the laptop under my t-shirt, picked up a waterproof and climbed back up to my spot. I called again.

Menu — your call is important — hold music — sorry all our operators are busy right now — hold music — your call is important — hold music — "hello this is Sarah, how can I help?" — passed information — hold music -"hello this is Sarah, how can I help?" — "You're already helping me, I've been on hold for five minutes — "Oh, yes, sorry, please hold again."

Forty-five minutes of my life, standing in a field in the rain, mobile stuck to my ear under my hood, praying the signal didn't disappear. It didn't. We got there eventually. They told me they would post the form out within 24 hours. Once I'd returned the signed copy, the money would be in my bank account within 2 weeks.

As I slid and squelched back down the now sodden sheep field, cold, wet and thoroughly pissed off, my confidence wasn't high.

On 25th April Gail came back. Her brother Gav drove her down. This time she'd left her car behind. It was a gigantic step for her. The car had been her last connection to her old life. Her last bit of independence. Now she was committing, trusting. I knew what that meant.

Gav had bought his two kids Eva and Zak down with him. They were an assault on my ears after the days of peace. They never stopped running about, shouting over each other and us. Gav never stopped talking to them. We got Gail's gear aboard, then drove round to St Mawes, so we could let the kids run around on the beach. We all ate fish and chips on a bench overlooking the sea. It was nice. All too soon though, it was time to say goodbye. Gail got tearful watching them drive away. I hugged her, then we walked hand in hand back down to 'Gleda'. This was it. This really was the start of our adventure together.

We stayed in Messack for the rest of April and the first week in May. There were highs and lows. We had welcome visitors. Adrian and Janine Hall came to see us. They were fellow Tiki 38 builders a few years behind, but with the same dreams as us. They treated us to a lovely lunch in St Mawes, and we talked Wharram all day.

My daughter Nicole drove down and spent a few days with us. She bravely slept aboard despite the less than ideal weather. Gail had experienced her emotional wrench a few weeks before, watching her brother drive away. I got mine watching Nicole leave.

Long time follower of the project Jon Kutassy and his wife Julie came to visit in their camper van. It was great to show him

'Gleda' on the water, and his parting gift of a bottle of rum was much appreciated.

In between times I worked hard on the boat, making preparations to leave Messack.

We now had a plan. As soon as the weather settled down we'd sail over to Alderney to pick up Jake before heading south.

I was confident enough about crossing the Channel with just Gail and I. Neither of us had ever been to Alderney; it sounded like a splendid plan.

I'd considered leaving directly from Messack, but there was a problem with that. The creek is shallow and dries out at low water. I wasn't sure we could get out on anything other than a high spring tide. I didn't want to miss any weather window that might appear. So I decided we'd go and anchor up the Fal where we'd be free to leave anytime. Apart from a change of scenery, it also meant we could easily do some sea trials.

MAGGOTY BANK

Winter hadn't finished with us yet. The first week of May gave us persistent rain, a Force 9 gale and single figure temperatures. There was ice on the deck the morning we left Messack, but no wind.

That made it easy to untie the lines for the last time and motor round to St Just Pool, where we anchored for breakfast. After that we lifted the hook and motored up the Roads, around the dog-leg of Turnaware Point, and into the river. It was good to be moving. Over the winter, Tony on 'Cape Cornwall' had told me about a nice little anchorage off the wonderfully named Maggoty Bank in the Truro river, a little way up from where the Fal splits off to the east. Good holding in mud, and beautifully set in a curve of the wooded valleys surrounding the water. An hour later we were there, safely anchored, drinking a cuppa and admiring the scenery.

Maggoty bank seemed a million miles away from the rest of the world. But next morning the radio brought news. The General Election result was in. David Cameron and the Tory Party had won. The polls had predicted a hung parliament. They were wrong. The Conservatives took power with a majority. The first time that had happened since 1992. I didn't give a toss. But that election started us down the road to Brexit. That election would, ultimately, change our lives.

The scenery that morning matched the bleak political outlook, shrouded from view by sweeping bands of rain. We hunkered down and did little.

Just up river from the anchorage was the tiny village of Malpas. A picture post card place with a jetty where we could leave the dinghy. A pub called the Heron where we could get Wi-Fi and walking distance from Truro where we could get supplies.

Once again the weather dictated everything.

16th May: Feeling down as I write this. The wind today has been cold and fresh again. My fingers are numb. Cabin temperature 10 °C. They forecast the weather to stay unsettled, unseasonably cold, unseasonably windy. The long-term forecast means that even if we got to Alderney, it's likely to be the end of the month before we got favourable winds to head south. I just don't know what to do, I've felt tired and listless all day. Another kick in the balls is that the Revenue have unexpectedly deducted £300 from my pension draw down. I'd thought we'd be able to leave with a decent cushion in the bank. Now it's gone.

Unbelievably, yesterday marked the one-year anniversary of 'Gleda' leaving the barn in Wroxhall. Back then I'd thought we were weeks away from our escape. Now here we are a year later and still stuck. I know it'll happen. I should be happy, I should be excited, I should feel pride in what we've achieved so far. But I don't. Instead, I just feel empty and numb. I feel like I've let Gail down, that I've let everyone down. Will I ever make this dream work? Right now it doesn't feel like it.

This book is called 'A Foolish Escape' for a reason. From the moment I started building the boat, the theme has been 'escape'. That idea was everything. Escape from the job, escape from the crowds, escape from the bullshit. I believed changing my environment was the key to it all. I believed the sun always shone in that distant Shangri-La, that I just needed to get there.

Looking at that journal entry now, I can see how wrong I was. I believe it was Confucius who once said "Wherever you go, there you are." It's true. You can't escape yourself. So obvious and yet so easily missed.

Back then I'd escaped the barn, I'd escaped the job, and I'd escaped my old life. Yet, like a donkey following that carrot on a stick, I couldn't see the reality. I couldn't stop chasing.

THE VOYAGE BEGINS

20th May 2015: The decision is made. The weather has finally settled down. The boat is ready. We're ready. The alarm is set for 5am for a 6am departure. I won't believe it till we're away, but if the Universe is kind, we'll be in Alderney in a few days. I'm excited, nervous, maybe a little anxious. But it's way past time to do this thing.

The following morning dawned fine and calm. After a quick cuppa, I got the anchor up. No simple task, given how firmly bedded into the sucking Maggoty Bank mud it was. Weeks of powerful winds had seen 'Gleda' pulling hard on her anchor chain.

As we motored down river towards the Carrick Roads, I sat calmly at the wheel smiling. Inside, I wasn't so pleased with myself. I had no worries about the weather. I had no worries about the boat. But I felt a little guilty. I'd lied to Gail. I'd told her that if we left early in the morning, we'd be safely tucked up in Braye Harbour by nightfall. That would not happen.

It's some 120 nmi from Falmouth to Alderney. The forecast didn't have a lot of wind in it. I'd decided that for Gail's initiation into offshore sailing, a slow light wind passage in calm seas was preferable to a fast choppy one. In fact, even the 'fast' option would likely have taken around 15 hours. I knew that we would probably take around 24. A full night at sea. I knew it was unlikely I'd get the wind vane steering working in the light winds, so I would have to stay alert and awake for the duration. That was OK. I had only one overriding concern. Keep Gail safe.

As we exited the Fal and into the Carrick Roads, Gail took the wheel and I got the sails up. There was a nice gentle breeze blowing just over the port stern quarter, so I switched the engines off, and we were soon sailing along at 4-5 knots headed straight out to sea.

There was little else on the water, the sun had come up and it was getting warmer. I sat at the helm and looked around. We were soon passing the entrance to St Just and Messack. To starboard, Falmouth and the Penryn river. Places we now considered home. As we passed between the Pendennis and St Mawes castles my mind raced back to leaving on 'Mor Gwas' all those years before. Heading for the horizon with no idea when, or if, I'd ever return. Just as before, there was no one waving goodbye. But this time there was an enormous difference. This time I wasn't alone. This time I had someone to share the adventure with. I looked across at Gail. She was sitting in the corner cockpit seat. Woolly hat on her head, warm in her big coat and gloves. She smiled back at me, looking happy and relaxed. She trusted me completely. I would not let her down.

The morning passed quickly. The winds were even lighter than forecast. But they kept blowing from the right direction at least. With a smooth sea 'Gleda' kept moving, albeit slowly. A few hours later we were out of sight of land. Once we'd passed a few beam trawlers and some NATO warships on exercise, we soon found ourselves the only vessel in a 360° horizon. I love that feeling, but it was another first for Gail and understandably she wasn't sure how she felt. I was happy. Content to steer our course. But I had to be alert. The English Channel is a busy stretch of water. We were crossing the first of two sets of shipping lanes. Sizeable vessels to and from the Atlantic keep to the North, passing by Lizard Point before rounding Land's End and heading into the ocean. There were plenty of ships in view as we crossed their paths. With good visibility, it was no problem. I knew there was a greater challenge ahead. As we closed the French coast, we'd have to cross the much busier traffic separation lanes for shipping heading north and south. I also knew that we'd be doing it in the dark. But for now, it was just us, a few fishing boats and the sea.

By late afternoon we were halfway across. Gail asked what time I thought we'd arrive. I was deliberately vague. I figured it would be around dawn, but the winds were now becoming lighter and more variable. I wasn't ready to put the engines on yet. We'd have to see.

As dusk fell, I could see Gail staring ahead looking for land. It was time to tell her.

I blamed the winds. Told her that passage timings always change, we'd just been unlucky with the winds. She seemed OK with the news. I told her it was no problem. I could stay awake for 24 hours. There was nothing she needed to do. She could go to bed if she wanted and wake up in Alderney. I knew she wouldn't.

James Wharram, the designer of my boat, has spoken and written many times about the strength of women at sea. And how much they support us macho males. The first time I'd taken Gail to meet James and Hanneke, he'd gone out his way to tell Gail that she'd surprise herself. Understandably Gail lacked confidence. There was much she didn't understand. Even more she knew nothing about. There'd been a time, many actually, when I'd thought she'd choose not to come with me. But here she was. Keeping me fed and watered as I navigated our floating home across the open sea towards new adventures. Her presence eased any worries I had about the coming night. She might have felt like a passenger, but she wasn't. We were a team already. Looking after each other. Looking after 'Gleda'.

It was a black night despite the relatively clear skies, with a new moon and an inky sea the horizon all but disappeared. The wind picked up a little, and with it the sea. Every now and again a foaming wave would rise and hiss past 'Gleda's' quarter only to vanish into the darkness. Gail went down for a sleep and I started thinking about the challenge that lay a few hours ahead of us. Already I could see the navigation lights of enormous ships ahead. We'd be crossing the separation lanes at a 90° angle. It was all about timing. Like crossing a dual carriageway full of cars. You have to pick your moment to get across to the central reservation, take a breather, then look the other way and cross again.

For those that don't know, this is probably a good time to explain something about the 'rules of the road' out at sea. The main theoretical and overriding rule is that powered vessels give way to sailing vessels. That doesn't always work in practice. There will be many instances when a powered vessel can't give way. A narrow channel may restrict it, or shallow water. Regulations may restrict them, such as in the separation lanes we were about to cross. The larger the ship, the harder it is to change course quickly. So, I keep my own rule. When it comes to big ships, I keep well clear. I have a second rule that particularly applies to the situation we were about to face. When I need to cross the path of a large ship I always cross behind her. That way there can be no miscalculations. In comparison to motor vehicles, ships are slow and lumbering.

Generally, they will move at around something like 20 knots, which is a little less than 25mph (ca. 40 km/h).

But even at that speed, it's surprising how quickly a distant dot on the horizon can turn into a massive steel bow towering over you.

Get it wrong and you're in big trouble.

There's another reason I keep clear. One rule stands out above all others at sea. Ships should always keep a good lookout. Once again theory and practice differ. Most vessels at sea these days won't have someone steering. They'll be on autopilot. The person on watch doesn't have much to do. They can get distracted, they can nod off to sleep, they can just not bother. Apart from that, big ship watch-keepers are looking out for other big ships. Vessels like 'Gleda' aren't on their radar, sometimes literally. That's why I have my own rule.

'Gleda' didn't have radar and not so many years ago I'd have had to rely on the Mk1 eyeball. But technology these days has given us a helpful system called AIS (Automatic Identification System).

In 2004, the International Maritime Organisation introduced a regulation requiring most commercial vessels to carry AIS equipment. A transponder automatically transmits information such as the ship's identity, type, position, course, speed, navigational status and other safety-related information.

AIS receivers are not expensive. I'd fitted one to 'Gleda' over the winter. This meant that on my computer screen I could see all the larger vessels around us. More than that, I could see what course they were on and whether we were in any danger of getting too close.

But whatever tools are available, you can't take the human element away. As we approached the first shipping lane, I heard a call come over the VHF. It went something like this. In a well-spoken voice: "Cargo vessel 'Rust Bucket' this is sailing-vessel 'Rich Man's Toy of Hamble', are you receiving? Over". No reply.

"Cargo vessel 'Rust Bucket'......." repeated. No reply. "Cargo vessel....." repeated.

Eventually, a heavily accented, slightly slurred Eastern European voice replies. "Da, sailing-vessel 'Rich' dis is 'Rust Bucket'". "Ah, good evening 'Rust Bucket'. We are the 12-metre sailing yacht close on your port bow. Can you confirm that you can see us on your radar? We intend to cross your bow shortly". 'Rust Bucket' replies. "Wait please". I'm incredulous. I can just make out the navigation lights of what I assume is 'Rich Mans Toy'. I'd been watching 'Rust Bucket' for a while and had already changed course slightly to starboard to pass her astern, and well clear of the ship following her. That this posh yachty wasn't doing the same baffled me. Delegating his boats safety to someone else. Why take the risk? Crazy. After a minute 'Rust Bucket' came back on. "'Rich Man', I can't see you. Cross if you want". By this time I was too busy looking out for us to care any more. I guess they got away with it, but like I said, crazy.

It was intense to get across both lanes, but all went well apart from one minor incident. We'd cleared the southbound side of the separation zones, then I spotted a northbound vessel coming up fast, I wanted to take the usual action and alter course to starboard to pass astern, but this time there was another smaller vessel, probably a fishing boat apparently doing the same as us and crossing the TSS at right angles. He was a mile astern, off our starboard quarter and gaining on us. Turning to starboard would have put us under his bows. I was running with just the masthead tricolour light, but to try to ensure he'd at least seen us, I switched on the lower level nav lights as well. We both carried on along the same track for a while and then, just as I was getting ready to bail out to port and make a big circle astern of him, he altered course to starboard which gave me sea-room to do the same, and soon after I watched the lights of a huge tanker fade away northwards. We'd made it across.

A FOOLISH ESCAPE | 35

After crossing the shipping lanes, the wind picked up again. It was still from astern and 'Gleda' started moving along well. We hit 10 knots at one point and I began to think we might arrive well before dawn.

It's normally best to arrive at a new harbour or anchorage in daylight. Everything is so much easier when you can see what's going on. But with an accurate chart plotter I could see exactly where we were, and I knew that the entrance to Braye harbour was wide. Once in we'd be picking up a mooring buoy, and I didn't think that'd be any problem. We'd been at sea for 18 hours already, Gail had slept a little, but I'd been at the wheel pretty much all the time. I felt fine, my shoulder ached a bit, and I was yawning often, but crossing the shipping lanes had raised my adrenaline levels, and now we were sailing fast in a lively sea they'd gone higher still.

Sadly, it didn't last.

At around 03:00 the wind died. We gradually slowed until we were struggling to make 1 knot. Normally, I'm reluctant to put the engines on. 'Gleda' is a sailboat. But spending hours floating around in the Channel with a fatigued skipper isn't a sensible thing to do. We'd done well, we'd broken the back of our first big passage. It was time to get in.

The next couple of hours were the hardest for me, after the adrenaline had faded, tiredness started hitting home and although I never once felt my eyelids drooping I found it harder to steer a straight course, and even hallucinated that one of the deck dorades was a little hooded Eskimo waving at me!

A few hours later, as dawn broke, we could see the light on Burghou Island to the east of Alderney. I'd opted to take a slightly longer route and pass around the north of Burghou to avoid the strong currents known as the 'Swinge' that runs between Burghou and Alderney. A better skipper than I would have calculated the tides, and it may have been possible to sluice north through the gap. I kept things simple and 100 percent safe.

On the other side of Alderney, between the island and the French coast, lies another area of water known as the Alderney Race. At the biggest spring tides, the water can flow through there at anything up to 12 knots. That's faster than a lot of cruising boats can move, even under power. Both can throw up steep, confused seas. Get it wrong and they are dangerous places to be.

I'd hoped some nice warm sunshine might greet us, but sadly not. The day dawned grey and misty. Grey sea, grey sky, little horizon.

Unbeknown to us, Jake had been ringing my mobile throughout the night trying to find out how we were doing. All he knew was that when he got the mobile unavailable message, we were still in the middle somewhere, but around 04:00 we got back into mobile range, and we could give him an ETA. I could see the loom of the Casquets light on the horizon. I told him we'd be a few hours yet.

As we approached the harbour entrance a big orange RIB came screaming out towards us. It was Jake in the Mainbrace water taxi. The last time I'd seen him had been when he'd left the boat in Messack after our aborted departure. That seemed a lifetime ago now.

Jake guided us to a mooring buoy well into the harbour and helped us tie up. I switched the engines off at 08:15. According to the GPS we'd been on the move for 26 hours 8 minutes and 15 seconds. We'd covered 123.85 nmi at an average speed of 4.74 knots. It'd been a pedestrian passage, but I didn't care. Nothing had broken, we'd had no dramas, we'd arrived safely. More than that, Gail and I had done it together. My tiredness all but vanished, replaced with a wave of satisfaction and relief as I hugged and kissed Gail. We'd finally got this adventure properly started, we'd done it.

It took a good hour to wind down with a cuppa as I tidied the boat and told Jake about the trip as he dropped by between taxi runs. But soon we were down below and crawling into bed, and I can tell you this, it felt damn good. I was asleep before my head hit the pillow.

4

ALDERNEY

I shouldn't assume you know anything about The Channel Islands and Alderney, so here's a bit of 'Wikipedia' type info.

The Channel Islands are an archipelago in the English Channel, off the French coast of Normandy. They include two Crown dependencies: the Bailiwick of Jersey, which is the largest of the islands; and the Bailiwick of Guernsey, comprising Guernsey, Alderney, Sark, and some smaller islands. They are not part of the United Kingdom, but the UK is responsible for the defence and international relations of the islands.

Alderney is the northernmost of the inhabited Channel Islands. It's about 3.5 miles (5.63 km) long and 1.5 miles (2.41 km) wide, so about 5 square miles (13 square km). That makes it the third-largest of the Channel Islands. It lies only 8 miles (ca. 13 km) from the French coast.

The islands have gained a reputation as a tax haven. There's a 20% income tax rate, and no VAT, inheritance tax or capital gains tax.

All the islands have their own unique character. During my

time in the construction industry, I visited Jersey and Guernsey more than a few times. I didn't like Jersey at all. The first thing I saw when I landed at Jersey airport were rows of small jets, some private, others bearing the names of large banks and financial institutions. As I drove down the main road from the airport to St Helier, a Ferrari, several Porsches and a couple of top-end Range Rovers overtook me. The island is 9 miles (ca. 14 km) long and 5 miles (ca. 8 km) wide. I found out later that Jersey has car ownership figures of around 650 for every 1000 of population. This on an island with half a dozen 'main' roads, the longest of which is about 5 miles (ca. 8 km) and with a maximum speed of 40 mph (ca. 64 km/h). In town every other shop was selling Rolex's, jewellery, designer this, designer that. The place seemed to revolve around money. Jersey seemed to send an obvious message. If you've got it and want to spend it you're very welcome. If not, you can come and do all the low-paid work that needs doing. Come and serve us our food and drink. Come and cook for us, clean for us, run around after us. But don't expect to stay.

Maybe I'm being too harsh. The scenery is beautiful, I'm sure there are some very nice folks living there. It's just that the place rubbed me up the wrong way. Guernsey wasn't so in your face, but it's still restrictive. Incomers get vetted and approved before being allowed in.

On Alderney things are more relaxed and unpretentious.

There is a distinct 1950s feel to the place. There's next to no crime, it's small enough to be friendly but not intrusive. It seems everyone looks out for one another.

The population is around 2,000, with a reputation for being a friendly, sociable bunch.

Residents of Alderney have a well-established drinking culture. There is a common expression elsewhere in the Channel Islands that Alderney is composed of 'two thousand alcoholics, clinging to a rock'.

The coastline of Alderney is like the other Channel Islands. Sheer cliffs, broken by stretches of sandy beach and dunes. The highest point is on the central plateau of the island at 300 feet (ca. 91 m).

There aren't many trees on the island, as they cut many down in the 17th century to fuel the lighthouses on Alderney and the Casquets. There's plenty of wildlife though, particularly birds. The sound of Skylarks is predominant during the summer and all around the coast there are colonies of Gannets and Puffins.

The most striking features of the island are man-made. Alderney was a fortress island for centuries. In the Victorian era they built 13 forts. They're imposing structures even today. They have restored some and turned them into accommodation. Some are derelict. They are all fascinating. Towers, moats, vast stone walls with crenellated battlements, tunnels, courtyards, all open to exploration.

During the Second World War, the authorities evacuated Alderney. The Germans landed on a deserted island and set about fortifying it even more. Hitler had issued orders that it should become part of his 'Atlantic Wall'.

They built two work (slave) camps, and two concentration camps. They set about constructing bunkers, gun emplacements, tunnels, air-raid shelters and many other concrete structures. All this on an island of only a few square miles.

When the islanders returned in December 1945, it shocked them to see how their beautiful island had been devastated. Many homes were uninhabitable. The Germans had ripped away doors, window frames and anything made of wood to use as fuel. Later they uncovered the graves of hundreds of mainly Jewish workers who had died from hunger and the harsh conditions.

Today it's impossible to walk anywhere without seeing

evidence of the German occupation.

The island is surrounded by rocks, which have caused hundreds of shipwrecks. As I've already mentioned, there are treacherous tidal streams on either side of the island. Just to add to the fun, the tidal range at springs is huge. Somewhere around 40ft (12.5 m). It's a challenging place to sail around.

Braye is the only sheltered harbour. It's protected by a huge break-water 807 metres (2,650ft) long. The British Admiralty built it in the 19th century. It does a decent job when gales blow in from the west or south sides, but from the northeast the harbour is open.

To give you some idea of its effectiveness, consider this. In January 2018 storm 'Eleanor' barrelled across the Atlantic. It battered Ireland and the UK, then crossed the Channel. When it hit the breakwater in Alderney, around 12 huge granite blocks broke off the seaward side of the breakwater and got washed over the top by the force of the water. Each of those blocks weighed between two and three tons. Most of the island's freight comes in via the quay in Braye. Once a week the little ship from Poole on the UK south coast arrives and off-loads anything and everything the island needs.

That breakwater keeps Alderney habitable.

A mile up the hill from Braye lies St Anne. It's the capital and main (only) town on the island. In fact, the locals just call it 'Town'. Victoria Street is the principal thoroughfare with picturesque houses and plenty of pubs and restaurants.

Here the 1950s vibe is strong. Few cars, people strolling about, waved greetings, conversations in the street. Just a pleasant place to be.

We stayed in Alderney longer than expected.

The weather window I'd used to cross The Channel didn't stay open long. The unusually cold and windy May weather returned, and lasted right to the end of the month.

For the first few days though, we got a break. The sun shone, and we got to see the island in all its beauty.

I fell for the place.

I don't do crowds, and I don't do cities. Alderney has neither. I'd visited once before, many years ago. That was on a sailing school yacht whilst doing my RYA Competent Crew course. We'd crossed from the Solent and spent only a day on the island before a night sail back. But the place had made an impression on me nonetheless. Now, with more time to spend, I could see why.

The marketing slogan Alderney uses is 'So Close, So Different'. Regarding the first part I'd add the rider, it depends on how you get there. We could have flown to Australia in the time it took us to sail there, but as for the second part there can be no dispute. Alderney undoubtedly has a very different feel from anywhere else I've been.

It's hard to pin down, but there's something unique about the place.

As a member of the Channel Islands Alderney is not part of the UK and neither is it part of the EU, they pick their laws as they see fit. For example, you don't have to wear a crash helmet on a motorcycle, there are no MOT tests, road tax is paid with a surcharge on fuel, there's no public health service, you can't buy alcohol in shops and supermarkets. And yet English is the language, they drive on the left, and they have real ale in the pub, and in jugs with a handle! I for one liked the difference.

The island has been populated for thousands of years and there are Iron and Bronze Age sites dotted around the island. On the northeast side of the island next to Longis Bay is the best preserved small Roman fort in Britain, but even this treasure bears the scars of the German occupation during the Second World War. Overlooking our anchorage in Braye Harbour, the massive fortifications of Fort Albert, and the remains of the arsenal and harbour gun batteries left behind by the Germans dominated the skyline. Longis Bay mentioned above, features a huge concrete anti-tank wall that curves around behind the golden sand of the beach like a giant parenthesis.

   In the distance the still imposing tower of the German fire direction post stood sentinel, like an alien spaceship that's landed on the highest part of the island. Everywhere we turned we saw concrete emplacements for guns and searchlights. Many of them were unfenced and invited exploration. As we descended into the gloomy tunnels and alcoves, the echoes we heard could have been those of the young German soldiers sent to occupy and defend the island.

   It's not only the Germans that have impacted the landscape. The fort that overlooks the harbour wasn't built by the Germans, it was just one of 18 forts and batteries the Victorians built in the 1840s and 50s when, fearing war with the French, they turned Alderney into a fortress island and Naval base.

   But by the time they had finished the work the world had moved on, and iron-built battleships made them all redundant. Some of these forts are now derelict, some seem almost intact, some have been converted into little castles for millionaires to hide away in. On such a small island there's no escaping these colossal stone buildings constructed from blocks of the very granite that make the island, something to which the many disused quarries lay testament.

   One day, we explored the second largest fort on the island, Fort Tourgis. It was incredible to walk through the stone-arched gateway into a vast overgrown courtyard surrounded by the hollow windows and doors of countless rooms.

   There's one Victorian construction here that's far from redundant though, and it's the half mile long breakwater that allows Braye Harbour to exist.

   I mentioned it before.

   Even with its gift of welcome shelter from the prevailing winds of the west and northwest, anything further north or east can open the moorings and anchorage to some uncomfortable conditions, apparently the Germans wanted to extend it to give full shelter but never did. I think that's a good thing. If they'd done it, there'd probably have built a marina development and everything that goes with it by now, and the 'so different' tagline wouldn't be as true. Without Braye Harbour, Alderney would most likely be unpopulated. The small airport can bring people and light cargo, but anything of substance has to come by sea from mainland UK, via the weekly ferry 'Valiant' and offloaded in Braye.

On the mainland we take it all for granted, but you don't order from Amazon and get it next day on Alderney. Some online stores won't deliver there at all. Cars, food, gas, fuel, building materials, you name it, everything comes aboard the 'Valiant' and, as a local said to me one day, "if that big green crane on the docks breaks down we're buggered".

There's a glaring paradox on this island though, this insignificant piece of land so abused by man over the centuries also contains countless natural wonders. Blonde Hedgehogs, almost 2% of the world's population of Gannets, there are Puffins, rare butterflies and wild plants, not to mention a host of land and seabirds. The beautiful and unusual birdsong was one of the first things we noticed as we walked around the island. The senses come alive in other ways as well. The scent of wild garlic and perfumed dog roses was a constant as we walked.

The year 2014 marked the 70th anniversary of the population's return to the island after being evacuated to Weymouth in 1940. During the occupation thousands of workers were imported from all over Europe to work on the defences, they were housed in 4 concentration camps and there's a memorial on a hill just up from the harbour. The plaques are in French, Polish, Russian, Hebrew and Spanish among others, and it's sobering to think of the hardships they endured.

The lives of today's residents are far removed from those lived in those dark days, yet in some respects the way of life there is still as it was decades ago, I didn't see anyone use a key for front doors or lock their cars, and I suspected that the two policemen on the island (driving a car with the registration AY 999) weren't particularly busy. Unsurprisingly everyone seemed to know everyone else, but unlike other small communities I've visited they are friendly and very hospitable to strangers. This openness seems to reach even the governing Committee of the Island, as unlike the other Channel Islands there are no over zealous restrictions on buying property and residency.

There was an Arts Festival going on when we arrived. In St Anne, there was music in the streets and a big open air book fair we spent a good while browsing round. At lunchtime the following day we sat and listened to a live band on the quayside whilst eating excellent 'street food' paella. I figured it was a taste of things to come.

Jake was born and bred on Alderney. His lifestyle seemed idyllic. As I've already mentioned, he was working for a little business called Mainbrace. They had a small chandlery on the quayside of the inner harbour and also ran the water taxi that ferried people ashore from the moorings. During the summer he spent most of his time in the harbour, he did shifts on the taxi and worked in the shop.

When he wasn't at work, he was aboard his little Tiki 26 'A Roamer'. Tied to a mooring buoy, 'A Roamer' was the place he loved to be.

He and a few friends had started a video channel called 'Barefoot Boat Bums'. It was a perfect description for his lifestyle. He spent more time in or on the water than on land. I became convinced he was part fish. I'll provide more evidence for that later.

The longer we spent on the island, the easier it was to see where he got it from. We met his grandad in the sailing club. He had a beautiful CSY-44 called 'Ragtime' moored in Braye. He'd sailed the world in her and was just about to set off on a long cruise down the French canals. Jake's mom had a fast RIB she used as most of us would use a car. Weather permitting, she'd use it to pop across to Guernsey or France to do some shopping. Jakes mom and dad had built 'A Roamer' many years before. That's why he loved her some much, he'd grown up with her.

    We couldn't miss the opportunity to get our two Wharram boats rafted up together. So one afternoon we dropped 'Gleda' off her mooring buoy and moved a few hundred yards closer into Braye Beach and anchored. Then Jake brought 'A Roamer' round and tied up alongside. He'd invited his friends Ben and Helen plus a few others to join us. We sat around, chatted, drank and generally had a splendid time. It was fun. A proper Barefoot Boat Bums get together.

    The Alderney sailing club sits just above the harbour. It has a patio with amazing views across The Swinge and over to Burghou Island. It has excellent beer, and a great social atmosphere. We spent a few evenings there meeting folks and enjoying ourselves. There were decent showers and a laundrette with what Gail thought were the slowest washing machines she'd ever used. I figured they just worked at the same pace as the entire island.

    On days when the rain held off, Gail and I walked all over the island. We walked over to the east side and walked on cliff tops looking over the Race to France. We walked on shell covered beaches with crystal clear rock pools. We explored old German bunkers and gun emplacements. We drooled over some fabulous homes. One in particular caught my eye. It was one of the old Victorian forts built like a little castle. It even had a moat and drawbridge. I'm not big on expensive houses, but if I were to live anywhere, a place like that would do nicely.

    After a few days of exploring and recovering from our long passage, my thoughts started turning to the next leg of our adventure. Jake was ready anytime we were. It was all down to the weather. And surprise surprise it wasn't helping.

It was clear from the forecasts we wouldn't be going anywhere for at least a week. The winds blew fresh to strong most days, and it felt cold.

31st May 2015: This is ridiculous. It's been howling all day. It's 10 °C in the cabin. My feet feel like ice. We've not been off the boat all day. The forecast predicts that we've got at least two more days of this, and it's June tomorrow. How much longer!!

1st June 2015: It's just past 8pm, and we're in bed. The wind is rising, and the rain is just starting. The forecast says that until lunchtime tomorrow we're in for winds anything up to Force 9. So, here we are, hunkered down, all hatches battened, mooring lines doubled and fingers crossed.

2nd June: Well, it wasn't a peaceful night. I recorded a 40 knot gust at 4am and the wind didn't start easing until this afternoon. I photographed some spectacular seas coming over the breakwater. The boats on the mooring trots nearest the wall were getting dumped on now and again. I'm mighty glad to be inside. We spent most of the day in bed.

The following day dawned sunny and calm. The storm had broken and at last the forecast looked good. There was a bit of sloppy residual swell rolling into the harbour, but it soon calmed down.

I called Jake on the VHF. I told him to get sorted and to get his kit onboard. Gail and I spent the day on errands. Washing, shopping, fuel, water, stocking up on duty free. That night we went up to the sailing club for a farewell supper. A couple of pints and fish and chips were shared with new friends. The perfect end to a perfect stay.

Alderney had been amazing. But now it was time to move on. To head south. To chase that elusive sun.

FRANCE

DOWN CHANNEL

The following morning we made our last preparations to leave. The destination was L'Aber Benoit on the northwest tip of Brittany. In effect, that marked the corner before we turned properly south. I'd chosen it over the more popular and therefore more crowded and expensive harbour at L'Aber Wrach.

It was likely to be a challenging sail. L'Aber Benoit lay about 140 nmi away, to the southwest of Alderney. Our course took us straight down The Swinge between Alderney and Burghou, then just to the north of Guernsey, before heading out directly across the large open mouth of the Gulf of Saint-Malo. The Gulf extends from the island of Bréhat (west) to the peninsula of Cotentin of Normandy (east). It is 60 miles (ca. 97 km) wide from east to west and 20 miles (ca. 32 km) long from south to north. The Golfe includes the bays of Saint-Brieuc and Mont-Saint-Michel, site of the rocky islet of Le Mont-Saint-Michel, which is famous for its medieval walls and towers and its ancient abbey. I've mentioned the tides in this part of the world before. At the Gulf's principal port, Saint-Malo, the tidal range is 7-8 metres (ca. 26 ft normally, and as much as 15 metres (49 feet) at spring tides). We'd not be going anywhere near these ports. But we were leaving the night after a full moon. The height of springs. There'd still be a lot of water moving under us. Just how much became obvious later in the trip.

For those that don't know, I should quickly explain something about tides. 'Spring' tides occur when the sun, moon and earth all line up. So, when there's a new or full moon. This happens twice a month, and that's when the highest (and lowest) tides occur. It has nothing to do with the time of year. 'Neap' tides are the tides that occur during the first and third quarter moon, when the moon appears half full. During neaps the tidal range is far less, i.e. higher lows and lower highs!

As always, our departure time depended on the tides, once out of Braye Harbour we needed to turn SW and down through The Swinge, the tidal race running down the West side of Alderney. With a tidal stream of 6/8 knots, it's another obstacle a sailboat can't fight. The forecast for the next 24 hours suggested we'd get easterly winds of force 4 or 5 initially, but that they'd then veer to the west. After that, things became more uncertain. Variable 3-4 was the best they could offer.

On Thursday morning, with Jake and his kit aboard, we dropped off the mooring after an early lunch and motored out past the breakwater. Alderney had been amazing. We'd made new friends, explored the place thoroughly and grown fond of it.

The only downer had been the weather. I kept saying it. Let's get south. If the sun won't come to us, we'd better go find it.

The first hours of the trip were fantastic, The Swinge was kind, the sun shone and with a fair tide and a fair wind we sailed along nicely. By 14:50 the silhouette of Alderney had disappeared astern, and we could see Guernsey, Sark and Herm off our port bow, those too soon faded though and once again we sailed along with a 360° horizon. Jake and I had a play with 'Lewis' the self-steering and after a while, we got him helming for nearly an hour as we ran downwind with the main and foresails goose-winged. Now and again though, he'd lose the plot, and we'd have to take control, but it was an encouraging start.

As we headed out across the Gulf our excellent progress continued. There wasn't much to see. A few fishing boats and that was about it. It made such a difference having another pair of hands aboard. Gail's confidence was growing, but she was reluctant to get too involved with sailing the boat just yet. That was fine by me. I was just happy she'd been brave enough to come along. I'd told her she needn't worry about anything. That's why Jake was with us. We'd sail the boat. She could just sit back and enjoy.

After a delicious evening meal of pre-cooked chilli, Gail retired below to her bunk whilst Jake and I stood 2-hour watches overnight. As night fell, we'd all but crossed the Golfe and were approaching Les Sept Isles (The Seven Islands). This little group of small rocky islands are uninhabited except for huge colonies of seabirds. We'd be passing about 5 mmi to the northwest of them, and they'd be impossible to see in the dark. But as we closed the Brittany coast again, we could pick out the lights on shore. The lighthouse on the Isle-de-Bréhat loomed up over the horizon. In these days of electronic navigation it's easy to think lighthouses like these serve no actual purpose. But they do something no electronic navigation aid can ever do. They touch the soul. Ask any sailor who's been at sea in a small boat on an inky night off a treacherous coast. That sweeping, regular, reliable beam of light provides comfort and a visible reference in an otherwise black world. I'll never tire of watching them. That said, I nearly tired of watching this one.

I was on watch at dawn as the lighthouse off Les Sept Isles morphed out of the distant milky horizon, by which time the light wind was bang on the nose, forcing me to tack back and forth across our rhumb line course. By the time Jake came on watch I felt thoroughly pissed off, not to say totally befuddled. With the distant lighthouse the only point of reference I knew the direction of our two windward tacks was OK, but the plotter kept showing us going the other direction, back towards Alderney at 2 knots. I even went below to check the other plotter, convinced there was something wrong with Jake's little Garmin we'd fitted in the pod. When the main plotter gave me the same info, I just couldn't compute it, until Jake realised what was happening.

"We're going backwards," he said.

With a resounding clang, the penny finally dropped. Here we were, sitting off one of the major headlands of Brittany. With the spring tide, millions of gallons of water are rushing in from the Atlantic to fill the Golfe de St Malo, and float thousands of boats 50 feet (ca. 15 m) higher than they been floating just a few hours before.

I'd made a rookie error thinking we were far enough offshore that it didn't matter. I was wrong.

Now I knew why things felt odd. The tide flowing against us had created the illusion of forward motion. The strange ripples and eddies in the water should have been enough to tell me what was happening. But fatigue and darkness had blinded me. No wonder that lighthouse on Isle-de-Bréhat was still so visible. My eyes were telling me we were sailing along in one direction, but we were actually moving the opposite way, pushed by a powerful foul tide. The GPS was telling the truth; we were indeed going backwards. I'd been tacking back and forth for hours, and we were now 15 miles (ca. 24 km) further back than when I'd started. I like to think I'd have solved the puzzle myself at some point, but all credit to Jake. With the benefit of 2 hours sleep and a younger brain, he got there first.

Well, we fought for a while longer but when Gail got up

expecting to see L'Aber Benoit on the bows, I had to admit that we were still a long, long way off.

Ultimately, we admitted defeat and dropped the engines; we motored for 6 or 7 hours, dead on our course and straight into the wind. I felt bad, I should have factored in the tide, I should have planned better, I should have had a plan 'B'. At that point though, there was only one thing to do, and we did it.

By mid-afternoon we were navigating the tricky channel leading into the river and L'Aber Benoit. We'd travelled 139.45 nmi in 28 hours. We'd averaged 4.67 knots with a maximum speed of 10.4. Given we'd spent a few hours going backwards, I thought that was OK!

L'ABER BENOIT

We motored up the river and picked up a mooring just off Stellach quay, in a peaceful wooded valley just after 17:00 Friday. After something to eat, we all slept the sleep of the dead until the following morning.

I'd picked up the buoy because, despite what the pilot book said, I couldn't see anywhere I was happy to anchor. I figured if anyone came along and complained, we'd just move.

I'm always a little wary of mooring buoys. When you arrive in a harbour, they look like an easy option. Just motor up close, grab the little pickup buoy, haul in the line and tie it to the boat. Job done. Once secure the boat doesn't swing far and you can just untie and leave quickly and easily. That's got to be a far better choice than finding a space, dropping the anchor, hoping it holds. Then before you leave, you have to haul up all that chain, clean the mud off the hook etc. That's not to mention having to keep an anchor watch if the wind gets up. But here's the thing. Pick up a mooring buoy and you've delegated the security of you and your boat to a third party. You trust that the buoy is securely attached to something heavy on the seabed. You trust that someone has maintained it. You trust it's positioned away from hazards.

I'd checked the mooring I'd chosen as best I could. The buoy itself looked relatively new. So did the rope and chain I could see. It seemed fine.

The pilot book warned that L'Aber Benoit was very very quiet, even listing the many facilities the place lacked. It was no surprise, and just what we needed to recover from our long passage. I'd fuelled the boat fully before leaving Alderney, and although we'd knocked a sizeable hole in our reserves, I figured we'd got plenty for the next leg south, making any expeditions for more unnecessary. Out of the cool breeze the day was warm, and so we just chilled out and relaxed, taking in our beautiful surroundings. Just after lunch as the spring tide ebbed away fast, we realised that a huge unmarked oyster farm was appearing out of the water not far astern of us. Although the pilot mentioned them, no specific locations were given, and neither were they marked on the charts. I thanked the Universe I'd decided we'd pick up a mooring rather than anchor, because the spot I'd have chosen would have been right on top of them.

However, as the tide ebbed further, 'Gleda' listed to starboard more and more, and soon, through the clear water, we could see that the port keel was sitting nicely on top of some solid-looking rocks. For the next few hours we pondered the logic of laying mooring trots over underwater rocks, and how embarrassing the situation would have been had we been sailing a deep-keeled monohull rather than a shallow draught catamaran. Knowing that the strong flood tide would soon return with the wind behind it, and in order for 'Gleda' not to be pushed further aground as she floated, I got a long warp flaked down in the dinghy and ran it out to another mooring buoy downstream from the starboard quarter. With this line pulled taut we could hold 'Gleda' in position as she re-floated, and then warp her up to the more distant mooring to avoid a repetition. The plan worked well and with no damage done. But be warned, if you ever find yourself in L'Aber Benoit I'd suggest you go in at low water so you can see what's what!

We spent two days in the river. For the first time it felt as if we were 'properly' abroad. Alderney had been a transition. Everyone spoke English, same currency, same food, same drink.

Now we were most definitely in France.

Apart from polite greetings with a few passing dinghies we spoke to no one, no harbour master, no customs, nothing, there were no fees to pay. We were flying a French courtesy flag, but despite not being in the country officially, no one seemed to care.

'Gleda' had worked well on the passage down from Alderney. We'd only had two issues. First, the sheet winch had come apart a few hours before we arrived. We'd just tacked, and I was hauling in the sheet when the entire body of the winch jumped off its spindle and onto the deck. Miraculously, none of the bearings went overboard. When I looked at it in daylight, I could see the cause. The nylon retaining key had worn through. Luckily, I had a complete spare winch aboard, so I just changed the whole thing. I also replaced the toilet fan. We had a composting toilet in the starboard forward compartment. It needed a small fan to pull air through the waste container. The fan vented out onto the foredeck, and I'd fitted what I thought was a waterproof ventilation cover. I now knew it wasn't. We'd taken a sloppy wave over the bow and it had let water through and drowned the fan. It was an easy fix. We also replaced the lines on the self-steering. Whilst we'd had it working for a few hours, there was some friction in the system and the line had stretched slightly. Again, an easy fix.

With us rested up and all maintenance done, we could relax. We rowed ashore to the quay at Stellach and had a wander round. It was pretty and peaceful. Not a bar, not a shop, few people around. We stretched our legs, then headed back to the boat. The sun shone, and it was a pleasant walk. But there was still a chilly wind blowing. It still didn't feel like summer. It mattered not; I needed to sit down at the nav station. There was some serious passage planning to do.

Our next challenge was to complete a 52 nmi leg down to Sainte-Evette in southern Brittany. St-Evette looked to be the perfect departure point for our Bay of Biscay crossing. But to get there we had to navigate some of the most treacherous and notorious waters in the world.

I probably spent too much time reading the Pilot books. These books always seem to focus on the worst aspects of the places they cover. I guess it's understandable. Their primary purpose is to make folks aware of potential hazards and to guide them safely to their destination. But read any Pilot book for the northwest Brittany coast and you'll be reading about dragons and monsters, ship-eating seas and saw-toothed rocks.

The route to Sainte-Evette required that we head west for a short distance, before turning south to pass between Le Conquet on the mainland and the Islands of Ushant (Ouessant in French). This narrow stretch of water is known as the Chenal du Four. Once through there we'd cross the wide open bay to the west of Brest, and then into another narrow gap known as the Raz de Sein between the Île de Sein and Pointe du Raz on the coast. Both narrow passages are notoriously rough with even moderate winds against the tides.

I'd spent hours pouring over the tide graphs, charts and pilot book. I'd miscalculated the tides on the passage from Alderney. That had caused minor inconvenience. Getting them wrong now would be downright dangerous. To get this passage completed safely, the weather had to be right, and the tides had to be right. By my calculations, we'd have that combination if we left at 07:00 the next morning.

The waypoints and courses were all plotted. We were ready.

We'd been cursing the wintry north wind for days. Now I wanted it to stay awhile. Now I wanted it to blow us south.

FLYING SOUTH

Our passage plan meant that our courses boxed the compass, and with a F5/6 NE blowing I knew that for some time at least we'd be in for a bumpy ride. As is so often the case, passage making means taking a bit of pain to enjoy a lot of gain, and so it was here. As I've already mentioned, our route took us through the Chenal du Four inside the Isle of Ouessant, down past the entrance to the Rade de Brest, on through the narrow Raz de Sein and then a further 10 nmi round the corner to Sainte-Evette. Strict timings and sailing make poor bedfellows, but on this leg there was no choice. Either we got them right or we'd have to turn round and beat back to our departure point.

The reason for the strict timetable was simple. As the tide ebbs and flows, huge amounts of water get squeezed through the narrow gaps between mainland France and the outlying islands, not only does this create tidal streams running at anything up to 11 knots, but the shoaling seabed throws up eddies and overfalls that can build large confused and breaking seas. This can be the case even with wind and tide running together, but put them against each other, and they can ruin your day. My plan was to time our trip to ride this tidal conveyor belt south, with the northeast wind pushing us from behind. We had a 5.5-hour window of fair tide to cover around 35 mmi of potential danger, and although I'd pre-planned some escape routes, I didn't want to put them to the test.

Our first major waypoint lay abeam of Le Four lighthouse at the entrance to the Chcnal du Four. We needed to be there by slack water at 10:00 to be in the optimum position for jumping on that conveyor south. First, we had some 15 nmi to cover from our mooring in L'Aber Benoit, and so we were up at the crack of dawn. By 07:00 we were motoring down river towards the entrance. I knew that we'd be in for a bit of a bashing as we made our way out; the wind was almost on the nose and as the pilot book had warned, the NE direction was pushing bigger and bigger swells into the entrance. We had no choice but to take it as we motored into them at 4 knots, following a zig-zag track from buoy to buoy through the narrow channel. Soon though we could turn to port in slightly clearer water, and with the sails up and engines raised we picked up speed. We covered the distance to Le Four in half the time I'd expected as 'Gleda' regularly hit double digit speeds, it was an adrenaline pumping downhill blast, but a little too exciting sometimes, particularly for Gail and there were a few occasions when I too thought things might be getting a bit out of hand. Jake was loving it though as he switched between sail trimming and filming video. I just hung onto the wheel and tried to steer a steady course, something I found increasingly hard as 'Gleda' started surfing down the swells.

The conditions meant a lot of water pressure on the rudders. I noticed that the boat didn't seem to respond to my steering input as well as I thought she should. I realised shortly afterwards that the steering drum behind the wheel was slipping on the shaft, so that the rudders weren't always doing what the wheel was asking them to do. There were a few occasions when I had to get Jake to pull on the tiller bar to stop us broaching.

Later, in Sainte-Evette, I solved the problem by drilling right through the steering drum and shaft and bolting everything together.

Soon we were passing over shallower areas of water that threw up some confused seas, and every now and again the boat would drop into a bit of a hole and then come up like a dog shaking itself after getting wet. Water came sluicing up over the foredecks and several times got forced upwards between the aft side of the centre beam and the forward side of the engine boxes. This caused a sheet of water to push up the battery box lids like the opening sluices of a canal lock gate. On one occasion this happened as Jake was sitting alongside the pod on the port side filming on his little Go-Pro. We dropped into a trough, water lifted the starboard side battery box lid, then the port side, and immediately afterwards the forward beam slammed into a wave and sent a huge gopher over the entire deck. The deckpod screen protected Gail and me, but Jake copped a face full. We all had a good laugh about that one.

Not long afterwards though, I put my sensible head on (yes; I have one). I realised that if we continued as we were, then either something would break or the batteries would get drowned; I realised we ought to slow the boat down by reefing. A quick check of the navigation however showed us to be rapidly approaching our Le Four waypoint, after which we could again turn to port, and so bring the wind and waves more over the quarter. We'd arrived over an hour ahead of slack water despite sailing into a foul tide for an hour, but with the flood easing I had no qualms about pushing on. Within the hour, the stream would turn, and we'd be away.

In some respects the next 5 hours were a bit of an anti-climax, we hit all our waypoints early or on the button; we creamed along at near double digit speeds most of the time, and what a change it made to see the landmarks moving past at speed rather than staying in view for hour after hour. We went through some areas of disturbed water but nothing compared to what had gone before. Now and again the wind would gust up near to F7 and 'Gleda' would take off. At the end of the trip, my GPS showed a maximum speed of 15.48 knots over the ground. The other little GPS plotter showed a maximum of 17.6 knots. I don't know which was right. Of one thing I'm certain though, our floating home had never moved faster.

In between the gusts there was plenty of time to enjoy the

spectacular sights of this part of the Brittany coast. They describe the Isle of Ouessant in the pilot book looking as a mighty ship hull down on the horizon, and so it does. There are many massive stone lighthouses along the way, sat on dark forbidding rocks. Looking closely at areas of seemingly clear water, we could see points of rock sticking up with white foaming water swirling about their bases. If you've ever seen one of those enormous photo posters of a lighthouse being enveloped by gigantic waves, the chances are they took it on this part of the Brittany coast, I can't imagine being anywhere near the place when a winter storm sweeps in.

By 11:00 we were sliding past La Fourmi buoy which marked the exit of the Chanel du Four, and the land dropped away to port as we crossed the enormous bay leading to the Rade de Brest. If you've read my first book 'A Foolish Voyage' you may recall that Brest is where my story ended. It was there that I'd had to sell 'Mor Gwas' and return to England. As I stared across the water I couldn't help wondering if she was still there somewhere, giving pleasure to some new owner, or if she'd long since been broken up. These waters held some harsh memories for me. When I'd been working on the passage plan, I'd realised that our destination, Sainte-Evette, lay less than 15 miles (ca. 24 km) from Le Gulivenec. That's where the fishing boat L'Zephir bought me ashore after abandoning 'Mor Gwas' in Biscay.

So much had changed since then, but the sea never changes. I'm writing this chapter at the nav desk aboard 'Gleda'. Just above my head, screwed to the aft bulkhead, sits the hand-carved name-board I unscrewed from 'Mor Gwas's' washboard in July 1984. I'll never forget that lovely little boat. She looked after me to the end, and leaving her was one of the hardest things I've ever had to do.

As I continued to gaze towards Brest, my eyes watered. A wave of sadness swept over me, just as the waves had swept over

'Gleda's' decks not long before. But just as my boat had risen, so had I. Those days with 'Mor Gwas' had made me the person I was, the guy that built a boat and found a way back to the sea, the guy that was doing it right this time.

Wow, sorry, that got heavy there for a while but I needed to get that off my chest. Now, where were we?

Right, OK, next up was the Raz de Sein. Once again we were aiming for what seemed a ridiculously narrow gap, passing just to starboard of the squat solid La Plate lighthouse. At less than a mile wide and not much more in length, the Raz is a squeeze point but one we couldn't avoid, it is the gateway to The South. Once again it was a little anticlimactic, although we could see the water bubbling and churning away close to our bows. We were through within 30 minutes and once again turning to port to beat against the same wind we'd already motored against, run and reached with. The gusts had picked up and with 'Gleda' pointing better than she'd ever done we could just lay our course straight to the approach waypoint off Audierne.

By 15:30 the engines were off, and we were secured to a visitor mooring feeling extremely satisfied with ourselves. We'd done it, we'd passed another big test, and now La Coruña and Spain beckoned.

Passage Distance: 54.75 nmi
Passage Time: 8hr 18min
Average Speed: 6.58 knots
Max Speed: 16 knots

SAINTE-EVETTE AND AUDIERNE

To be honest, our first impressions of Sainte-Evette weren't that good. We rowed ashore that evening anticipating showers and something to eat. But the showers were locked, and there were no restaurants or shops in sight. We had to make do with a cold beer in the solitary little bar on the quay. The northeast wind continued to blow at F5/6 for the next three days. It felt chilly and there were frequent showers. It was more than a little disappointing. We'd left Alderney with the clear aim of chasing the sunshine south, covered many miles and worked bloody hard. It was now the second week in June. We were now in southern Brittany. It didn't seem fair. The following day Jake ventured ashore to explore. Gail and I stayed aboard. He'd had a tough time getting onto the beach because of the wind. We weren't so enthusiastic about a wet ride in the dinghy.

The weather might have been a negative, but there were some positives. We were safely moored to a nice new buoy. They had laid the mooring field out in a pretty sheltered bay protected by a long breakwater. It was here that the Isle de Sein ferry, 'Penn ar Bed' docked two or three times a day. As a bonus, there were no mooring charges until July.

We spent a week in Sainte-Evette. The weather improved eventually. We got ashore and spent a morning walking round the port of Audierne and had breakfast at a pavement café. Coffee, pain au chocolate, pain, confiture. There was a big open air market. Stalls crammed with fresh vegetables, crabs, lobsters, fish, meats, pâté, breads, charcuterie, the place was authentically French.

That evening we ate on deck. After we'd finished eating, Jake hauled up a bucket of seawater to wash the dishes as usual. The Tiki 38 has a handy little deck hatch perfect for this chore. Using seawater for rinsing off saves precious freshwater when we're at sea. Jake swilled everything off, then poured the bucket of dirty water back into the sea. Gail was down below heating some water when Jake stuck his head down the hatch to pass down the plates and sheepishly asked. "Gail, did I have the forks as well?". To this day three items of Gail's expensive WMF brand cutlery lie on the seabed just off Sainte-Evette. And for the rest of the trip we regularly reminded Jake of his error.

We frequented the little bar on the quay at Sainte-Evette

periodically. It served excellent coffee and had decent Wi-Fi. I needed the latter to check the weather. The passage down from L'Aber Benoit had demanded my attention. But this next one demanded more. Until this point, I'd always had an escape plan. If the weather had changed or I'd made a mistake, we could have bailed out. But now we had some 350 miles (ca. 563 km) of open sea in front of us. And not just any old bit of open sea. The Bay of Biscay, with its well-earned reputation for the most ferocious of storms. Feared by sailors throughout history. Sure, gales are much less prevalent in summer, but not unknown even in June & July.

We'd be out there for at least 3-4 days with nowhere to run. I knew from bitter experience what getting it wrong meant. I couldn't afford to make the same mistake again.

We'd arrived on Monday, and by Wednesday the weather had settled. I kept watching, and it kept improving. I decided Sunday was the day.

We needed fuel, and enquiries at the café revealed that the petrol station was several kilometres away. The owner drove me there and back. The first of many times we were to experience the kindness of strangers.

The next day we got a taxi up to the big Carrefour supermarket and did a major provisioning shop.

We were ready.

Jake and Gail were excited. So was I. But excitement wasn't all I felt. Fear and self-doubt still lurked within me.

There's an old African proverb that goes something like this;
"If you escaped the lion's den, why go back for your hat?".

But I wasn't going back for my hat. I was going back for something far more valuable. I was going back to rescue myself, and I was going back for 'Mor Gwas'.

6

BISCAY

DAY ONE — SUNDAY 14TH JUNE

We dropped off the mooring and left Sainte-Evette at 07:50. The forecast predicted predominantly northerly winds of light to moderate strength for the next few days at least.

That suited me perfectly. We were in no hurry. This leg was all about safety and enjoyment.

The engines stayed on only until we'd cleared the mooring field. We soon had the sails up and were heading south at a leisurely 2-3 knots. The sun rose higher in the sky. It warmed up. Our 4th crew member 'Lewis' the wind vane, was steering well. We had a breakfast of coffee and croissants and gazed around as we glided across the glassy Atlantic swells.

We were a happy crew.

By mid-morning the Brittany coast had disappeared astern. The wind picked up slightly and our speed increased to nearly 6 knots.

Another small yacht had departed Sainte-Evette at the same time as us but had changed course soon afterwards, back towards shore. Since then, we'd seen no other vessels. It stayed that way until mid-afternoon when we crossed paths with several cargo ships. I figured they were headed for La Rochelle, which now lay on our beam.

It was easy to stay out of their way.

'Gleda' was performing brilliantly. 'Lewis' continued to keep us on course. I'd tweaked his settings a few times, but that was all.

We ate lunch, we relaxed, we ate supper. It was wonderful to be properly offshore. After the stress of coastal passages through treacherous waters, this was easy. We had a single course to follow, and all we needed to do was to keep a lookout. That was it.

I'd decided that Jake and I would work 3-hour watches from 21:00 until 09:00, with the daytime hours left flexible. Gail would take responsibility for keeping us fed and watered during the day. She'd be free to sleep all night.

I took the first watch. Gail stayed with me for an hour before retiring. As darkness fell, we headed into our first night at sea since the channel crossing. There were no secrets this time. Gail knew we'd be out here for a while. It was just us and the sea. I asked Gail if she was OK. She said yes and smiled. I hugged her, and we kissed. It still felt surreal. Yet here we both were. Doing what many, including ourselves, had once thought impossible. The sun was setting on a spectacular red horizon. It was a special moment.

Once darkness had fallen and Gail had gone below, I settled into my watch. With 'Lewis' steering, there wasn't much to do. The wind stayed fair, the sails stayed filled. A little later I spotted the lights of a fishing boat astern and a yacht off to our port side. The yacht seemed to be on a parallel track to us, but she soon disappeared astern. Just before midnight three large ships crossed our path. I'd been watching them on AIS for a while. They were several miles in front of us though and of no concern.

From 08:00 to midnight we'd covered 95 nmi. It had been the perfect start.

Jake woke just before his watch and I didn't waste any time leaving him to it.

I crashed out in the deckpod berth. It was close to the wheel so that in any emergency I could be awake and on scene immediately without disturbing Gail. It'd been a long day, but sleep was elusive for a while. This was the first time I'd been able to fully relax while the boat was underway. It felt odd lying there with the ocean swooshing past just a few feet under my bunk. The wheel creaked as 'Lewis' made minor course corrections. The mainsheet blocks clicked and clacked on their fixings. The red compass light glowed just above my head. I could see we were on course. All seemed well. I trusted Jake, and I knew he'd call me if needed. My eyes closed, and I drifted off.

DAY TWO — MONDAY 15TH JUNE

I slept soundly until about 01:00 when Jake shook me awake like a kid brother on Christmas morning. "Everything's OK" he said, "But you've got to see this". Still half asleep, I followed him up onto the foredeck. I rubbed my eyes as I looked in the direction of his pointing finger. Then rubbed them again as I tried to figure out if I was still asleep and dreaming. Another explanation entered my sleep addled brain. I must have taken too many Stugeron seasickness pills and was tripping. It seemed the only logical explanation for the psychedelic vision in front of me.

The water between 'Gleda's' bows was being criss-crossed with bright luminous green dolphins. They streaked past, cutting through the water, leaving bright glowing trails of luminescence fizzing behind them. For 50 to 100 metres, all around the boat, the water glowed. As I watched, a single large dolphin started coming in at 90° to the bow. Looking for all the world like the torpedos you see in the old war films, it was incredible. I knew Gail had to see this. I dashed below, calling her to wake up. The urgency in my voice panicked her at first. She thought we must be sinking. I told her everything was fine, helped her into her jacket and pulled her up the companionway onto the deck. She, too, was still half asleep as she lay down with her head over the forward beam.

I watched the puzzlement in her face as she too tried to process what she was seeing. The three of us lay there for what seemed like hours, mesmerised by this magical spectacle. Oohing and aahing like we were watching fireworks on November 5th.

We got a repeat performance the following night. It was just as captivating.

All three of us will take the memory of those glow in the dark dolphins to our graves.

For those that don't know, this bio-luminescence is caused by algae suspended in the water. Much like fireflies flitting through the air, the algae (of a wide variety of species) emit a glow whenever they are disturbed.

During the voyage Jake captured some incredible daytime footage of our dolphin visitations. But even his sophisticated equipment couldn't capture the nighttime show. Talking about it afterwards, we decided that was the best thing. There's no way any video could do it justice anyway. And somehow it seems fitting. Fitting that only those who pay the price of admission to the deep waters of Biscay get to experience the magic.

I wasn't at all annoyed at losing some valuable sleep. The rest of Jakes watch was uneventful.

Jake woke me again at 03:00 with a welcome cup of coffee.

He was sleeping in the port forward cabin, and so I was soon alone in the pod.

The glow in the dark dolphins returned around 04:00. I left Jake and Gail sleeping. This was only day two. Sleep is important. I didn't want us all suffering from fatigue just yet. But truth be told, I wanted to be alone. I sat on the foredeck and emotion rolled over me. It's doing so again as I write. The enormity of my interminable journey finally hit home.

This was what I'd dreamed of when I left Falmouth on 'Mor Gwas'. Now here I was. On the open ocean. On a beautiful boat I'd created with my own two hands. There were stars in the sky above my head. There were luminous green dolphins playing around the bows. I was sailing south towards the sun. The pre-dawn hours at sea can be chilly, but I was glowing warm inside. Finally, I could be satisfied. Finally, I could be proud.

During the night the wind had shifted by a few degrees, and we'd gone slightly off course. When Jake was awake, I adjusted 'Lewis' before putting my head down again. Jake wrote in the log that the dolphins returned around dawn. By the time I woke just after 08:00 the sun was shining and Gail was making breakfast.

During the morning, the wind died away, and it stayed light all day.

We covered only 15 nmi between 09:00 and 15:00. By that time Sainte-Evette lay 163 nmi astern. Cabo Ortegal, our first Spanish landfall, 128 nmi ahead. With the French coast over 100 miles (ca. 161 km) away to the east and America thousands of miles away to the west, we were truly on the open ocean. We were also in deep water. Literally. It's daunting to notice that on the chart the centre of the Bay of Biscay bears the words 'Abyssal Plain' and an abyss it is, with the water nearly 6000 metres deep in places.

Think about that for a second. 6000 metres is 6 kilometres, (c.a. 3.7 miles). I've often thought a small boat at sea is similar to a spacecraft. They are both survival capsules for humans travelling through an alien environment. Apart from the dolphins, we'd seen no evidence of life in the surrounding sea. Yet below our tiny boat there was a vast strange world. Teaming with life. Much of it unknown, much of it unexplored. And all just the other side of the thin wooden sides of our spaceship.

I thought it best not to share that last thought with Gail.

For me though, as I sat at the chart table, those water depths meant something else.

Biscay's shoaling seabed can have a dramatic effect on the sea when the winds blow strong. In a few days I knew we'd be closing the coast of Northern Spain. Here the depths would go from 5000 metres to less than 150 metres over a distance of only 5 miles (ca. 8 km). In a gale this sharply rising seabed forces the water upwards into large swells and steep waves. I'd picked up a weather forecast on the Navtex. It mentioned the threat of near gale force north or northeast winds around Finisterre Tuesday night into Wednesday. It was a concern, but no surprise. Biscay is Biscay. We still had some miles to do, and at this speed we might be nowhere near. I put it to the back of my mind.

As we continued to drift along slowly that morning. I caught sight of a pigeon circling the boat. After a couple of abortive landings he eventually dropped onto the forward deck and I could see some tags on his legs. I figured he must be a racing pigeon. Although seemingly in good health he gulped down some water we put out for him and later gobbled up some broken biscuits. He gradually got braver, hopping around the deck and looking down the hatches into the boat. He even hopped onto Jake's legs as he lay sunbathing.

We named him Percy. He stayed with us nearly 24 hours, spending the night huddled down in front of the deckpod, but as dawn broke the next day, I decided it was time he got on his way, not least because we'd tired of washing pigeon crap off the deck. I figured he'd had a good rest and been fed and watered. It took 10 minutes of waved arms and chasing around the decks before he finally got the message and headed off towards Spain.

Strangely, on our third or fourth day in A Coruña, as Jake and I sat in the pod, a racing pigeon suddenly fluttered down and perched on the starboard guardrails. Jake and I looked at each other, mouths open. The pigeon cocked his head and looked at us both. Then flew off. It looked like Percy. Could well have been Percy. Was he just saying thanks? We'll never know.

Not much else happened during the day. That evening Jake thought he saw a large fin and spouting water off in the distance that might have been a whale. The wind picked up for a while before I came on watch at midnight.

When I checked the log we'd covered just 60 miles (ca. 97 km) in 24 hours. I couldn't help but wonder if things would get a bit livelier sometime soon.

DAY THREE — TUESDAY 16TH JUNE

The early hours of day three were uneventful. Around 01:00 the wind dropped again, and with it our speed. A large pod of dolphins played round the boat for over an hour. It helped keep me awake. Just before Jake came on at 03:00 the wind returned. The updated forecast confirmed what I'd suspected. This was the changeover point. From now on, it would keep increasing.

As dawn broke on our third day, we could just make out the outline of the Galician mountains in the far distance. At 10:00 I spent some time on the navigation to confirm our progress. Sainte-Evette was now 233 nmi behind us. Our Spanish landfall, Cabo Ortegal, 58 nmi ahead. By 18:00 that evening we had it in sight.

Gail and Jake were excited. We raised our Spanish courtesy flag just before dark. In their heads we'd made it. I was excited too, but I knew we weren't there yet. It would be a dark, windy night. I knew that we were clearing the abyssal plain I mentioned earlier. We were still in 5000 metres of water. But in a few hours we'd be in only a few hundreds. I didn't expect that to go unnoticed. Shortly afterwards we just missed running over an orange pot marker complete with pole, float and rope. Given the depth of water we were in, it couldn't have been attached to anything. It floated away past the port hull. Soon afterwards a wooden pallet floated past the starboard hull.

Man's detritus littering the pristine sea again. The previous day we had run dead centre over an orange life ring. We'd spotted it early on and tried to catch it with the boathook, but we were moving too fast.

It's a curious phenomenon I've experienced any times before and since. I'm talking about the magnetic attraction that small boats at sea seem to have for random floating objects. I've read somewhere that from the deck of a yacht you can see about 35 square miles of water, so how is it that within that 35 square miles it's possible to almost hit three small floating objects head on?

The night was moonless and pitch black. The wind continued increasing. We were now closing the coast fast. This would be our last night at sea and it would likely be a testing one. There was no way I'd be sleeping until we arrived safely in port.

DAY FOUR — WEDNESDAY 17TH JUNE

Not long after midnight we saw the lights of a fishing fleet dead ahead. A lot of these boats use bright floodlights to attract sardines, their decks are well lit, it's hard to miss them. The problem is that from a distance all these lights completely drown out any navigation lights they may or may not be carrying, and this makes it difficult to figure out which way they're headed. It's kind of academic anyway though because they alter course constantly, and although the AIS helps not all of them have it. As we got closer, we disconnected 'Lewis' and took manual control, so we could alter course quickly if necessary. It was a sensible decision as we then spent several hours playing dodgems. On more than a few occasions I thought one of the fishing boats was deliberately trying to hit us. Every time I altered course to avoid him, he'd change direction and put us back on a collision course. It certainly kept me awake.

Now we were much closer into Cabo Ortegal I had a decision to make. The cliffs at this Cabo are some of the highest in Europe. It marks the most northerly point of Spain. The pilot book had warned that these cliffs can funnel the wind in different directions, mainly east or west, irrespective of the forecasted direction. More than that, they can produce wind strengths far higher than those offshore. I'd planned for this. If we found the winds blowing from the west, we'd head for a place called Vivero. If they blew from the east, it'd be Coruña. As it happened, it was the latter, and we changed course accordingly.

The wind continued to increase. The seas started building. We were now riding sizeable waves with foaming crests. The crests were about all we could see in the pitch black. When 'Gleda' began touching mid-double figures boat speed regularly, we dropped the jib and foresail to make things a tad more comfortable. But despite that, the F5/6 and choppy seas made for a rough ride. Even with just the mainsail up, we were still making 12 knots. Things turned even bumpier when we came abeam of Cabo Prior and turned southwest towards the Ria de La Coruña and the bright shining light sweeping out from The Tower of Hercules. This fresh course had us beam on to the seas and in the dark it wasn't much fun. Jake helmed as I continually checked the plotter. The motion had woken Gail and I could see she was frightened. I did all I could to reassure her. I knew that once we got into the lee of the land things would quieten down. So it proved. Our final approach was straightforward, and once in the lee and everything had calmed down, we dropped sails and motored towards the well lit breakwater that protects the marina. When I say well lit, I mean well lit. An incredibly bright-green LED arrow strobe flashed to point us in the right direction. As we turned around the breakwater the enormous marina complex came into view. There was a long pontoon just to starboard with two catamarans moored alongside. I wasn't going to mess about. I said we'd just drop in behind the last one in the row. Jake and Gail soon had lines and fenders ready and I bought 'Gleda' gently to rest alongside. It's a shame they couldn't have lit the pontoon as brightly as the breakwater. Jake and I jumped ashore into darkness. Within seconds, we were both sat on our arses. It wasn't because we'd been at sea for days. It was because they had covered the pontoon in a huge net to stop the seagulls roosting on it at night. The holes in the net were just the right size to take a sea-boot and snag it. Oh how we laughed.

I switched the engines off at 05:55

We'd been at sea for 70 hours. We'd covered 343.43 nmi at an average speed of 4.9 knots. We'd crossed the Bay of Biscay.

I had finally laid the ghost to rest.

A Coruña
A Coruña
○ Ares
○ Pontedeume
○ Sada
○ Cambre
○ Betanzos
○ Carral
○ Guiti

Laxe
○ Ponteceso
○ A Laracha
○ Caristanco
○ Carballo

Camariña
Camariñas ○ Muxía
○ Zas
○ Ordes
○ Frades

○ Dumbría
○ Cee
○ Fisterra
Cape Finistere

Santiago de Compostela
○ Arzúa
○ Melide
○ Pa

○ Carnota
○ Muros ○ Noia
Muros & Portosín ○ Porto do Son
○ Padrón
○ Vedra
○ Vila de Cruces
GALICIA

○ Rianxo
○ Catoira
○ A Estrada
○ Silleda
○ Lalín
○ Rodeiro
A Pobra do Caramiñal
○ Caldas de Reis
○ Forcarei
AP-53
○ Ribeira ○ Vilanova de Arousa

○ O Grove ○ Cambados
○ O Carballiño
○ Moside
AG-53

Pontevedra ○
Sanxenxo & Combarro
○ Marín
○ Ponte Caldelas
○ Avión
○ Ourense
○ Ribadavia
○ Ba
○ Buen
○ Redondela
Vigo
○ Mondariz
○ A Cañiza
North Atlantic Ocean
Ría de Vigo
○ Ponteareas
AG-31
Bayona
○ Nigrán ○ O Porriño
○ Baiona
○ Gondomar
○ Crecente
○ Celanova
○ Monção
○ Melgaço
○ Tui

7

GALICIA

A CORUÑA

We spent a full week in A Coruña and it was memorable. We'd sailed south to find the sun and at last we'd found it. I wrote in my journal *'It's been hot today. Beautifully, wonderfully hot'.*

Berthed in front of us was a lovely Broadblue catamaran called 'Friendship'. The English couple who owned her, June and Garry, lived up to the name of their boat. They were also heading to the Algarve. We were to cross paths with them a few times on the voyage south later. We became good friends during our time in Portugal and are still in touch today. It was our first opportunity to meet others who shared our dreams of the cruising lifestyle. Gail had just spent 4 days at sea with two guys. June had spent a similar amount of time with her husband, She and Gail were soon off shopping and chatting.

It was here we met another couple who also became friends. I was working on deck one morning when a fellow came walking along the pontoon up to the boat. He stopped. Looked at the boat. Looked at me, and said. "You're Neil, and this is

Gleda". His name was Ian. He and his wife Jackie were also sailing their Rival 36 'Rivalady' to the Algarve. It turned out that Ian had followed my 'Gleda Project' blog early on. When I'd stopped building to focus on my business, he figured I'd given up and didn't visit my website again. That's why he'd stopped and stared with such surprise on his face. He'd found himself looking at a boat he thought he'd never see.

We walked a lot in Coruña. It's a beautiful city. Wonderful architecture, vast plazas, shops and restaurants. There's a real buzz to the place. We splashed out and hired a car to drive the 80 or so kilometres to Santiago de Compostela. For those that don't know, Santiago de Compostela is the famous destination of the Camino de Santiago (the Way of St. James). The 'Camino' is an extensive network of ancient pilgrim routes stretching right across Europe, coming together at the tomb of St. James (Santiago) which lies in the cathedral.

The history of the Camino de Santiago goes back to the beginning of the 9th century (year 814). It would be no exaggeration to say that millions of people have made the pilgrimage over those centuries. There's no sign of the tradition dying out anytime soon. It's estimated that some 200,000 still do it every year.

I'm no pilgrim and I have no religion. But being this close to Santiago de Compostela and not visiting seemed wrong. Gail wanted to go there, and she deserved a treat.

I'll admit to being a little less than enthusiastic about visiting such a tourist trap, but I was pleasantly surprised, The old town and cathedral were spectacular, and although there were a lot of tacky souvenir shops selling tat, they blended with some more authentic shops bars and restaurants that balanced things out; we ate an enjoyable lunch in one such tapas bar. It was there we gained a long-lasting taste for 'patatas bravas'.

Whatever your religious views, I'd recommend visiting Santiago. I sat and watched some arrivals in the square in front of the cathedral. These folks had walked or cycled many miles to get there. Some were limping, most looked exhausted. But there was joy in their faces. They'd succeeded in what, for many, must have been a long-held ambition. Whatever their reasons for doing the 'Camino' they'd achieved their goal, and it had changed them.

Sitting there in Plaza de Obradoiro I realised that in some ways I'd been on my own 'Camino'. The destination had been less specific. But I'd had a path to follow, and I'd followed it. It had bought me to Santiago in a way much different from the 'peregrinos' around me. But I too had succeeded, I too had changed. And none of us would ever be the same again.

There are places in the world where centuries of human spirit seem to have soaked into the very earth on which they're built. Santiago de Compostela is one such place.

We'd originally planned to leave A Coruña early on the 24th June, but we found out that the night of the 23rd was the night of The Bonfires of San Juan, and everyone we spoke to said it was unmissable. It was a simple choice to stay on, and I'm so glad we did. As we walked through the city at 21:00 things were just beginning to get going. The roads were grid locked with traffic, every bar seemed to have a BBQ going on the street cooking sardines, thousands of people thronged about as we made our way towards the main beaches. As we walked across the promenade and looked out around the huge crescent-shaped bay, it was hard to take in what we were seeing, Every inch of the miles long beach was filled with people sitting around prepared bonfires of all shapes and sizes. Some just small pyramids of uniform sticks, others towering creations of pallets, doors and old furniture. I couldn't imagine what would happen when all these hundreds of bonfires were lit. As darkness fell and the midnight firework display drew nearer flames started appearing, and by midnight most were alight. It was an incredible spectacle, one they would not have allowed in the UK. Smoke and flames fanned by the sea breeze covered the entire beach, rising to scorch the onlookers gazing over the promenade railings. We could only bear it for a few minutes as I used my hat to shield our faces from the heat.

Gail and I headed back to the boat not long afterwards. Jake stayed until dawn.

Unsurprisingly there was no way we were leaving for any sort of passage making the following day. But to avoid paying another night in the marina, we motored out and over to the other side of the Ria to drop anchor close to the beach in the Ensenada de Mera. We spent a lovely peaceful night there, free from squeaky warps and fenders and fishing boat wash, and woke fresh the following morning to head out for our next port of call, Laxe.

LAXE & CAMARIÑAS

We lifted the anchor at 09:00 and motored out of the bay, headed for the Ria de Come and the town of Laxe some 35 nmi away. It turned into a frustrating passage. The gentle onshore breeze in the forecast never materialised. What wind there was came straight at us. We also got our first experience of two things we'd become familiar with over the coming weeks; big Atlantic swells and fog.

When winds are light and the sea flat, the sails can still provide enough drive to keep the boat moving at a few knots. But when there's a big swell, it doesn't happen. The boat moves about so much that the wind gets spilled out of the sails and the boat stops. In those conditions it's best to put the engines on. That way you keep up enough speed that the sails stay filled and 'help' the engines.

Fog is just a pain.

It's difficult to forecast. There's nothing you can do about it. And it's potentially dangerous.

'Gleda' didn't have radar. So apart from the AIS we drove 'blind'. On a coastal passage even the AIS loses its effectiveness. That's because most of the vessels around will usually be too small to be carrying a transponder. Eyes and ears become hyper-sensitive. Trying to pick up on any clue to what's going on around the boat.

The fog stayed with us for a few hours. We only saw one other vessel. It was a small coaster laden with timber. It crossed directly across our bows about half a mile ahead. Like a ghost ship, it appeared and disappeared in less than a minute. I'd like to think they knew we were there. Our radar reflector should have given a good signal for them to see on their screen. We'll never know.

We dropped anchor off the beach near the tiny town of Laxe just after 7pm. It'd been a slow slog. 39 nmi in 10 hours at an average speed of 3.9 knots.

Laxe was pretty, but with little to offer ashore there was no point staying. And Jake was now running out of time. He had to get back to Alderney sometime over the coming week. Ideally, I wanted him aboard until we rounded Cape Finisterre. To me, that marked the point at which we'd be clear of the Biscay weather and coastal passages would get easier. Until then, we'd be sailing along Galicia's pleasantly named Costa da Morte. (Coast of Death). The Costa da Morte is so called because there have been so many shipwrecks along its treacherous rocky shore over the centuries. The similarities of this Northern Galician coastline to Brittany and Cornwall are striking. But for scale La Costa da Morte wins hands down.

I'd planned the next passage to take us down to a place called Camariñas. En route lay Cabo Villano (The Villainous Cape) not far to the southwest. It marked another turning point as we gradually rounded the corner down towards the south. We had a leisurely start to the day. A decent breeze meant we could sail off the anchor, and we were soon sailing nicely out of the bay and towards the Cabo. Once clear of the anchorage the swells once again began rolling under us. As we passed the towering black cliffs of The Villano with its outlying shoals and rocks, it looked suitably foreboding.

The first half of the passage gave us some good sailing, but once again the wind headed us. It was impossible to lay the course we needed to enter the Camariñas bay. Once again I had to fire up the engines. I felt bad every time we did this, but when you've already had a long day, the swell is large, darkness is approaching and a calm safe haven lies just a few hours away to windward, it's impossible to resist temptation.

We'd done 28 nmi in 6hrs 25 mins at an average of 4.4 knots Camariñas was nice. We spent three nights there. We could have anchored just off the small Puerto, but it was cheap to lay alongside the pontoons and saved us inflating the dinghy.

The little Club Nautico had decent showers and a little bar/café where we could get Wi-Fi. After a bit of research it became apparent that this would be the best place for Jake to leave us. The airport at Santiago de Compostela wasn't far away by taxi. From there he could get a direct flight back to London and an onward connection to Jersey. Once there, his Mom could bring the RIB and ferry him back to Alderney.

After having used the engines so much, we needed fuel. I asked the club café owner if there was a petrol station nearby, but he told me the nearest was about 10 kilometres away. When I asked about a taxi, he shook his head and said "Pas de problème, je vais vous y conduire" (No problem, I'll drive you there). Now it may puzzle you why this proud Galician Spanish gentleman was speaking to me in French. Well, he didn't speak any English, and I didn't speak any Spanish, but we both spoke a bit of French. Between us we communicated pretty well, and even managed some conversation as we drove to the garage and back. I offered to pay him for the trip, but he refused to take any money. "Nous sommes tout amis" (We are all friends) he said.

We had a farewell meal with Jake in the Club Nautico the next night. A lovely pork and mushroom dish washed down with an excellent Rioja (something else we'd gained a taste for). It was a special treat, and we all enjoyed it. Beneath the surface though, we were all sad. Jake had been onboard for nearly a month. We'd spent two weeks with him in Alderney before that. We'd been through a lot together. He'd become part of the family. It'd been an absolute pleasure to have him aboard and I knew I would miss his energy and enthusiasm for sailing. Not least because I'd now be the one hauling halyards sheets and anchor chain again.

I think it'd be fair to say that 'Gleda' worked some magic on Jake.

I wrote in my journal that night that I knew he'd be following in our wake soon. As I write these words today (August 2018). He's aboard his grandads boat 'Ragtime'. He and his girlfriend Lucy have sailed her from Alderney, following almost the same route as we did aboard 'Gleda'. Right now they're anchored in the Ensenada de Muros. And here's a weird coincidence; That's the next port of call for this story.

On Monday morning we were up at 05:15 to get Jake away by 06:00. He had a lengthy journey in front of him. There were a few tears as we waved his taxi off into the mist.

The forecast predicted a nice northeasterly wind force 4/5. I didn't feel like sailing and Gail was apprehensive about us being on our own again. But I'd already planned the next leg. Out past Cabo Torinana, the most Western point in Spain. Then south at last towards Cape Finisterre before turning in towards the sanctuary of the Ria de Muros.

After that we'd be clear of the death coast and into much more relaxed sailing. We were up and awake; the boat was ready. We could sit around all day thinking about it. Or we could just go. I told Gail to stow for sea and got ready to untie the lines.

MUROS

I felt a little apprehensive as we motored away from Camariñas with a forecast of N winds F3-5. Whatever the forecast, the winds around Finisterre do their own thing, so I knew things could be different once we got out there. But with the winds forecast to move south, we had to go.

In the event we saw F6 for a time and it made for some exhilarating downwind surfing. We flew past Cabo Torinana and were soon on our heading to clear Finisterre. But with the wind came that other Finisterre feature…. Fog. We had a couple of hours when visibility was poor; we were averaging over 7 knots, and we maxed out at just under 13 knots, and unlike our last fast passage through the Chanel du Four there was no tide under us this time!

It was the first, and I hoped the last time, that we'd get a strong breeze and thick fog simultaneously.

I pushed 'Gleda' as hard as I'd ever done. She lapped it up. We'd spent far too many hours on engine since we crossed Biscay. It felt good to be properly sailing again.

After a while the sun finally burned through, the fog cleared and there, off the port beam, lay the famed Cabo Finisterre.

Once round the Cape and closer to land the wind died almost completely, the day became hot, and we ended up motor-sailing the last 3 hours into the Ria de Muros. As predicted by the pilot book, this large open Ria had a much softer feel now that the coast of death lay behind us.

On the north side of the Ria lies the town of Muros, a pretty little place nestled under the mountains. With only a small marina I opted to anchor in the Ensenada de Ria, just off the beaches a little way from the town.

We soon had the anchor down and the kettle on. We both felt well satisfied. Gail had been amazing. This had been her first proper coastal passage with just the two of us. And what a passage it had been.

It was a huge landmark for us, physically and mentally.

With Jake gone, all thought of any timetable had disappeared. For the longest time it had seemed that there had always been an obvious target ahead. Leaving Falmouth. Getting to Alderney. Brittany, Biscay, Finisterre. Now that had all changed.

Yes, we wanted to get south. Yes, we wanted to reach the Algarve for the winter. But we had months to do that. It felt as if the freedom we'd been seeking for so long had finally arrived.

That evening I got the fishing rod out. Within minutes, I had two gorgeous Mackerel on deck. We ate them as the sun went down. We opened a bottle of white and just sat, soaking it all up. It was magical.

The peace didn't last.

There was yet another Fiesta of some sort going on ashore. The sounds of fairground rides and music echoed across the bay that night. We were woken at midnight by fireworks, which to be fair were spectacular.

We were less impressed by the incredibly loud maroons fired off early the next morning.

The Spanish seem to have a thing about fireworks. One morning I was sitting on deck with a coffee when I saw a little car come driving down the quayside. It stopped at the end and two guys got out. They opened the boot and brought out two huge rockets. One guy held out the first at arm's length while the other lit it. A few seconds later it shot up into the sky trailing blue smoke, before exploding above the town with a noise similar to a clap of thunder. They repeated this procedure with the next, before getting back in the car and driving off. We got to hear a lot of these 'random maroons', as we started calling them.

We spent three nights on the hook at Muros with one

dinghy trip ashore for a look around, the highlight of which was a visit to the church of San Pedro de Muros where we climbed the bell tower and took in the incredible vistas.

Muros is known as 'a town of sea and salt' and it seemed everyone fished or gathered shellfish. Early on the first morning it treated us to the surreal sight of hundreds of people wading in the water, gathering prawns off the beach. They used small handheld nets to scoop up the fish before dumping them in baskets on their backs.

With the winds still not fair for a passage south, we changed the scenery with a 5-mile sail across the Ria to Portosín. We opted for the small marina at the Club Nautico. As we pulled in towards the pontoons a familiar face appeared to take our lines. It was Ian from 'Rivalady' who we'd last seen in Coruña. Portosín was nice but expensive. But it had good showers and a laundry. Looking ahead, I thought it might be our last opportunity to get them for a while.

As we were both ready for a temporary break from the boat we hopped the bus for a ride into the town of Noia at the head of the Ria. It was interesting to walk around this ancient Galician town with its mix of new and old buildings.

There was also a big indoor market with an enormous space dedicated to fish and shellfish. It's fair to say that the Galicians like their seafood.

Right in the centre of town we found a lovely tiled avenue of palm trees edged with cafés. We stopped at one and ordered some drinks. They came with complimentary nibbles and little tapas. All for €3. We were just beginning to realise that food and drink costs were significantly lower than what we'd become used to in the UK.

Annoyingly, though much of Western Europe and the UK had been experiencing unusually warm weather for us, it remained mixed. The cause was the Jet Stream and its position to the south. What it meant for us was that the winds for the previous 4/5 days had been predominantly from the south or southwest. The Ria de Muros had been the perfect place to hole up while they passed.

On our last afternoon in Portosín the wind picked up a lot and blew in some rain. I wondered just how far south we'd have to sail before we got a break.

The following day we motored out of the marina and headed down towards the entrance of the Ria. I'd spotted what looked like a nice little anchorage off the beach in a place called San Francisco. I figured that we could spend a restful night there, and be in the perfect spot to head back out to sea first thing the following morning.

It was a mistake. I ended up dropping and lifting the anchor four times. The water was deep for an anchorage. Nearly 10 metres. The first time I dropped the hook we dragged immediately. It took a lot of effort to pull the anchor back up. I couldn't do it by hand. It puzzled me. Even once clear of the seabed the anchor was ridiculously heavy. I had to use the manual windlass to haul it up inch by inch. Once the anchor broke the surface, all became clear. Wrapped around the anchor were huge black glistening sheets of kelp. It took ages to pull it all off with the boathook. I made three more attempts, all with the same result, until I realised it was useless. So, we motored the nine miles back to our original anchorage near Muros. As a final kicker, it took me two attempts to get the anchor to bite there. Not the most restful way to spend the afternoon before a passage.

RIA DE PONTEVEDRA

We were up early the next morning and sailing off the anchor just after 08:00. There was hardly a breath of wind, and we drifted out towards the open sea at a leisurely pace. I'd hoped for more wind once we got clear of the bay, but it didn't materialise. With a 40-mile passage in front of us, we couldn't wait for it to arrive. It was back to motor-sailing. As things turned out the wind didn't arrive until after lunch and then started blowing freshly. We finished the trip under sail and at a decent speed.

We anchored off the beach at a place with the tongue-twisting name of Sanxenxo.

Ria de Muros had been very much a 'working' place. It seemed everyone there was making their living from the sea. Our first impression of Ria de Pontevedra was that we had entered an entirely different world. Here everyone on the water seemed to be there for pleasure, pedalos, jet skis, canoes, swimmers and a beach packed with sun worshippers until late into the evening.

We'd had an easy passage 37 nmi, average 4.28 knots, maximum 8.6 knots, nearly 9 hours. I felt shattered though. Maybe all that hauling of anchors the previous day had taken more out of me than I'd thought.

I wasn't long out of my bunk.

The next morning we weighed anchor and motored down the Ria to a little marina in a place called Combarro. Once again there was no wind, the waters of the Ria glistened mirror-like in the sunshine. A movement on the water caught my eye. It was a huge pod of dolphins heading out towards the sea. Several leapt right out of the water.

As compared to Portosín, Combarro marina was cheap. But the facilities were still excellent and the staff friendly. I'd chosen to go there because it was Gail's birthday the next day. I figured she deserved the gift of some shore time.

The principal attraction in Combarro was the restored fishing village with its granite houses, narrow streets, ancient crucifixes and many Horreos. Horreos are raised stone storage buildings used for grain, fish and anything that needs keeping safe from the sun, pests and rodents. They're a common sight all over Galicia, but Combarro has more than anywhere else.

Combarro turned out to be perfect for celebrating Gail's Birthday. We had a chilled, relaxing day, and that evening walked into the village to find a restaurant. There were plenty to choose from. We picked one serving BBQ meat cooked on a wood fire with views over the water, ordered a nice bottle of Rioja and celebrated.

We stayed another night in Combarro, partly because we'd had a disturbed night thanks to strengthening wind and a large Guardia Civil patrol boat. It came alongside the pontoon right astern of us at 02:00. Its enormous engines rumbling away, its crew shouting with no consideration to the hour. I thought it best not to complain.

We spent the day relaxing. I did some more passage planning. Next up was Baiona.

BAYONA

We had a challenging day of sailing to reach it.

The winds stayed mainly light. But I was determined to sail rather than motor. That meant near constant work trimming the sails and trying to get the best out of the boat. The last couple of hours gave me my reward. The wind increased significantly as we closed the shore. The approach to Bayona is navigationally tricky. I'd opted to go outside the off-lying Islas Cias, and by the time we'd swung round to our easterly approach we were flying. We touched 12 knots several times. Our average for the trip stayed under 3 though. Nine hours to travel 27 nmi tells the story.

We anchored off the beach well within the sheltered bay. Among the other boats already there we spotted 'Friendship'. We'd last seen them in Coruña. Garry and June rowed over that evening for a few drinks onboard. It was nice to catch up and swap stories of our respective journeys.

The pilot book for Northern Spain lists Bayona (Baiona) as a long-time favourite stopover for British yachtsmen. As we sat chatting on deck with the panorama of the Ensenada de Baiona all around, it was easy to see why. I'd been to Bayona once before. Those of you who've read 'A Foolish Voyage' may remember. Back then I was working as mate on the 35ft (ca. 11 m) steel junk-rigged 'Abraxis', which the skipper and I delivered from Falmouth to Tenerife. I mentioned the tricky approach to Bayona earlier. On the 'Abraxis' trip we'd nearly come to grief trying to get in at night. That all seemed a long time ago now. But I remembered how much I'd liked the place, and how I'd dreamt of sailing my own boat there one day. And now I was here.

My recollections of Bayona were unsurprisingly vague. The place was far less developed and a lot quieter back then. The castle of Monte Real overlooking the harbour was the same, but the marina had become far larger. I remembered some streets in the old town too, but that was about all. What hadn't changed though was the atmosphere. It was still welcoming and full of life.

I decided we'd spend a few days in Bayona exploring, relaxing and enjoying the place. With no timetable, there seemed little reason to push on while we were having an enjoyable time. Being anchored for free made it a straightforward decision.

I also knew that Bayona would be our last easy port of call in Northern Spain. From here all the way down to Cape St Vincent, the coast wouldn't be so welcoming.

That night we were again disturbed by loud live music and fireworks that went on well into the wee small hours. As I've said before the Galicians like to make a noise, but you know what? It's great to see (and hear). There's something of value in the fact that their traditions and personal freedoms seem to have remained undiluted by rules and regulations. One of the phrases I'd started using a lot was "they'd never allow that back home". The longer we spent in Europe, the more we saw how controlled and regulated life back home was. The police in Spain may have carried guns, but they wore T-shirts not stab vests, petty 'enforcement officers' and traffic wardens in hi-vis were absent, as were CCTV cameras. Some folks wore seatbelts and helmets on the road others chose not to. Somehow things just seemed easier going, more live and let live, and I liked it.

I'd only planned to stay in Bayona a day or two, but it turned into a week. Our anchorage was in a brilliant spot. We could land the dinghy on a nice sandy beach. There was a good Carrefour supermarket nearby and a café where we could get internet. Pretty much everything we needed for cheap, easy living.

Not a lot happened. We chilled, sat in the sun, swam. It seemed we were at last adapting to our alternative lifestyle.

There were only two incidents worth mentioning. Early one morning Gail woke me to say she could hear a strange knocking and scraping noise on the hull. As usual, I'd heard nothing. To humour her, I groggily went up on deck to look around. I could see nothing and came back to bed. Later, as we were sitting on deck having breakfast, I looked down through the slatted timber deck beneath my chair. There was something large and yellow right under the boat. I jumped down in the dinghy to get a better look. There was a large lozenge shaped mooring buoy wedged between the engine boxes. Gail calls them 'Minions' after the characters in the animated film. Incredibly, during the night, this buoy had come adrift from somewhere, drifted down on us, avoided the anchor chain and bridle, then got wedged. Obviously, that's what Gail had heard. She spent some time making sure that I now understood who'd been right about strange noises.

It took me a while to free it from its position. It had to come out the way it'd gone in, and so I used the dinghy to tow it. There were several metres of extremely rusty chain attached to the bottom. It took me 15 minutes to tow the whole lot slowly across the anchorage to the marina. There I tied it up to a vacant pontoon.

Remember earlier when I wrote about the magnetic attraction boats seem to have for objects at sea? Here was further proof. The attraction continues even when stationary in harbour.

The second incident wasn't so amusing. We'd been over to 'Friendship' for a few beers, come back and eaten a risotto Gail had made, then gone to bed. A few hours later I woke feeling nauseous and needing the loo badly. I got up on deck, heading for the toilet compartment. Next thing I knew I was sitting in a strange position on the compartment floor, with Gail calling my name from the hatchway above with a concerned look on her face. It seemed I'd passed out as I was halfway down the companionway steps. She'd heard me fall and rushed to help. She found me crumpled awkwardly at the bottom of the steps, unconscious. As I came too, I was sick. I sipped some water and Gail helped me back to my berth. After that I slept but woke feeling groggy the next morning. We'd considered leaving for the next leg south. That was now impossible. Whatever had caused my ailment passed quickly. Gail and I had eaten the same thing, yet she felt fine. It was the only time in my life, before or since, that I've passed out. Hopefully, it'll stay that way.

It was hard to leave Bayona in more ways than one. Not only was it a pleasant place to be, but I knew that the next legs of this trip wouldn't be as enjoyable as those that we'd had since Finisterre. Safe harbours along the Atlantic coast of Portugal are fewer and farther between than in Spain. Gone are the relatively sheltered Rias and good choice of anchorages and marinas, the pilot book warns that when the Atlantic swells roll in even previously viable harbours may become dangerous to enter. An added hazard is fog. As we'd already experienced rounding Finisterre, it can descend without warning. During our last few days at anchor in Bayona we watched banks of it roll in across the bay whilst we were sitting on deck bathed in sunshine.

    We planned to leave early on Wednesday morning, the 15th July, but one of these fog banks delayed us. When it cleared after lunch I decided we'd leave anyway, figuring we could comfortably get the next 40 or so nmi south to our next port before dark. We followed our friends Garry and June on catamaran 'Friendship' out of the bay, they were heading back north to Cangas to meet up with family, so at the fairway buoy we turned in opposite directions as we headed out to clear the outlying dangers of Cabo Silleiro. The pilot books all talk about the 'Nortada' winds that blow down this coast in the summer months. Whatever else the wind may do in the morning, it's usual around noon for the wind to switch round to the north and blow at anything up to F6 until sundown. I'd been banking on this to speed our afternoon passage south. But as we came abeam of Silleiro, the wind stubbornly stayed right on the nose and then, after a mile or so of beating into it, the horizon disappeared, followed in short order by the land. Another thick band of fog had rolled in. We carried on for about half an hour, but frankly it wasn't fun. I was concentrating hard on sailing the boat. Then I looked across at Gail. She was huddled in the corner of the pod with tears in her eyes. It caught me off guard. She was upset and scared. I made an instant decision. I hit the button on the GPS that reverses the plotted course 180°, hauled the helm round and ran right back into the sunshine of Bayona Bay. An hour later we were back on the hook drinking a glass of Vino Cheapado.

    Making decisions in the fog is a total gamble, wait 10 minutes and you could find the fog clearing and the wind turning, or things could stay the same for hours, it's anyone's guess. It's a gamble in other respects too, thanks to GPS you may know exactly where you are, but without radar you're blind to other vessels, even with it there's no guarantee you'll see smaller vessels in the large rolling swells and that meant 'Gleda' would likely be invisible too. As I've mentioned before, I had an AIS receiver aboard, but only larger boats carry transmitters. It has to be said that short of being caught in a full gale close inshore, being caught in fog is the worst sort of weather to experience. Sometimes you don't have any choice but to make the best of it. Other times you can bail, just as we had. Sailing can be tough, but when you have no timetable, it's well worth remembering that you're out there to have fun. And if you're not, then change something.

    We stayed where we were the following day and watched another fog bank roll in during the morning, but by mid-afternoon the Isla Ciés were clearly visible offshore, and the sky stayed clear as the sun went down, with a decent evening forecast things looked good for an early morning depart.

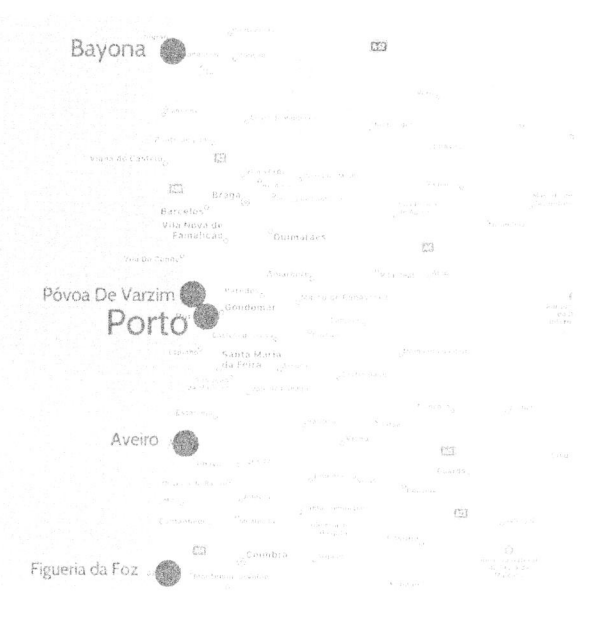

8

NORTHERN PORTUGAL

PÓVOA DE VARZIM

We weighed anchor just after 08:00 and motor sailed out towards Cabo Silleiro once more; the wind stayed stubbornly out of the south right through the morning though, so I kept one engine on to keep us moving. I was on fog alert the entire time. Scanning the horizon for telltale signs. There were none. Around noon, as we drew level with the Portuguese border off a place called Garda, the 'Nortada' arrived, and before long 'Gleda' was creaming along downwind at 6-8 knots with 'Lewis' the self-steering back on the helm for the first time since Biscay. The sun was shining, and we spent the time watching the coast glide by and enjoying the ride. We even spotted two sunfish with their strange single flipper sticking up out of the water as we passed them.

As I mentioned, we'd moved into Portuguese waters about the same time as the wind arrived. A bright new Portuguese courtesy flag was now flying from the shrouds, and with decent progress being made, I decided to press on past the first viable harbour of

Viana de Castello, towards Póvoa de Varzim some 53 miles (ca. 85 km) south of Bayona. It would mean a late evening arrival, but even a night approach wouldn't be a problem there. We'd heard that Varzim was much nicer than Viana, and we weren't alone in our choice. Some way astern of us I could see 'Breezer', another Broadblue catamaran like 'Friendship', and owned by another UK couple Gary and Chris. We'd chatted with them in Bayona and discovered we had the same plan. I could see 'Breezer' flying a nice big cruising chute, but pleasingly they didn't seem to be gaining on us by much. In the event they arrived in Varzim minutes ahead of us, having left Bayona two hours after us, so they did well. It's fair to say I had some cruising chute envy.

The wind continued to blow steadily and even increased a bit as the evening approached, we topped out at 9 knots downwind, with 'Lewis' doing a grand job holding our course, although I had to disconnect a couple of times to steer around one of the dozens of pot markers scattered along this coast. All seemed well for a relaxed arrival then, around 19:00 I noticed that 'Breezer' had disappeared astern, then the slowly rotating vanes of the huge floating wind turbine a few miles off on our starboard side also disappeared, and I realised that once again fog had come to play games with us. It was a bit of a worry, Varzim is a small but busy fishing harbour, it was likely there would be other boats around, the plotter chart covering this part of the coast didn't have large-scale detail of the approach, and with a narrow entrance and poor visibility I knew getting in would be testing. I briefly considered staying offshore, but with no sign of the fog thinning, the wind increasing, darkness coming on and the next large port being another 50 nmi down the coast, the dangers of staying out were greater than the risks of going in. I knew I had the approach and entrance waypoints double-checked and programmed into both the laptop chart plotter and the GPS, so we'd just have to trust to the satellites orbiting up above, and the two pairs of MK1 eyeballs straining down below.

Two miles out, I got the sails down and the engines on whilst Gail steered in the increasingly choppy sea then, once I had everything sorted I took over, and with Gail keeping her eyes peeled on the port side and me on the starboard I steered tightly to the course leading us in. We didn't see the breakwaters until we were virtually between them, then the water calmed down, the glow of a few lights on shore became visible, and there, just ahead of us I saw the stern of 'Breezer' making her way in…… we'd made it.

The stress wasn't over though as I then had to get 'Gleda' into a tight finger berth against a fresh breeze in what was by then next to zero visibility. Thanks to some helpful folks on the pontoon, including Gary off 'Breezer', we got alongside without mishap. Gail went below to get the kettle on as I sorted out the springs and warps and gradually wound down. The weather was downright weird, the atmosphere seemed saturated, everything on the boat was dripping wet, yet there was no rain, the wind was fresh but warm and it was now almost dark. As we sat below drinking our tea and eating a hastily warmed meal of tinned chicken and rice, it felt good to be in Portugal at last, but I think it's fair to say we didn't expect arriving as we did and not being able to see anything!

It'd been a long day. 12 hours at sea. 54 nmi travelled at an average of 4.5 knots.

After dinner, we toasted our arrival with a fitting glass of Port and then turned in. I slept solidly for 6 hours or so but woke well before dawn still buzzing from the previous day's events. It was still dark and still foggy, but I figured the dawn would bring some warm sunshine and the Portuguese welcome we'd been looking forward to.

The next day did indeed dawn sunny. Our welcome in the marina office was just as bright. As this was our first landfall in

Portugal there were a few more formalities to complete. They were easy enough. A form to fill out, photocopies of passports and boat registration documents taken. That was about it.

We had an advantage of course. We were citizens of the European Union. The agreements between member countries meant that we had freedom of movement within the Union. As I write these words in September 2018, the UK is but a few months away from leaving the European Union. I thought then, and I think now, that it's a monumental mistake. It may well be that our children won't find it so easy to travel as we did.

The amiable lady on the desk spoke good English and gave us a map marked with all the supermarkets and places of interest. Finally, we had our fingerprints taken for the locked and gated access to the pontoons.

After a cuppa, we walked along the promenade towards the adjoining town of Vila do Conde. It was nice. We passed many old buildings, all beautifully tiled with the predominantly blue and white decorative ceramics famed in Portugal.

All along the promenade there were large decorative tiled plaques depicting the history of Póvoa de Varzim. Whilst fishing has always been the dominant industry, it's also been a resort town for nearly 300 years. Many of the plaques contained what to me looked like Egyptian hieroglyphics or runes.

I discovered afterwards that these symbols are unique to Póvoa de Varzim, and have been used since time immemorial.

Known as 'Siglas Poveiras' the symbols were used primarily as a kind of family signature to mark ownership. We also saw them painted on some local fishing boats.

This ancient written language wasn't the only new one we came across. Our ears were now having to get attuned to Portuguese. If you've never heard it, the best description I can give is that it sounds like Spanish, but spoken with a Russian accent!

Take the name Póvoa de Varzim. When the Portuguese say it,

it sounds nothing like we English speakers might expect. Strung together as one word and spoken fast, it sounds something like 'Pabodewazeem'.

We may have only moved 50 or so miles further south, but already it felt very different to Spain.

I hadn't planned to stop in Póvoa for long, but as it was relatively inexpensive, pleasantly positioned and, as we discovered, well-connected for visiting Portugals second city Porto, we ended up spending five nights there. The weather also made it easier to stop. Throughout our stay the winds were persistently coming from the south, and with them we got frequent fog. It seemed to appear at anytime during the day, sometimes disappearing again, sometimes thinning and thickening repeatedly for hours. Other times it just stayed. It got to the point that every time we came up on deck after a spell below, we didn't know if we'd be able to see anything.

For the first few days we chilled and explored locally. We both liked the place. To be fair, the area immediately around the marina was shabby and rundown. But the town itself was a different story. The main town square with its beautiful City Council house built in 1790 was just one of the many attractions.

The city of Porto had been high on our list of 'must see' places for a while. I'd originally thought to take 'Gleda' up the Douro river and into the small marina close to the city. But once we discovered the fast tram that ran from Póvoa directly into Porto city centre, that seemed a far easier option.

A LITTLE TASTE OF PORTO

So, the next day we turned tourist, bought our tickets and used the excellent Metro service to get us into Porto.

As I've said before I'm not a fan of big cities and Porto is big, too big to see in a day, so we had to be selective. We got off the

Metro at the central station and sauntered downhill towards the river Douro. This gave us a chance to take in the atmosphere and get a good view of some impressive architecture along the way.

Once down by the river, the scale of the place made a real impact. The valley sides are steep and the city seems to rise to the sky away from the river. We walked along the north bank of the river and crossed the 'Ponte Luis I' bridge, one of the six that cross the Rio. It's a two-level bridge, and as we walked alongside the roadway, we could hear the trains rumbling across on the second level way above us. Above that, a cable car ran from the riverbank near the Port Wine Cellars up to the highest point of the south Bank.

The Port Wine Cellars were our key reason for crossing the river, as they are all clustered together on the South side. We visited the Calem Cellar and had a fascinating guided tour during which we learned a lot about the famous Porto Wines, not least that they don't come from Porto and that they're not wines!

We finished the tour with the obligatory tasting; we sampled a nice Branco (White) and a vintage Tawny, both went down a treat, but we left with a bottle of Rose as we fancied something a little different to take back.

To clear our heads, we took a slow walk back over the river and up through the town to visit the 'Livraria Lello'. It's a bookshop reputed to be one of the most beautiful in the world and is a World Heritage site. I'd never been to a bookshop with a queue before. Most of the visitors weren't there to buy books, but to take photos. It was indeed beautiful. The dominant feature a wonderfully crafted double curved staircase right in the middle of the shop.

We came away from Porto with a good impression of the place, bolstered by something that happened whilst standing on a corner studying the map and trying to get our directions back to the Metro station. Some local youngsters came up to us and asked in excellent English if we needed help. We explained that we needed to find the station, and rather than give directions they walked us there. It's perhaps indicative of the state of our own country that Gail's first thought was that they planned to lead us down some backstreet and mug us. We may forget some of what we experienced, but one thing is certain, now and forever we'll toast the city of Porto and remember our visit every time we raise a glass of their most famous export.

When we got back to the boat, we discovered that the wind had finally moved round to the north and freshened. The forecast said it would remain so for a few days. I started thinking about the next passage. The damn fog still hadn't gone completely though. When we'd returned a few hours previously we'd had bright sunshine, but before sunset I watched the town skyline as it began to vanish into whiteness once more. It would make leaving a tricky decision, but one I'd have to make at some point. Ahead of us lay some longer coastal passages with fewer ports of refuge to run into if things went wrong. We'd not left our sailing challenges behind just yet.

AVEIRO & FIGUEIRA DA FOZ

After leaving Póvoa de Varzim we sailed down to Aveiro. It was another 50 miles (ca. 80 km) south and a fairly uneventful passage. But the wind dropped again, and I put the engines to use once more. Well, the starboard one at least. When we're underway, I periodically lifted the engine box lids to check that a jet of cooling water was coming from the engines. One of these checks showed the port one had reduced to a trickle. I stopped the engine and raised the leg so I could check for blockages but couldn't see anything obvious. That's when it's an enormous advantage having two engines. We just ran on the other one until the wind returned, and later that evening I was able to sort the problem out. It was just weed that had got shredded and sucked into the water inlet.

There's no marina in Aveiro, so we anchored in a sheltered lagoon close to a military airfield. There were several other boats there but plenty of room. Aveiro is a busy industrial port, and we encountered a bit of ship traffic on our way in. Once again the AIS helped. Pleasingly though, the fog stayed away this time.

9 hours. 49.76 nmi. 5.45 knots average.

We left early the next morning. It was cloudy and drizzly but that hadn't deterred dozens of locals from clogging the harbour entrance in their tiny fishing boats. I had to pay attention to get through them and into clear water. They were a friendly lot though, waving cheerfully as we passed by.

There's always a twinge of guilt when leaving a place without taking the time to explore. The town itself looked interesting and apparently has a touch of Venice about it with its canals winding between the streets. But we were now halfway down a 100-mile stretch of coast with no all-weather harbours. The entrances to both Aveiro and our next destination, Figueira da Foz, are frequently closed because of swell. These swells originate from storms hundreds of miles away across the Atlantic, They then travel east and, as they arrive off the coast of Portugal, the shallowing seabed can push them up into enormous waves. It's hard to predict when that might happen. I knew that even though the weather locally was fine, we could still discover our chosen harbour closed.

Our trip to Figueira was also uneventful. We had drizzle, cloud and little wind to start with, then it brightened, and we got enough wind to sail. The coast most of the way along comprised low-lying dunes, so there wasn't a lot to see. Gail likes to read as we're going along anyway, so she hardly noticed!

As we rounded Cabo Mondego towards Figueira, the wind picked up even more and the cloud came down, which made for a lively last hour. It was still warm enough to work on deck in a T-shirt though.

7 hours. 36 miles (ca. 58 km). Average 5.2 knots.

We moored to a pontoon close to the marina office and showers. Well, at least as far as the crow flies we were. But to get there we had to walk about half a mile along the pontoons, right around the head of the marina and then down the quayside. It took about 15 minutes. But by that time we hadn't stepped off the boat for 40 hours, so we needed a walk.

To be honest, Figueira wasn't anything to write home about. It's a beach resort, but the town itself wasn't particularly interesting, although we found an amazing indoor market opposite the marina.

The marina was expensive, 42 Euros per night. With no anchorages and no other ports close by they had somewhat of a monopoly so could get away with it.

The last marina we'd been in at Póvoa de Varzim had been 18 Euros per night. This was an erratic pricing pattern we were to experience all the way down the coast.

Expensive though it was, we stayed two nights. I was feeling low on energy. Our previous night at anchor had been peaceful, but I'd been up several times during the night to check on things, so hadn't slept well. I was finding these coastal passages hard work. There was so much to think about. Would the harbour be open? Would the fog come in again? We're there any ships close by? Was everything OK with our engines and sails? Were we on course and clear of hazards?

It may seem strange to non-sailors. You'll have seen from my log figures that we were moving along at not much above walking pace. Yet I'd have been more relaxed doing 80 mph (ca. 129 km/h) hour in my car on the motorway. I figured I was still adjusting, still learning. I figured things would get easier with time.

So now we were over halfway between Cabo Finisterre to

the north and Cabo de São Vicente to the south. Since Baiona we'd been moving along pretty well. July was drawing to an end, and I felt like we needed a holiday. I'd looked at the charts and spotted what looked like the ideal place to spend a bit of time. It was an enclosed bay called São Martinho do Porto just south of our next port of call, Nazaré. But we weren't there yet.

Figueria da Foz

Nazaré
São Martinho do Porto

Sintra
Cascais Lisbon

Sines

CENTRAL PORTUGAL

NAZARÉ

Nazaré is unique on this coast because the harbour entrance is straightforward in most weathers and at night, It's also one of the few that don't get closed by swell. I'll explain that in more detail later. Nazaré lies some 38 miles (ca. 61 km) south of Figueira da Foz, with the next viable harbour at Peniche another 23 nmi on.

It's for these reasons that so many boats stop at Nazaré, we weren't going to do things any differently.

Given the forecast of NW 3-4 occasionally 5, I'd banked on a swift passage, but as with every other leg of this trip down the coast it wasn't to be so straightforward. Things started well enough. We hoisted sail as soon as we were clear of the harbour entrance and for a decent time we were cruising along nicely with 'Lewis' at the helm. We just lazed in the pod, Gail reading as usual, whilst I watched for the floats of lobster pots as the unbroken line of dunes and pine forest passed by to port.

I'd expected the wind to freshen as lunchtime approached but it did the opposite, and by midday we were struggling to keep steerage way as 'Gleda' rolled gently on the glassy swells. We tried to chill out and be patient, and managed it for an hour, but with no sign of wind anytime soon I cracked and dropped an engine. Patience wouldn't have been rewarded, it stayed calm for the rest of the trip. An hour out of Nazaré the coastline changed to rocky cliffs backed by gentle hills running inland, but we didn't get to see much more because surprise surprise, our old enemy the fog came to haunt us again. Like a damp blanket it dropped farther and farther until we could see no more than half a mile.

Once more it forced us to rely on the satellites and MKI eyeballs to get us in. It was stressful, and just as with Póvoa de Varzim we saw nothing until the two harbour entrance breakwaters appeared slowly out of the gloom. Already I was failing to be impressed by Nazaré. I'd read in the pilot book that there were two small marinas close to the fishing boat dock. The Club Nautico ran the larger of the two. But the pilot said it had limited space for visitors, and only for monohulls. That meant we had to aim for the smaller one at the far end of the fishing harbour. As we approached, I spotted a vacant hammerhead pontoon where we could easily come alongside. With no wind it was an easy manoeuvre. But as Gail jumped off the boat onto the pontoon with our lines, she nearly went for a swim. Some planks were missing, as was one of the fittings that attached the entire thing to the piles. After we were tied up, I walked some distance across a semi-industrial wasteland towards the security shack where, the pilot book said, I could book in. On the way over a small pack of stray dogs marauded me. They ran towards me snarling and barking and for a minute I thought I was in real trouble. But I stayed calm, ignored them, and kept walking. Eventually, I found the security guard in a small gatehouse, paid €30 deposit for a key and got directions to a shabby office corridor leading to even shabbier 'facilities'. I think it's fair to say that 'failure to impress' had turned into 'what a dump'.

Back on the boat with a cuppa I noticed there seemed to be a few permanent residents both afloat and ashore, and I couldn't help wondering what misfortune had left them stranded here, given that no sane person with a choice would surely stay here voluntarily.

I told Gail that barring a storm we'd be leaving early next morning.

Later that evening however, some shore-side residents came down to say hello. Alec and Dodi were the first. It turned out they had been there for 7 or 8 years; they told us that there was a friendly little long-term ex-pat community, they almost begged us to stay and explore the town and not to judge the place by what we'd seen so far. Apparently, Alec was working towards taking over the pontoons and improving the place. They told us we must visit the old village up on the cliffs, see the lighthouse, the beaches, the seafront. Their words tugged at my conscience, we were after all on a voyage of discovery; we were supposed to be searching for new experiences, new places, new people. We'd skipped seeing Aveiro recently. Leaving without seeing more of Nazaré would be wrong. We decided to give the place a chance.

Forty-eight hours later we both agreed it'd been the right decision. The next morning we walked the mile and a half into town and explored as Alec and Dodi had said we should. The seafront and beaches were super touristy, but it was peak season and it was good to see a place buzzing with a holiday vibe. There were some strange sights mixed in with the predictable ones. Fish drying on racks right behind the sunbathers. A display of traditional fishing boats on the sand and, most bizarrely, elderly women in traditional dress touting rooms to let, they held up small signs advertising their rates and mostly sat in plastic chairs on street corners. Apparently, most are widows and it's a tradition going back years. As I said, most bizarre.

Once through the town we found the lower station for the 'Ascensor de Nazaré', a funicular railway that climbs the 110 metres up to 'Sitio' the cliff top village above the town.

It was a fantastic ride and as we gained height, the spectacular views hinted at what was to come at the top. Once there, the breathtaking vista laid out below was truly stunning.

After soaking up as much as we could, we walked down away from the village towards the old fort and lighthouse that we'd been unable to see on our way in.

It may well be that you've seen pictures of this lighthouse yourself.

In January 2013 Garrett McNamara rode what is believed to be the biggest wave ever surfed, and it happened in Nazaré. Incredibly, that wave was nearly 100ft (ca. 30 m) from trough to crest. There's a peculiar set of geological, oceanographic and climatic circumstances that come together just off this promontory that, during the Winter, can generate truly phenomenal waves. I mentioned earlier that Nazaré is unusual because the harbour doesn't get closed by swell. This is because there's a deep underwater canyon that starts offshore and runs straight towards the harbour entrance. This means that the swells don't build into dangerous waves as they do elsewhere. But move half a mile or so north, just around the headland on which stands the lighthouse, and it's a different story. Here the seabed shelves steeply and that's where these incredible waves are generated. Locals told us that in theory it would be entirely possible for a boat to enter the harbour safely whilst almost within sight of those gigantic waves.

I'd seen some video of Garrett riding that wave. But standing by that lighthouse I couldn't imagine the scene. As I gazed out, I realised that just the day before, we'd motored 'Gleda' right over the spot where these waves appear!

The next day we went back into town for a bit of shopping and to sort out some propane. In the afternoon I spent a bit of time exploring around the marina. A quick walk across the yard whilst looking out for stray dogs and then through some dunes took me out onto the beach overlooking the bay and harbour entrance. I enjoyed stretching my legs and even with the brisk wind, the heat, sand and plant life gave my walk a distinctly Mediterranean feel.

On the other side I got another view of the harbour entrance and bay that'd been hidden from us on the way in.

I even found a wall full of 'cruiser graffiti' left by folks who felt a need to leave their mark on a place that had left a mark on them. It was more proof that this place had something about it. It may have been rough around the edges, going through some hard times, but we'd given it a chance, and it had rewarded us well.

The weather was looking right for the short trip down the coast to our anchorage in the bay of São Martinho do Porto. But, unlike Nazaré, the conditions had got to be perfect to go in. I decided to check again the next morning.

As I drifted off to sleep that night I thought more about Nazaré. Yes, the marina is tatty, yes there's a smell of fish in the air sometimes and yes, it's a walk into town, but…… The marina is sheltered and free from swell and wash, Nazaré was by far the most spectacular place we'd visited so far, everyone we'd met had been friendly and helpful, and we'd be taking some happy memories away with us.

Bottom line, I'm glad we stayed.

SÃO MARTINHO DO PORTO

Nazaré had been fun, but we were ready to move on. Our three nights tied to the tatty pontoon cost us €91. Too expensive by far.

We'd now been on the move for a few weeks and both of us felt ready for a break. It's perhaps worth taking a minute to explain why. You must wonder why we'd need to take a holiday from a holiday.

Whilst it's true that we were under no actual time pressure, we still had to make sure we got down to the Algarve before the autumn weather kicked in. How long we could stay in one place depended on two things; weather and cost. Baiona had been the last place where we'd been able to anchor for free somewhere safe in all weathers. So, since then, as soon as we arrived anywhere, I was immediately thinking about the next leg. Constantly watching the weather, looking for an opportunity to move on. Knowing that if we got stuck, we'd have to keep paying the marina fees.

Even on passage I could never relax fully. I've explained that already.

By the time we got to Nazaré the idea of sitting on the boat in a gorgeous sheltered anchorage for free, and being able to stay for a few weeks without worry, was extremely appealing.

I thought I'd found the perfect place for us to do it. São Martinho do Porto, about eight miles south of Nazaré.

I'd read that it had one of the most beautiful beaches in Portugal. In a sheltered bay, shaped like a scallop, with calm waters and fine white sand. And some of the warmest swimming water on the west coast of Portugal.

Too good to be true?

Well, there was a catch. The problem with a small circular cove in the cliffs is that it must, by definition, have a narrow, shallow entrance. The pilot book was clear. There could be breakers at the entrance, even with a modest swell. It could be dangerous.

It said that this anchorage should only be entered in calm weather in daylight and should not be attempted at all if you couldn't afford to wait for suitable weather before leaving again.

The shallow depths within the bay prevented most monohull boats from entering anyway. At least that was one thing I didn't have to worry about. 'Gleda' only needed about 1 m of water to float.

I was keen to get in there. But I knew it was completely weather dependant. I'd been watching like a hawk. From the beach behind the marina in Nazaré I could see how much swell was coming into shore. I knew I had to get it right. It's easy to be deceived when approaching an entrance like this from the seaward side. That's because you can only see the backs of the waves, and the backs are much smoother than the fronts. That can fool you into believing that the water is much calmer than it is. And by the time you realise it isn't, you're in trouble.

I'd thought to leave Nazaré on Wed 29th July. But we woke to drizzly rain and yet more fog. There was no way I could tackle the entrance into São Martinho do Porto in zero visibility, so we had to wait.

It was mid-afternoon before the fog thinned and disappeared. There was still no wind, but that was fine. I was happy to motor the short distance needed.

It was pleasant to be out of the harbour. By now the sun was shining and the sea calm. Perfect conditions for our approach. I'd plotted all the waypoints and paid close attention as I followed them in. The entrance was exactly as the pilot book described; narrow. It felt intimidating as we passed through the narrowest point with breaking waves and high cliffs on both sides of us. But once through, wow.

The bay opened up in front of us. Beautiful calm clear water, fringed by yellow sand, the town nestled into one corner. There were a few boats on mooring buoys just off the town quay. All local fishing and small leisure craft. I chose a spot just clear of them and not far off the beach. The anchor dropped through a couple of metres of water and bedded first time in the sand. I wasted no time in jumping over the side for a cooling swim. Soon afterwards we had the sail covers on and the boat snugged down. That evening we sat on deck and watched the sunset right in the narrow entrance. It was beautiful. For the first time in a long while I started winding down. This was more like it. The weather could do as it pleased, we could stop here as long as we wanted. This really felt like a proper escape.

We spent eleven nights in São Martinho do Porto.

It took a few days to adjust though. Bizarrely I felt a little lost with no passage making to occupy my mind. I didn't realise it, but this lack of activity would lead me to a new occupation that would change my life; writing.

For some time I'd had it in mind to write down my experiences aboard my first boat 'Mor Gwas'. I'd even considered it might become a book someday. I'd given it a title; 'A Foolish Voyage'. São Martinho do Porto turned out to be the place where a fresh adventure started. I set up a little writing space in the forward cabin. I spent a few hours a day in there writing. The only disturbance, an occasional beach pedalo bumping into the hull. That was one slight annoyance we hadn't thought about when anchoring close to a tourist beach. 'Gleda' became a 'destination' for curious holidaymakers on their own little voyages of discovery.

After a few days of hot sunshine, the weather went downhill. Looking out at the harbour entrance we could see a line of white breaking water. Powerful gusts of wind came racing across the bay, but we remained pretty much undisturbed. I saw online that many of the harbours up and down the coast had been closed because of swell. It seemed I'd made a good choice to hole up in the bay. The São Martinho fishing fleet stayed put. I knew we wouldn't be leaving until they did.

Interestingly, the 'fishing fleet' wasn't truly a fishing fleet. I'd noticed that most of the boats had large air compressors on the stern and big hydraulic grabs aboard. We found out why a few days after our arrival when we saw the boats come alongside and offload vast amounts of kelp seaweed into waiting trailers. Apparently it's used for agricultural fertilisers, animal feed and even diet supplements. The compressors pump air down to divers on the seabed overseeing the harvesting.

During our stay we explored all round the town and bay. To be honest, there wasn't a lot to the town. The seafront comprised mainly bars and cafés. We found a good supermarket a short walk away. The walk took us past an amazing abandoned hotel. It looked as if its heyday may have been in the 1920s or 30s. If it hadn't have been for the bright sunshine, it would have made the perfect setting for a horror film.

Along the quay was another unique feature. A long tunnel cut through the rock under the cliffs. It had been built long ago by fisherman who wanted to see what the sea conditions were like outside the sheltered harbour without having to climb to the top of the cliffs. Even on a calm day, the tunnel provided a spectacular contrast. You entered on the warm, calm and sunny side nearest the harbour. Then exited on the shady dark rocks close to the rolling surf of the Atlantic. We heard stories of winter storms that had sent large rocks rolling along the tunnel and out onto the quay.

One day, we took the dinghy over to the southern side of the bay. Here we found a giant sand dune, once one of the largest in Europe. Called Salir do Porto (Dune of Porto) it stands some 50 m high and 200 m long. Amazing.

São Martinho do Porto had done its job perfectly. We were both rested and ready to move on. Next stop Lisboa (Lisbon). Portugals capital and another place on our must see list.

CASCAIS & LISBOA

Leaving São Martinho wasn't easy. We'd enjoyed relaxing in such a fantastic spot.

It wasn't easy in other ways too; the anchor got fouled around an old DIY mooring that took a lot of heaving and untangling to sort out. I was hot sweaty and frustrated even before we reached the harbour entrance.

Despite the swells having died down in the entrance, they were still running large. With both engines on three-quarter throttle we motored into them at 6 knots until we were a few miles offshore, at which point they died down a bit and it became more comfortable as we turned south heading towards Cabo Carvoeiro.

I had one moment of panic on the way out though. I suddenly heard the anchor chain running out as we came off the top of one particularly large wave. Shouting at Gail to grab the wheel, I ran forward to see what was happening. I found that the wave had pushed the anchor off the bow roller and left it hanging just below the water on its retaining rope. The anchor chain was now rapidly headed for the bottom under its own weight. I grabbed some slack and jammed it into the windlass to stop its escape, before hauling it back aboard as quickly as I could. It happened because I'd bent the retaining pin while trying to unfoul the anchor. It seemed unimportant at the time, so I hadn't bothered to put it right. I made a mental note to prioritise the repair as soon as we stopped again. If the anchor hadn't been tied on we'd have been in a right mess.

Once things calmed down a bit Gail went below to put the kettle on expecting to find stuff all over the place because of our bumpy ride but amazingly nothing had moved; more evidence of the stability of a Wharram catamaran.

The next possible refuge down the coast was Peniche, just around Cabo Carvoeiro. But I gave it a miss. I'd read that there was no anchorage, the marina was small, and that the large fishing fleet seemed to relish sending as much wash into moored boats as possible. It was a good decision. We later heard from some friends who'd spent one disturbed night there and come away with a damaged hull. My decision meant we had some 65 miles (ca. 105 km) to run down to Cascais, so I was hoping the 'Nortada' would pick up and give us some speed. It didn't happen. To avoid spending the night dodging pots and fishing boats, we needed to average 5.5 knots, and it was only possible by motor sailing on one engine. Despite the lack of wind, the swell stayed with us though. We motored along as if on a roller coaster.

The wind picked up as we rounded Cabo da Roca later that evening, but by then it was a bit late. Cabo da Roca is the most western point of the European mainland. It felt significant to pass it. The wind dropped again as we cleared the Cabo and started our approach to the Rio Tejo and Cascais, and both Gail and I noticed how much warmer it felt despite the setting sun.

We dropped anchor in the bay of Cascais after some 12 hours at sea, exhausted but pleased to have completed another leg of our journey.

We spent two nights anchored in Cascais; I had some preconceptions about the place being a playground for the rich. Brash, noisy and up itself. The marina has the highest prices and the worst reputation for service anywhere on the Portuguese coast; the anchorage has patchy holding and suffers from swell and strong katabatic winds. Our stay there did nothing to change my view, not least because we didn't go ashore and the anchor dragged once, then fouled as I was lifting it. Our friends Gary and June on 'Friendship' anchored there for over a week not long after we left and loved the place, so maybe I should have given it a better chance. As it was, we spent some time enjoying Lisbon instead.

So on a sunny and calm Tuesday morning we set off to

motor the 18 miles (ca. 29 km) upriver to the Parque das Nacoes Marina on the north bank of the Tejo. Lisbon is a busy port and the currents run fast in the river, so I had to be on my toes regarding navigation. But luckily, we seemed to have picked a fairly quiet morning and I could enjoy what turned out to be a spectacular trip. A little over a year before, we'd sailed 'Gleda' down the Tamar river, under Isambard Kingdom Brunel's railway bridge and out past Plymouth into The Channel. Now here we were sailing into one of Europes most beautiful cities, and from the river we got to see many of its most famous landmarks, the Belém Tower, the Discoveries Monument, the monastery of St Jeronimo. We passed under the '25 de Abril' bridge, which is similar in design to the Golden Gate Bridge in San Francisco, and on our port side we could see the city laid out on the hillside. The bridge is so named in remembrance of the so called 'Carnation Revolution' of 25th April 1974, which overthrew the dictator Antonio Salazar.

Even with the tide running with us, it took over 3 hours to reach the marina, and my next challenge was to manoeuvre 'Gleda' into the outer basin and through the 8 m (ca. 26 ft) wide sluice gates. 'Gleda' had a beam of 6.5 m (ca. 21 ft) so there wasn't a lot to play with. It took me two attempts to slot her through. My heart rate was high by the time we got in I can tell you. Once alongside our berth the 'marineros' helped us tie up and gave us a warm welcome and later, when we went to the office to check in, they invited us out onto their little patio overlooking the marina entrance and the river estuary. In the distance we could see the Vasco de Gama bridge. Crossing the Tagus estuary it's the longest bridge entirely within Europe, with a total length of 12.3 kilometres (ca. 8 miles). We drank cold beer with them and chatted. One of them had played football with the famous Mourinho at Sentebal FC. He said he'd never have believed the guy would become one of the most famous Portuguese in the world. It had taken some effort to get there, but undoubtedly PDN was the nicest marina we'd been in so far.

I'll let Gail tell the story of our stay in Lisboa.

Day 1 – We just went out to the local butcher and mini-market to get something for tea and I used the laundry facilities

Day 2 – We planned to go to the Oceanarium, but the queue was massive, so we went to the shopping centre — Vasco de Gama — instead, and had McDonald's for lunch. You can get a beer at McDonald's here. Don't know why UK McD's don't do the same. Very civilised. However, I didn't notice this until I had started on my Sprite.

Day 3 — A visit to Sintra by train and shopping centre.

Day 4 — The Oceanarium and shopping centre

Day 5 — Lisbon city

Other days — The Shopping Centre and boat jobs

Sintra

To get to Sintra from the marina was easy. The train station is just the other side of the road to the shopping centre and trains to Sintra ran 3 times an hour. As Sintra is the last stop on the line, you can't go wrong. It was about a 40-minute trip and cost €5 return.

Sintra is known for its many 19th-century romantic architectural monuments and is a UNESCO World Heritage Site. There are many royal palaces and castles to visit in this one town and it is very much a tourist destination. It has been described as Disneyland for adults. I'm not sure I'd describe it as such but it is busy with day trippers. We visited the palace which is in the centre, so we didn't need to get a bus. Some of them are just outside the town itself and the Moorish castle is right on the cliff top. It reminded me of Carcassonne with the cobbled steep streets and artisan shops. We had a glass of vinho verde (green wine) along with cake and cherries doused in port at The Painters Garden, sat on a terrace built up near the canopy of a tree. They offered people purple blankets if they were cold. It wasn't cold up there as such but the wind did gust occasionally.

The Oceanarium

This was fabulous. I have never been to one before, poor really considering the Sea Life Centre in Birmingham wasn't far from home. However, I was impressed. The main tank is just huge and there are so many viewing areas at different levels. Some are a big expanse of curved glass which looks into the centre, there are small windows looking into one particular area and the types of sea life in there is amazing.

There are over 450 species of sea creatures, and they concentrate on raising awareness towards the conservation of nature. I was wondering how they managed to feed such a diverse range of creatures, as I would expect the sharks to eat everything else. There was a video which explained this and how the Oceanarium works, which was good to be included as it answered my questions. This is one of the few aquariums in the world to have Sunfish, as apparently they are notoriously difficult to keep. We have seen the small flapping fins of Sunfish on the surface of the sea a few times as we have been sailing down this Atlantic coast. These are the fins that are on their sides, just behind their eyes. I had no idea what was underneath though. They can grow to weigh up to 2 tons and are ugly. The ones here were massive. The gift shop did manage to make a toy one look cute though, and Neil bought me the keyring version as a memento. Can't imagine that they'd sell many if they were as ugly as the real thing.

They also had puffins, penguins, otters, other seabirds whose name I have forgotten, as well as many tanks with other sea creatures in. No piranhas though. They had a tank with sea dragons, which reminded me of the Soup Dragon from the Clangers.

In addition, there was a temporary exhibition which was also fabulous called Forests Underwater designed by Takashi Amano. Takashi is a landscape photographer who has explored forests all over the world. He introduced Japanese gardening techniques into the design of the planted aquariums. It was beautiful. What I liked was the fact there was a bare patch in the display. It wasn't necessary to fill the space. There was some harmonious music playing and raised seating areas. The idea being you could sit and enjoy quietly. However, that was never going to happen with scores of people passing through chatting, and kids running up and down the seating area. Neil thought the experience could have been enhanced by listening to the music through headphones to zone out the background noise. Some facts: the aquarium is 40 m long and 2.5 m wide and used 4 tons of sand, 25 tons of volcanic rock from the Azores, 78 tree trunks from Scotland and Malaysia, 10,000 tropical freshwater fish from 40 species and 46 species of aquatic plants.

After the Oceanarium we continued to the shopping centre, as we were halfway there. Because of the problems with refrigeration, we have been buying fresh meat and produce as we are using it.

Lisbon

No rest for the wicked as they say, and we took the bus to Lisbon old city, Commercial Square. Again, transport from the marina was easy. The bus stop was close and went straight to the square and cost €1.30 each, return. We had seen the square from the boat and were impressed with the size and the archway leading to Augusta Street behind. As we had motored in I commented on how clean the buildings looked. The old stone churches and basilicas looked spotless considering the age of them. As we went through the archway to Augusta Street, which is the main shopping street, I met Captain Jack from Pirates of the Caribbean and had my picture taken.

We wandered up the street looking up at the architecture of the old buildings and it opened out into Rossio Square where there were two big fountains. We sat down for a beer at Café Nicola and stayed for some lunch just people watching. People kept coming up and taking photos of the front, and I wondered why. Turns out it was a famous café where literary and political meetings were held when it opened in 1929. It maintains part of its past in its art deco facade. There seemed to be endless ways of touring Lisbon. On foot, open-top buses, an amphibious vehicle, small buses, horse and trap and trams but my favourite was the TukTuk. There were loads of them in different designs and styles. Some only sat 2/3 in the back, others were designed for 6 or even a limo style one for 8. They looked fab, and they had been drawing up outside Café Nicola. We decided to take a tour in a TukTuk. I wasn't going to walk up the steep hills, and this was a great way to see the old city as a few of the streets only TukTuks can get down as they are so narrow. A couple of them were only just wide enough for us to fit through. Jorge our driver gave us a good tour and wasn't too chatty or pushy when it came to "trying" the local cherry liquor or ports — obviously locals with an agreement with the TukTuk firm to get sales. I loved the TukTuk and have added one to my virtual home in Portugal. We were tatting on the internet looking at cheap property to buy in Portugal and you can get a ready to move in 2 beds, 1 bath property with 4,000 m of garden in the country for £24k. In fact, if you want a doer-upper then £15k is not unheard of. So naturally, in my head, I am living in a house with an allotment and selling my excess fruit/veg from my TukTuk at the roadside. Boy, do I have an imagination.

We had a great day in Lisbon and barely scratched the surface on things to do and see.

Map of Southern Portugal (Algarve region)

- Sines
- Vila Nova de Milfontes
- Odemira
- Southwest Alentejo and Vicentine Coast Natural Park
- Aljezur
- Monchique
- Silves
- Vila do Bispo
- Cabo de São Vicente
- Sagres
- Lagos
- Alvor
- Lagoa
- Albufeira
- Quarteira
- Loulé
- São Brás de Alportel
- Faro
- Olhão
- Aljustrel
- Castro Verde
- Ourique
- Almodôvar
- North Atlantic Ocean

10

THE ALGARVE

SINES & SAGRES

We stopped 8 nights in Lisbon and thoroughly enjoyed it, but we still had two more 60 mile (ca. 97 km) plus passages ahead of us before we turned the corner and reached the Algarve. It was time to get going again. Next stop was Sines, birthplace of Vasco De Gama.

We got out of the marina with the tide just after 08:00. With the motors on and the current with us, we ran out downriver at 7 knots. I'd expected some decent wind once we got into the estuary proper, and for a change it duly arrived.

We had a couple of hours of great sailing to get us on our way, and saw 11 knots on the GPS in one gust.

The rest of the day was mixed. Sometimes the wind blew, and we got sailing nicely. Other times it died, and we had to motor sail. It took us 12 hours to cover the 65 miles (ca. 105 km) to our anchorage close to the beach within the inner harbour at Sines.

I got the anchor to bite on the second attempt and wasn't long out of my bed.

Next morning we got the dinghy sorted, and I went ashore to find fuel, water and to check in. The marina office was shut. After a long wait, I finally got the fuel, and we were free to explore.

Sines is a busy commercial port but well hidden from the inner harbour where we were. The town itself is authentically Portuguese and surprisingly large. As we walked up the hill towards the castle, the place felt a little run down though. As we'd seen elsewhere in Spain and Portugal, graffiti artists don't leave many buildings untouched.

We found the statue of Vasco De Gama and paid our respects. Our own voyages of exploration had instilled a fresh sense of admiration for pioneers like Vasco. We'd seen firsthand what it was like to sail these dangerous Atlantic shores. To do so in vessels without engines, with rudimentary navigation and no knowledge of what lay beyond the horizon, left us in awe.

Back on board I checked the weather and told Gail all looked well for an early departure next morning. As we sat in the cockpit that evening a large black RIB with half a dozen border police aboard pulled alongside. One officer asked to come aboard. He checked our passports and ship's papers, asked a few questions, and left us in peace. That was the first time we'd had any direct contact with police or customs since leaving Falmouth.

On Friday 21st August we weighed anchor before dawn and laid a course for Cabo São Vicente 54 miles (ca. 87 km) to the south.

Cabo São Vicente. It still seemed impossible that we'd shortly be sailing around it. Cape St Vincent is the southwesternmost point of Portugal and of mainland Europe.

The place has been special for millennia. It was already sacred ground in Neolithic times. The ancient Greeks called it Ophiussa (Land of Serpents). The Romans called it Promontorium Sacrum (or Holy Promontory).

Ancient people believed the sun sank here, hissing into the ocean. To them, its towering cliffs marked the edge of their world.

These cliffs rise nearly vertically from the Atlantic to a height of 75 m (ca. 246 ft). It's a wind blasted and storm pounded headland that marks the turning point for any vessel travelling to or from the Mediterranean. Just off the Cape lies one of the busiest shipping lanes in the world.

It would be a turning point for us also. Physically and metaphorically. Once around it, life would get easier. The waters calmer and clearer. The weather warmer and sunnier.

We were more than ready.

We motored out of Sines before dawn. The sea was like a mirror. As the sun rose behind the mountains inland, bright orange beams of light shot out across the water. I'd have liked some wind, but it was spectacular.

Once we'd cleared the enormous ships anchored off Sines, we had the sea to ourselves all day. As on our trip down from Lisbon, the wind came and went. We sailed, we motored. By 3 in the afternoon I thought I could see Cabo São Vicente in the distance. But as I watched, it started fading from view. It seemed our old nemesis the fog wasn't ready to let us go just yet.

I should have guessed. Back in June, when we'd rounded Cape Finisterre and onto the Atlantic coast, the fog welcomed us.

Now, some 600 miles (ca. 966 km) and two months later, it had come to see us off.

Over the next few hours, the fog grew thicker. We lost sight of the horizon; we lost sight of land. Once again our world shrank to a few hundred yards around the boat, with only the little red triangle on the chart plotter showing us where we were on the planet.

Gail and I had visited Cabo São Vicente several times. Only a few years before we'd stood on the cliffs looking out to the horizon. I'd said to Gail, "Someday soon we'll be out there on 'Gleda'. Imagine how that will feel".

Gail will admit that her imagination isn't so great. But when I'd said those words, in my head, 'Gleda' had been under full sail, cutting through the waves as we gazed up at the sunlit cliffs above us.

Proud though I was that we were finally here. I couldn't help but feel a little let down as we motored along through the gloom.

It wasn't until I altered course to the east and closed within a mile of the shore that we finally saw the Cabo.

The iconic squat red lighthouse atop the low, red tiled roofed buildings loomed up out of the fog. The farther we moved east, the more the fog lifted and the more we could see.

A few miles later we rounded Sagres Point and turned into the bay to drop anchor off the beach, we'd done it, we were on the Algarve proper.

By the time we'd boiled the kettle and sat down on deck, the sun was shining. The sky was blue, and the wind had died completely.

I smiled at Gail.

Crossing Biscay had been a huge milestone for me personally. This felt different. This was why Gail had come. We had shared the desire to get here. We'd done it together.

It would take some time for it all to sink in.

The wind blew hard all night and well into the morning. Some gusts reached 30 knots. I hadn't planned to stay on in Sagres, but it didn't take long for me to decide to stop.

The anchor was well bedded in; we were safe and comfortable. I figured we'd just rest up. As the day went on, the wind gradually eased. That evening our friends Garry and June arrived on 'Friendship' and anchored close by. They came aboard for drinks and a chat. We'd last seen them in Baiona. It was great to share experiences with a couple who'd done what we had done, overcome their own challenges and made it south.

We had a shared next stop too. We were headed to Alvor, a little town just to the east of Lagos.

Not long after we arrived in La Coruña we'd been told about the anchorage in Alvor. Soon after we arrived there a Fountaine Pajot catamaran berthed astern of us. It was crewed by two Portuguese guys named Vito and Santos. Santos told me they had just bought the boat in France and were on their way home to Alvor in Portugal where Vito planned to use the catamaran as a day charter boat for holidaymakers. When I told him we were also headed to the Algarve, he got excited. "You must come to Alvor" he said. "It is my home, it is beautiful. I tell you, people only leave Alvor when they have too".

I'd made a mental note, but to be honest I'd taken his words with a pinch of salt.

I had no idea how true they'd been.

ALVOR ARRIVAL

The next morning we sailed off the anchor and started our short passage the 20 odd miles east to Alvor. It was a cracking downwind sail. What a difference it made being 'round the corner'. We'd finally left the rolling Atlantic swell behind. We ghosted along in flat water with blue skies above, a warm wind pushing us along, and not a hint of that damned fog. It was perfect.

'Friendship' left a little while after us. But once again my cruising chute envy surfaced, as they gradually gained and eventually overtook us.

We parted company off Lagos as they needed to go in for fuel and water. Unlike 'Gleda' they needed to get the boat alongside to refill. We used containers for both. That meant I could throw them in the dinghy and go ashore anywhere.

The wind freshened as we rounded the cliffs at Ponta de Piedade and into Lagos Bay. We reached across towards the Alvor entrance at 7-8 knots and were there by 15:00. I dropped the sails and got the engines on. We'd been sailing for nearly six hours at a leisurely 3.5 knot average. But what a different sail it'd been. I'd felt as relaxed as I'd ever done on the boat.

Now though, I needed to pay attention again. The Alvor lagoon is renowned for shallow depths and sandbanks. Every winter the sand gets moved around. I'd been warned not to trust the buoyed channel, but to use the depth sounder and go slow. The fun started just inside the breakwaters. In Europe, Africa, most of Asia and Australia the buoyage system is set up for entering harbour. To stay in the channel, you keep the port (red) buoys to the left and the starboard (green) buoys to the right. Not in Alvor. Here you kept to whatever side there was water.

It's perhaps worth mentioning that in North, Central and South America, Japan, Korea and the Philippines they do things the opposite way round. In those waters you'd be leaving the right-hand buoys (boo-ees) to the left!

Anyway, we navigated our way through OK, although the depth sounder dropped dramatically a few times and in inverse proportion to my heart rate. Again we had an advantage. 'Gleda' only needed shallow water to float, even if we'd gone aground, it wouldn't have been a problem. I've long kept a stiff broom handy on deck when entering harbour. If we go aground, I can jump over the side and start scrubbing the hulls. That way onlookers would think I'd done it deliberately. You can't do that in a monohull that's lying on its side.

Once through the narrow channel we reached the sheltered lagoon in front of the town. As expected, it was crowded with moored and anchored boats. Yet again, our shallow draft gave us an advantage. I spotted a nice little spot close to the outside of the lagoon. There wasn't room for us to swing, so I used two anchors, one off the bow and one off the stern. It kept us in position parallel to a sloping stone surrounding wall. It took a bit of effort, but once done, I knew we'd be able to stay put for as long as we liked.

The satisfaction I'd felt when we anchored in Sagres returned. But this time it felt stronger. This time I knew we really had done it. We'd already got our winter berth booked in Lagos marina just a few miles away. No more passage planning, no more weather watching, no more stressing about where we were going to spend the night.

I had planned this escape for so long.

When I'd left Falmouth over 30 years previously, it'd been my intention to get to Culatra, just up the coast. I never made it.

But now I was here. On a boat I'd built myself. My dream had finally come true.

ALVOR DAYS

In the back of my mind I'd wondered if Alvor might be too noisy, too touristy, too tacky. It was all those things. But somehow they seemed in balance. The place had authenticity. Tourist boats and working fishing boats, holiday apartments and people's homes. Our first impressions were good. Sure, the centre of town was packed with tourist tat shops and an unbelievable number of bars and restaurants, but walk a few streets either side and you discovered real Portugal.

We treated ourselves to a celebratory meal at the Casa Do Rio restaurant overlooking the harbour. We sat outside on the patio looking out over the anchorage, we could see 'Gleda' below us and look right across to Lagos. It was special.

As I've already mentioned, I'd tucked 'Gleda' close to the north side of the river, with a stern anchor out to stop us swinging too much. It was a good move, the anchorage was protected from the open sea by a narrow dogleg entrance and dunes, so no swell could enter. 'Gleda' only moved when an occasional power boat came past. We were close enough to the bank that we could hear the Cicadas chirping, and at night the clank of cattle bells. When the wind came from the east, we could smell the charcoal smoke from the harbour-side restaurants. A short dinghy ride across the harbour lay a nice pontoon for access to the town. There was no charge to anchor, and €10 paid to the fisherman's organisation meant we could get unlimited water from the fishing quay.

There was always something to see. Boats came back and forth constantly, and we'd met folks from the friendly little community of like-minded sailors anchored and moored around us.

I spotted the Fountaine Pajot catamaran we'd met in Coruña; I hadn't recognised it at first. When I'd last seen it, the hulls had been white. Now she was painted bright blue, with the words 'Alvor Sailing' in big letters down her side. When she came past us one morning, her decks loaded with orange canoes and a dozen or so tourists, I heard a shout and looked across. There were Santos and Vito waving with enormous grins on their faces. They'd recognised 'Gleda' immediately. "Hey, welcome to Alvor", they shouted, "it's great you came!"

For the first week I did little. I sat on deck; I sat in the pod; I took siestas; I worked hard at being lazy (easy for me). We took the dinghy ashore for shopping. We took a taxi with Garry and June into Portimão.

I hadn't realised how much I needed to rest and wind down. Perhaps you'll think we'd just been on one big long holiday, and I won't argue, but the challenges of sailing had run my energy levels low again.

I'd given no thought to when or where we'd go next. But that felt fine. We were both enjoying the peace, the sunshine, the restful nights.

This was what the escape had been all about. Now we really were living the dream, and we embraced it.

By the beginning of September, I'd finally wound down. My desire to move on and sail some more had evaporated. We had a booking to go into Marina De Lagos around the middle of October. Staying right where we were until then was just fine.

I'd realised that Alvor was the perfect location for us. It was just so nice to enjoy the weather, wander through town, swim, sunbathe, siesta, eat, drink and simply enjoy life.

There'd be time aplenty in the spring to cruise again. For now, we just wanted to make the most of the remaining summer.

We did some lengthy walks inland, exploring along the riverbank. The views were amazing. It was baking hot; the ground was bone dry (there had been no rain for 3 months); the Cicadas were chirping, and on a lake a mile or so inland we saw Flamingoes in the wild.

Garry and June on Friendship had also chosen to stay in Alvor until going into Lagos. Gail and June had become best friends. They went shopping together and got in the habit of swimming in the afternoons. Well, when I say swimming, what I mean is that they both floated around with their brightly coloured China shop swim noodles, nattering.

As for me, I lay on deck in the sun, watching the world go by. I realised this was the first time for years that I'd truly been content. Maybe even the first time. Of one thing I was certain. This felt like redemption. Thirty-one years since I'd failed and lost 'Mor Gwas'. Twenty years of trying to be someone I wasn't. Eight years of blood, sweat and tears making 'Gleda' a reality. Just 12 months previously I'd been exhausted, stressed and frustrated with my inability to sail south. Now, I'd crossed Biscay, I'd navigated my boat through 1300 nautical miles of treacherous waters. I'd got us safely anchored in paradise. It felt like I deserved to bask in some self-satisfaction for a while.

As the weeks went by we adjusted to our new life. The anchorage was frequently crowded. Too crowded on some days.

There was supposed to be a fairway between the inner harbour and the channel, but deeper draft boats fearful of going aground often anchored right in the middle of it. Many of the local fishermen used smaller boats with big outboards. They'd leave early in the morning and be forced to slalom their way through a minefield of anchored yachts. Some took their frustration out by doing so at speed, sending their wash to rock the offenders awake. Some days even that wasn't possible. One morning I saw a fisherman throttle back and throw his arms in the air in frustration. There were so many yachts veering about in the breeze, he couldn't see any way through.

One day whilst waiting for Gail on the quayside I was chatting to Santos. You'll remember him as the crew of the Fountaine Pajot cat we'd met in Coruña. He and Vito had got their business up and running quickly. They'd now got a shack on the quayside where they could target the holidaymakers and were doing well. They were filling the boat and doing one or two trips every day. Anyway, during a quiet spell I mentioned that some locals must resent their village being so overwhelmed with tourists. He said no. Born in Alvor, he'd lived there all of his 30 or more years. He remembered the village as poor, a little fishing, a few people scraping a living from the land, not a lot else. Now there were jobs. The place was prosperous and alive. OK, maybe a few fishermen didn't like it, but you can't please everyone. No, for him and most of the locals, life was far better. When he'd seen me in Coruña and pleaded with me to come to Alvor, he'd meant it. He thanked me for making the effort. His words both touched and amused me. He'd thanked me for coming to paradise!

Although many of the boats visiting Alvor only stayed a few days, there were others, like us, who stayed longer.

Apart from Garry and June on 'Friendship', there were two other boats we'd crossed paths with on the journey south. Jackie and Ian on 'Rivalady', Roger and Pam on 'Déjà vu'.

Gail and the three ladies started sharing a cab and making 'coffee and shopping' trips into the Aqua retail centre in Portimão.

We made some new friends, Jan and Baukjen, a Dutch couple on their boat named 'J&B'. Well into their sixties they'd been cruising full time for a decade, the Med, The Caribbean, Scotland, Ireland, Scandinavia. They've even had J&B tied up to the quay alongside Tesco in Truro, our old adopted home! Proper sailors.

Then there were some characters. Two in particular spring to mind. I'll call them Earle and Anastasia for reasons that will become apparent. American and Russian respectively, I'd describe Earle as loud and full of shit. Anastasia was quiet and mysterious. He'd apparently been cruising aboard his one-off aluminium (aloom-inum) motor sailer for 25 years and had circumnavigated twice. His much younger partner Anastasia, had joined him six months previously in Greece and planned to sail back with him to Earles home in Grenada. An interesting couple. He dropped not-so-subtle BS hints that he was ex-military or covert ops. She'd sit there and say little. The anchorage would occasionally echo to the sounds of them screaming at each other as they argued below decks. Often Anastasia would then abandon ship and take the dinghy ashore, leaving Earle to cool off. Given that in almost every conversation I'd ever had with Earle he'd mentioned firearms at least once, I'd been expecting to hear gunshots every time one of these arguments kicked off. He endeared himself even more as he'd acquired the delightful continental habit of standing on the stern and pissing over the side in full view of the entire anchorage. Gail and June were convinced Anastasia was a Russian spy trying to get to the States undercover; if so, she wasn't good at it. She couldn't even be consistent with her cover name. She told June her name was Natalie, and Earle referred to her as Olga at least once.

We woke up one morning, and the boat had gone. I wonder what happened to them. Their story would make a marvellous book.

There were many other friends around. We had our first deck party. Fourteen of us. Brit's, Dutch, American, Polish, French and Swiss, oh, and a Russian. It was fun.

We eked out summer as long as possible but time passed quickly, 'Friendship' left for Lagos on the first of October, followed by 'Rivalady', 'Déjà vu' and, with some poor weather approaching, 'J&B'. Gail and I hung on, enjoying the quieter days.

We watched a lunar eclipse lying on deck; I swam every day despite the cooler temperatures. The first autumn rains arrived with winds from the southeast. They left the decks coated in yellow sand from the Sahara.

Stronger winds blew through, catching some boats out. Early one morning a Dutch boat next to us, 'Ocean Goose', dragged her anchor. Gail saw it happen and called me up. I was just going for the foghorn to alert them when the couple on board popped up on deck in a panic. They got the engine started just in time, but came perilously close to the rocky breakwater.

It took them several attempts to get the anchor bedded again.

On Friday 9th October we left Alvor on a gorgeous calm morning. We'd spent 51 consecutive nights on anchor. The weather forecast for the weekend was lousy. My daughter and her boyfriend were arriving for a visit in a few days. It was time for our winter berth.

WINTER IN LAGOS

ADJUSTING

With the Lagos entrance only a few miles down the coast, it wasn't worth getting the sails up, so we motored along gently, just enjoying the view.

As always, I was on my toes as we entered the channel leading up to the marina; it was narrow and busy and I knew we'd be coming alongside the reception pontoon, passing under a lifting bridge and then manoeuvring into our berth, so I had plenty to think about.

In the event, with no wind and little current, it turned out to be straightforward, apart from one slight glitch when the starboard outboard kicked up out of the water as I went astern. I'd forgotten to lock it.

It was cool to call up on the VHF and have the bridge opened specially for us. Gail and I had walked across that bridge more than a few times in years gone by, and back then I'd never have believed that one day I'd be bringing my own boat under it.

We slotted into a berth right next to 'Friendship'. It felt strange to be back in a marina.

Here's what I wrote in my journal that night:

A year ago today I'd just heard that Jake couldn't crew for us and I'd decided to stay in Falmouth. Tonight we had drinks with American friends aboard their boat in a marina on the Algarve, then walked back to 'Gleda' in the warm night air with the sound of cicadas all around.... Incredible.

We spent the first few days getting settled in, we'd heard nothing but excellent reports about the marina and from what we'd experienced so far they seemed to be accurate. The last time we'd been in a marina had been in Lisbon back in the middle of August, so having hot showers, mains electricity, running water and washing machines proved to be a welcome novelty.

My daughter Nicole and her boyfriend Simon also appreciated the facilities when they came to visit for a few days.

The weather held up well, and we got out for an enjoyable day sail with them, although our old friend the fog came down to see us again.

Once out into the bay, we hoisted sail and drifted slowly down the coast in the fog before anchoring off Alvor beach for lunch. While we ate it the sun obligingly came out for an hour before another bank of fog rolled in. We sailed back to our berth in a warm fug.

The clocks changed not long after they left. I stripped the sails off the masts and bagged them, and flushed the outboards through with fresh water. I tied us to the pontoon with extra mooring lines. The season was well and truly over.

And what an incredible season it had been. Six months, 1327 nautical miles travelled, 4 countries. 22 days and 5 nights of sailing, 32 nights in marinas, 23 nights on moorings, 84 nights at anchor.

I counted back and discovered that I'd passed a milestone of

500 consecutive nights sleeping aboard 'Gleda'. Safe to say she'd become a home.

It'd been great spending precious time with Nicole. But after she left, I felt unsettled and down. There'd been a time when this had been my default state. I thought I'd shaken it off for good. I was wrong.

The Lagos Marina environment wasn't helping.

There was nothing wrong with the place really, people were friendly enough, it was in a safe and sheltered location, the showers and laundry were usable, and we were within walking distance of the town and beach.

For me though, it felt claustrophobic. On the anchor in Alvor, we'd had plenty of space around the boat. From the deck I could see for miles inland towards the mountains of Monchique. In Lagos we were hemmed in all round with boats. Everywhere else I looked was concrete. It's a strange thing. In a marina it's considered perfectly normal and acceptable to have everyone so close together, but if the boats had been caravans and the water concrete folks wouldn't have put up with it.

It was noisy too. The road opposite seemed to be the key route to and from Lagos Hospital, and a dozen times a day ambulances from the National Institute of Medical Emergency (INEM) came screaming along with their multi-toned sirens blaring. They're effective devices those sirens, they start with a deep single repeating tone that sounds like an electronic train horn, move through to high-pitched wailing, and finish with the more traditional UK 'nee nah' 'nee nah'. There's no ignoring them.

In Alvor the soundtrack to our lives had been cicadas, cattle bells and the call of terns. The contrast was glaring.

There were a dozen bars and restaurants alongside the marina. They hosted live music or karaoke most nights. I was usually in bed by the time they started. I hoped that these activities would die down as the season drew to a close.

Everyone we'd spoken to before we arrived raved about Lagos. But as far as I was concerned, it ranked as just OK. I realised that the folks who loved it the most were those that ate out a lot. Those who spent their mornings in the coffee shops and their lunchtimes and evenings in the bars. They loved the security and comfort of this floating suburbia with its social gatherings, the Mexican train dominoes, the yoga, the rambling. Many of these people had been here for years, they liked to know who was who and what was what. Nasty gossip or well-intentioned interest. However you described it, I found it intrusive.

There was another reason I was feeling uncomfortable. The place was shining a glaring spotlight on our lack of funds. Millions of pounds worth of yachts surrounded us. Tens of thousands of Euros passed through the tills up on the quay every day. There seemed to be plenty of people around for whom money wasn't an issue. I had no problem with that. Fair play to them.

But we simply couldn't afford to buy coffee and beer every day or eat out in the way they did. In Alvor that had been easy to forget, but not in Lagos. Not when you have to walk past the temptation many times a day. It's even harder when you have to turn down an invitation to eat or drink and folks take it as a social snub.

'Gleda' acted as a mirror for our finances. I'd grown used to her attracting a lot of attention because she looked so different. Since we'd started our journey, we'd had some genuine interest and more than a few compliments. But Lagos was the first place where I'd overheard words of ridicule about my boat. I didn't care what others thought about me or my boat, but these petty annoyances were all beginning to add up.

I knew it was just me being me again. But I couldn't help feeling what I was feeling. All I could do was to try to control my reactions to those feelings and do my best to stay chilled.

We were in Lagos because it was the best place to be for the winter. Had I been on my own, I'd have stayed on the anchor in Alvor and roughed it out. But that wouldn't have been fair to Gail, she was enjoying Lagos far more than me. She was enjoying being back in touch with 'civilisation' again. She deserved a break.

A DAWNING REALITY

But there was one element of 'civilisation' we weren't getting our fair share of. And that was Wi-Fi.

We'd been told it was good in the marina, but despite our berth being comparatively close to the office and antenna, I couldn't get reception inside the hulls, and even in the deckpod it was weak and patchy.

For me, good Wi-Fi reception had been one of the major attractions of coming into the marina for the winter. I'd been hatching plans for a few internet reliant activities, but this poor service had prevented me cracking on as I'd intended. Instead, I'd wasted a lot of time trying to get connected, and eventually had to give up and order a dedicated external antenna and black boxes.

Lack of funds held me back from doing it at first, but my hand was forced. It's obvious that decent internet connectivity is essential to any plan of creating some income online, so I'd treated the purchase as a long-term investment in my business.

And what business is this? I hear you ask.

Earlier in the book I talked about how relaxing Alvor had been, how I'd switched off and basked in the glory of my achievements. I was being somewhat economical with the truth.

Yes, my body may have relaxed, but the inactivity had started the little electrons popping inside the tiny bit of grey matter of mine that passes for a brain.

I'd sit on deck with pen and paper, staring across the water and occasionally scribbling away, trying to put some flesh on the bones of some random thought or idea.

Most of the time I'd fail, get frustrated, jump overboard and swim for a while. But later in the day my head would be buzzing again, usually when I was trying to get to sleep.

It'd been an age since I'd had the time and space to think like this. I knew I was blessed. For most folks, life is just too damn busy to leave room for such luxuries.

As with everything though, there are pluses and minuses. On the plus side, I was able to find a release for my creative urges by writing and taking photos. But there was something wrong. It took me a long while to figure out what it was.

The downside of having time to think is that all those thoughts will not be positive. There was plenty of time for negativity and doubt to creep up on me, throwing up questions I didn't yet have answers to. And there was one scarier than the rest put together.

How the hell do I sustain this lifestyle?

Funds for the past 18 months of living aboard, finishing the boat, and sailing south to Portugal, had come from two sources;

1) A cash draw down from my pension pot
2) Gail's redundancy money.

And that money was running out.

We'd got some breathing space. We had lived cheaply for months, and we'd put aside the money for our winter berth in Lagos.

But there was an inescapable fact.

Without generating some income, we'd be broke by the spring.

The words I wrote in my journal whilst in Alvor are telling:

I have no idea what the solution is, but here's the thing. My journey to get this far has taught me many things, the greatest of which is that I'm capable of far more than I'd believed of myself.

> Not so many years ago I'd have been sinking into a pit of depression, paralysed by the fear of what was to come, blaming life for kicking me in the nuts again, blaming myself for letting it happen.
> Now it's different, I've changed. I see things differently.
> Life is simple, it's just made up of choices, I chose to take money out of my pension; I chose to spend it in the way I have, and now the time has come, I've chosen to find a solution, and I will.

Easy to write, not so easy to do. I spent weeks thinking about it.

Back to my journal:

> It pains me to write about money, really it does. Why? Because I have no interest in it.
> See, I'm already wealthy, I have my health; I have people that love me (go figure); I have food and drink on the table and I have a floating home all my own. I'm living the life I've dreamed about for years.
> I've learned that money and possessions no longer hold any great attraction to me. What I value far more is quality of life and the freedom to pursue it.
> For all my dreamy aspirations though, I'm still a realist, I can't change the way the world works and it's money that keeps the wheels turning. Like it or not, there has to be some cash in the bank or the wheels will come off my own little bandwagon.
> But there have to be some ground rules, the money has to come via channels that are a comfortable and enjoyable fit with my values and lifestyle.
> I will not go back to the life I had before and give up my happiness, freedom and self-respect for a monthly pay cheque.

I'd asked my blog followers for suggestions. As usual, they came up trumps.

Cynthia and Jean Paul suggested laying 'Gleda' up for six months and heading back to the UK to work, I knew Beat, (Tiki

38 'Aluna') had just spent 18 months away from his boat to build up a war chest. A decent idea, but not for me, it just didn't appeal. It would seem like a betrayal of everything I'd worked for. 'Gleda' was my home, and I would not leave her.

Philip and Michael both suggested chartering but, as Philip pointed out, to do that legally would mean fighting with bureaucracy and red tape. Neither 'Gleda' nor I were up to that.

Exchanging my skills in return for reward was already on my radar and held some appeal. It was just a case of being on the lookout for opportunities and taking them when they arrived. An option to keep open, but not a plan.

We had an industrial sewing machine onboard and that, along with a lot of deck space, could be something to capitalise on.

Ken suggested teaching English. Yes, probably a possibility in some places, but on the Algarve they all seemed to speak it perfectly already!

I discounted other suggestions such as people smuggling, drug running, piracy and personal prostitution. Sure, there was money to be made in at least three of the four, but I filed them with my 'rob a bank' pension plan for possible later consideration.

But there was one idea in particular that kept coming back. It was the one I'd had back in São Martinho do Porto; writing.

It was something I enjoyed, I'd already started writing a book. Maybe that could be the answer. The book would be a long-term thing, but I'd read that writing articles for publication could bring in some money.

I knew that it was a competitive market, but perhaps I could bring something a little different to the table. How about an article about living with a composting toilet? Yeah, I could write about that shit!

I knew what I was looking for was a means to generate a modest regular independent income that wasn't location or time specific, ideally with a passive element to it. Writing seemed to tick those boxes.

THE WRITE STUFF

As the weeks passed, my thoughts about writing narrowed. I'd been blogging for years. Folks seemed to enjoy what I wrote, and I gradually came round to the idea that maybe writing was the way to go.

I stumbled across a website showing how people were earning income as freelance writers. Perhaps that was the answer. I dived into the subject headfirst. I found and purchased the domain name ClearWords.zyz and set up a website, then signed up to several freelance sites like Upwork. After posting my availability for work I waited. A couple of small jobs dribbled in. I spent hours on them. I got less than two dollars in return. My enthusiasm waned, again.

My mood was slipping into winter just as surely as the weather.

One particular Saturday night, the sky hinted that we were in for something unusual. We discovered that old saying 'red sky at night, shepherds delight' doesn't apply in Portugal. Because any Portuguese shepherd wandering about the fields the following day would likely have seen his flock being washed downhill at a rapid rate of knots, and I'm not sure he'd have been delighted about it.

It started raining in the early hours and, apart from a lull mid-afternoon, it rained for 24 hours, heavily. Afterwards, the Portuguese meteorological people said we'd had the whole of the month's average rainfall in one day.

When there's a lot of water about the best place to be is on a boat, we hunkered down and kept dry. The morning after this biblical downpour, we woke to find they had replaced all the water in the marina with milky tea. The marina in Lagos sits on the outlet of the river Bensafrim. The tea-coloured water resulted from mud washed in from the hills above the town.

Along the coast a little way in Albufeira, folks had suffered badly. One man had died in a submerged car. People lost their homes, businesses were destroyed. It made me reconsider my right to complain about life.

I reconsidered a lot of other things. Here's a blog post I wrote at the time.

> *So, here I am again, stabbing at the keys on my laptop in the vain hope that somehow I can turn the words churning round in my tiny little brain into something folks might read without losing consciousness.*
>
> *Writing's supposed to get easier the more you do it, that's what it says in all the writing books I've read (I'm sure my purchases of such books have increased Amazons share price these past few years), but I'm seeing no signs of it yet, and I've been writing a lot lately.*
>
> *I have plenty of time to write as I sit here in this floating caravan park waiting for spring and escape back to the open sea and peaceful anchorages.*
>
> *I have time to write and I have time to think, and the writing helps me think. It hurts my head to think though, I can see why so many of us try to avoid it. I'm an expert at not thinking, but I know I should do it more, not thinking has got me into a lot of trouble in the past and still does.*
>
> *Anyway, before the last of you falls into an unconscious stupor, what I'm trying to say is that all this thinking has led me to make some changes to my thinking. Hmmm, thinking changes thinking, that sounds almost clever...... Nahh, can't be.*
>
> *So, here's what's changed.*
>
> *I am now absolutely, 100%, rock solid certain what I want to do....... I want to write. I'd pretty much reached that conclusion before, but I made a mistake, I was focusing on the wrong writing. I was looking at writing as 'work', I defaulted to using what I already knew*

was a broken template, starting from a position of need and looking for a way to make money by doing stuff my heart wasn't in. Going back to working for 'clients' and putting up with all the crap that comes with them.

What was I thinking? (Strange phrase isn't it? We say it even when it's obvious that we weren't thinking at all).

But thanks to all that thinking, I can now see clearly that I was charging down a blind alley, destined to slam into a brick wall and do myself some serious harm...... Again.

That blind alley was ClearWords.xyz and all that went with it. So I stopped, backed out of there, and drew a new map.

Some might say they could see it coming, some might say they knew I was headed in the wrong direction, I might say well done them. Sometimes you can be too close to something to focus properly, sometimes you get it wrong. But if I've learned anything over the course of this build a boat and go sailing project, it's that you don't give up, you learn from your mistakes and move on, so that's what I'm doing.

So, here's today's news. I'm going to carry on writing, but I'm going to write what I want to write. I'm going to write books and I'm going to self-publish.

I know this is the right path. Why?

Because it allows me to be me.

That's what this project was about all along. It was about finding a path that allowed me to live my life as I wanted to live it, all the time.

Chasing money isn't me, I can't do it. All I can do is write what I want to write, put it out into the world and see if a few folks will pay to read it.

Maybe they will, maybe they won't.

It doesn't matter. What matters is that I'm true to myself. After that, it's down to the Universe.

I don't know why it took me so long to come up with this. The clues had been there in São Martinho do Porto.

Looking back, I realise now that for decades I'd been blocking my thoughts and emotions about 'Mor Gwas' and my failed voyage into Biscay. But now that I'd finally succeeded, laid the ghost to rest, I felt ready to tell the complete story. It felt right, it felt necessary.

I'd called the book 'A Foolish Voyage' and the first draft was well underway.

TIME PASSES

During the run up to Christmas, I was on my own for nearly three weeks. Gail took the opportunity to get back to the UK to see friends and family. It was strange. We hadn't spent a day apart in eight months. There'd been a time when I enjoyed being on my own, but not any more. I missed her.

The marina had gone noticeably quieter. There were fewer visitors, and it seemed lots of folks with boats also had 'homes' to go to for Christmas, so they'd already left or would leave soon. Now and again I found myself wishing that I too had a place ashore somewhere. I knew Gail did. But we both knew that it was something just not possible for us. For now, we were both happy that home was where the boat was. But at this time of year the attraction of a more traditional home and family environment is greatest.

I spent a lot of time writing while Gail was away. 'A Foolish Voyage' was close to completion. As well as editing and rewriting, I'd been getting my head around the self-publishing process and learning other skills like formatting and cover creation.

To mix things up a bit, I also spent time 'decorating' our cabin. There were jobs that needed doing that would have been difficult when we were both aboard, but with Gail away I could put the double berth out of commission and sleep in the single cabin while I got things done.

Apart from a fresh coat of paint, I added some more insulation and drilled holes in the plywood bunk base to aid air circulation. In Falmouth we'd struggled to keep the condensation under control, and even with ventilation mesh and timber slats under the mattress had still got mouldy. The milder drier climate of the Algarve meant we would likely have less of a problem, but I figured anything I could do to prevent further issues was worthwhile.

I also stripped off all the horrible foil and polystyrene insulation I'd stuck to the cabin top sides the previous winter. It had made no difference, and it looked crap. It was a horrible job to remove it and I even found mould underneath, so I was glad to be shot of it. I replaced it with cork tiling. A better insulator and better looking.

I only had one trip away from the boat. I took the train into Portimão, so I could go to the big Aki DIY store for paint and stuff I needed for the cabin work.

It was a 20-minute train ride along the coast and it was nice to see a different bit of the country. The train was clean and on time and the fare €2 each way.

I had some time to kill after my shopping, so I walked into the town for a look around. Portimão is the largest town on the Western Algarve and far less touristy than Lagos. I walked through the old town and down to the banks of the Arade river. Most of the buildings were old and pretty. There were a good variety of shops, bars and restaurants and some beautiful little parks. I found a huge wide promenade running along the river which, when I was there, seemed mostly deserted.

It was slightly surreal to walk through town in the warm sunshine looking at oranges hanging on the trees and Christmas decorations hanging across the street.

Gail got back on the 13th of December. I'd put Christmas lights up the mast and around the pod. I wanted to welcome her 'home'.

'A Foolish Voyage' was published on Christmas Eve. It was scary to push the button and send my work out into the world. But once done, I relaxed. What would be would be. Only time would tell.

I wrote in my journal:

Feliz Natal

A long time ago a wise man said;
"So here it is Merry Christmas, everybody's having fun. Look to the future now, it's only just begun".
That man was Mr Noddy Holder, the band was 'Slade' and the year was 1973. Who'd have believed that, 42 years later, I would hear his words repeated ad nauseam around a shopping centre in a town on the Portuguese Algarve? Mr Holder was wise indeed to pen those lyrics.
So here it is. The day is nearly upon us, with the year-end right on its tail. It seems that most folks are having fun, and although I too am enjoying the present, I can't help looking to the future.

We ate Christmas dinner at a small restaurant in town. We shared it with a multi-national group of about twenty from the marina.

The food was excellent; the company delightful; we enjoyed it,

On New Year Eve there was live music down on the quay and a huge fireworks display by the harbour entrance. Given my dislike of crowds, we walked down the opposite side of the entrance channel and found a spot in the beach dunes to sit. From there we could look across the water at the festivities. Hearing the music wasn't an issue. We could hear that in the marina.

We got a bit of a shock when it came time for the fireworks though. We discovered that our peaceful spot in the dunes was only a few yards from the firework launch site. They were spectacular, as was our view. The blanket we'd sat on became a shelter from sparks and spent rocket sticks falling from the sky.

After Christmas I stopped writing in my journal, and I stopped blogging. I just switched off and waited for time to pass. Marina funk had truly set in.

The rest of winter passed without event. It got cold in January. We had ice on the deck a few mornings.

That said, Gail's Mom Veronica, and her friend Barbs came to visit in January and had some decent weather.

Veronica came back in March with Gail's Step Dad Bryan. Gail thoroughly enjoyed showing them around and introducing them to friends. We even took them out for a sail.

We stayed in Lagos until the 14th April.

It felt good to leave. An hour later we anchored back in 'our spot' in Alvor lagoon.

It was cold that evening, but I didn't care. I sat on deck. Breathed in the fresh air, listened to the silence. I began to wake up again.

Aljustrel

a Nova de Milfontes

Castro Verde

Garvāo

Mértola
Guadiana valley
Natural Park

Odemira

Penha D'Água

Pulpis de G

Almodôvar

Alcoutim & Sanlúcar
Villanueva de Castillejos

Southwest Alentejo
and Vicentine
Coast Natural Park

Aljezur

Monchique

Vilablanca
Cartaya
Lepe

Silves

Vila Real
A-49

Alvor
Portimão
Lagoa
A22
San Bras de
Alportel
Tavira

Vila do Bispo
Lagos
Albufeira
Loulé
Quarteira

Faro
Olhao

Armona
Deserta
Culatra

12

EAST TO EDEN

ALVOR AGAIN

We spent the first couple of weeks back in Alvor doing little. We eased ourselves back into life on the hook, got used to using the dinghy to 'commute' ashore again, enjoyed the tranquillity.

The season hadn't yet started. We were the only boat on anchor most of the time. A lot of the bars and restaurants in town were still closed.

My laziness couldn't continue though. I had a big job planned.

I've mentioned already that the lagoon in Alvor had many sandbanks. As we'd come in, I'd noticed that the winter gales had shifted some of them. I'd been following the plotter track we'd used the previous year and nearly ran aground on a new sand spit that had extended out into the channel.

The sand may have been a navigational hazard, but for us, it provided an opportunity. As I've mentioned many times, one of the enormous advantages of catamarans is that they can 'take the ground'. 'Gleda' had been afloat for 18 months. Her hulls were dirty with weed and various other marine life. They needed cleaning, and I needed to apply some more of the special anti-fouling paint used to slow down such growths.

The firm sand of Alvor gave me a chance to dry out the boat and avoid the huge cost of having the boat lifted at a boatyard. I just needed the right spring tides. You'll remember those from our passage around Northern France.

The task also required some calm weather. I didn't want us to get blown about as we settled and lifted with the tide.

After spending some time in the dinghy I'd found the perfect spot just a short distance from the anchorage. After that, it was just a waiting game.

I watched the weather, and I watched the tides.

Then, right at the beginning of May, everything came together. No wind, dry and sunny. With high tide early morning and early evening we'd get the best part of the day dried out.

So, on the morning of 2nd May I got 'Gleda' sitting pretty on a lovely bit of sheltered firm sand. No more lazing around.

We filled the whole of the first day scrubbing the hulls clean of 18 months of mud and slime. No jet wash on the sand unfortunately, so it was elbow grease, a stiff broom and lots of seawater.

Actually, I was pleasantly surprised how easily the crud came off, almost as easily as the skin from my hands.

We came off the sand each evening back onto anchor. It was so much easier and more comfortable than letting her float and dry overnight, hoping to stay in the right spot.

Day two was a last scrub, rinse with fresh water and application of fresh anti-foul. I did that, while Gail did all the rubbing and lashing strakes with teak oil… twice.

Day three I changed engine and gearbox oil in both engines. It was a pig of a job. I didn't have much clearance to work with, and I got soaked and sandy in the process. After that we touched up the yellow paint on the hull sides (still bearing the scars of errant pedalos in São Martinho do Porto) and checked everything under the decks. I kept having to remind myself that if all went to plan, we wouldn't be able to do this again for a while. There are no tides in the Mediterranean.

It was hard graft for three days, but it had been a lovely spot to work. Sand, sunshine, Red-rumped swallows flying between the hulls and Fiddler crabs waving at us from the mud. And 'Gleda' looked much better after our labours. We treated ourselves to a meal in town the next night as a reward for saving all those haul out fees.

With the boat ready to go, my mind started turning to our next destination.

There wasn't any rush. We'd got a lucky break with the weather to get our jobs done. But now it was going downhill again.

My journal:

6am, first light. It's raining again.

The sloppy chop splashes and knocks against the hull a few inches away from my right ear. 9 mm of plywood is all that's stopping my warm cosy bed from sinking into the cold salty water just the other side of it.

I got up and wiped the condensation from the cabin portlight. I could just make out the lights from the villa up on the hill. I knew we were still anchored in our spot.

Last night was our 26th anchored here. Add on the 51 nights we spent here last summer and you can see how we've come to think of it as our spot.

It's been a different experience this time round though. For the last 5 days the wind has hardly dropped below 15-20 knots. Saturday into Sunday saw us riding out the strongest winds we've yet experienced on anchor.

Alvor is one of the few safe anchorages along this Algarve coast.

We're tucked up a dog leg estuary protected by sandbanks and over a mile away from the entrance, so sea swell can't reach us.

My 20 kg Manson anchor is by now buried deep in the thick mud below our keels.

With a 4 m tide we float in 2-6 m of water.

The anchor is attached to the boat by 15 m of chain. We don't have swinging room for more, so before the strongest winds arrived I shackled the spare 20 kg Bruce to the chain and slid it two metres down.

It's worked well, a better angle of pull on the Manson, no jerking on the bridle, less veering.

There were 3 other boats anchored with us during the worst winds. One of them dragged and took several attempts to get secure. One of the resident boats broke her mooring and ended up on shore.

If we'd dragged, we'd have been ashore as well, even if we'd spotted it was happening straight away, there wouldn't have been time to do anything about it. We were only about 15 m off the shore. The sloping mud would have stopped us at anything other than high water, but after that it would have been a rocky sea wall.

I'd bought that big old Manson anchor a couple of years before 'Gleda' launched. At the time I'd wondered if it was too big………. It wasn't.

Before the wind and rain arrived, we had four days of 100% cloud cover.

My single 100W solar panel became next to useless. The Rutland wind generator had seized up while we were in Lagos, so I'd been having to run the outboards for two hours a day just to keep the batteries charged.

After a search online and a phone call, I ordered another panel and arranged to collect it when we got to the river Guadiana up the coast.

Meanwhile, I'd just have to minimise our electrical consumption and keep using expensive petrol.

Yes, our next destination had been decided over the winter. We'd spoken to many who'd been there, it was unmissable we'd been told. We'd decide for ourselves, but it seemed well worthwhile to check it out.

All we had to do was decide when to leave.

Truth be told, we could probably have made a break for it in the week following our drying out work. Problem was that all the wind that week came out of the east, the direction we needed to go. At one point I was tempted, but not for long. We had no timetable; we were here to enjoy life, beating into wind and waves was something to avoid. I'd made the choice.

The forecasts looked as if the unseasonal and unreasonable weather might finally clear off by the coming weekend. I hoped so; we hadn't done any proper sailing since the previous August when we made the passage from Sagres. Eight months had passed. It seemed crazy.

A few decent days with the right winds was all we wanted. It was a 70 nmi passage from Alvor to Ayamonte at the entrance to the Guadiana river. Culatra lay 40 nmi away and offered a possible overnight stop en route.

Both had potentially dangerous approaches, sand bars, powerful tides, navigational hazards. I'd need to be awake and alert again.

But I was looking forward to it.

We didn't have to wait too long.

On 14th May, after 30 nights anchored near Alvor town, we picked up the hook and used the last of the ebb tide to motor the 1.5 miles (2.41 km) down to the lagoon entrance.

We said 'see you later' to Gary and June on 'Friendship' on the way past. They'd arrived a couple of days before and were staying a few days more. I knew we'd see them again down the way.

We anchored just inside the breakwaters, ready for a first light getaway the following morning. The plan? To head south and east toward the Guadiana River.

EAST TO EDEN

We motor-sailed for the first hour post-dawn. The sea was flat, the wind but a breath. I knew it would change. I was happy to start slow.

By 08:00 we had the engines off and were past Portimão with 20 plus knots of wind and a choppy sea. I'd forgotten what it was like to sail properly. 'Gleda' romped along on a reach at 9-10 knots, her foredeck wet with salt water for the first time in many months. It was fun.

We soon passed Albufeira, and I thought we'd have a far shorter passage than I'd expected.

We were aiming for the Guadiana river, but I had a stop in mind. There's a big lagoon just south of Faro. It's protected by the low-lying island of Culatra. It's fair to say the place is fabled in Wharram circles. I'd first heard of Culatra when I'd met Steve Turner up the Penryn river back in the 'Mor Gwas' days. He'd been there many times and planned to return. There'd been a liveaboard community there for years. A sheltered anchorage, a sandy beach, gorgeous weather, cheap wine and beer. Free and easy living. It sounded like paradise.

It became my Shangri-La. If I'd succeeded in getting 'Mor Gwas' across Biscay it's where I had planned to go. It never happened.

Now, here I was. Sailing my own Wharram with the lagoon entrance but a few miles away. How could I not go see?

But the wind is a bugger. Most of our previous passages had seen us going slow. We rarely averaged 5 knots. I'd planned for the same on this one. But that strong wind off Portimão had brought our average up to 7 knots. There's only one entrance to the lagoon. It's narrow, it has shallow areas, and the tide can run up to 7 knots through it. We were there earlier than I'd planned. The spring tide was still on the ebb. We couldn't go in until it turned in another couple of hours.

I didn't want to hang around that long. We'd got some wind, and I didn't want to waste it.

I'd waited decades to see Culatra. I could wait a while longer.

Sod's law came into play, of course. Not long afterwards the wind died, and we were back to motoring. But I'd now committed to make the Guadiana river entrance, and that was still some miles away. Although wider than the one into Culatra this entrance still had my attention. The pilot book warned of the possibility of steep seas across a sandbar, a tricky approach, strong tides.

I was paying even more attention as we got close. The wind had picked up again, and we made a bouncy entrance in some nasty cross-seas.

Our Dutch friends Jan and Baukjen on J&B had told us of a nice spot to anchor on the eastern (Spanish) side of the river just south of the town of Ayamonte. It was now dusk, and the light was fading, but I spotted the anchorage easily enough, not least because I could see another boat there. As we got closer, I realised it was J&B. They'd left Alvor a few weeks before us, and we thought they'd still be up river.

Once we'd got the hook down I inflated the dinghy and rowed over to say hi.

It turned out they'd dropped down river that afternoon and were headed back to Alvor. Jan told me to make sure our anchor was well bedded. He'd seen a forecast for some powerful winds to come in overnight.

He was right. I got up about 02:00 to check on things as 'Gleda' was pulling well on her anchor chain and veering about some. It was pitch black, the wind whistled through the rigging, there were some spots of rain in the air. I was glad to be anchored safe in this sheltered spot. I glanced across to see if J&B was OK. The boat had gone. Jan had said he might leave in the early hours "I don't like to waste a good wind" he'd said with a smile. I'd never have dreamt of leaving on a night like this. I wondered what that entrance sand bar would be like, thought about the darkness, the choppy sea, the lobster pots you can't see at night. I may have sailed my boat 1000 miles (ca. 1,609 km), but I still had a lot to learn. Like I said before; proper sailors Jan and Baukjen.

VILLA REAL & THE RIVER

We'd had a long day sailing from Alvor. Seventy nmi, nearly 13 hours. I'd used the engines more than I'd have liked, and we now needed fuel. Our next destination lay 20 nmi up river. We'd be motoring there and back again, and I wasn't sure how easily we'd get fuel once there, so I wanted full tanks to start with.

We also needed the tide under us. The Guadiana is a big river, and the tide runs surprisingly fast. To get up there in daylight we'd have needed to leave early in the morning. I figured we'd have a quiet day on anchor, get our fuel, explore ashore and leave the next day.

The Guadiana River defines a long stretch of the Portugal-Spain border, separating Extremadura and Andalusia (Spain) from Alentejo and Algarve (Portugal). It runs for a distance of 829 kilometres (ca. 515 mi) with 100 kilometres (ca. 62 mi) of it shared between the two nations. We'd anchored near the river mouth, close inshore on the Spanish side near to Ayamonte.

After breakfast, we got the fuel containers in the dinghy and motored across to the town of Vila Real on the Portuguese side.

This country swapping was something we'd get used to later. But for now, it felt odd.

Vila Real was an unexpected pleasure.

We knew nothing about the place when we arrived, but its layout and architecture sparked my interest.

When we'd been in Lagos, it had intrigued me to see some road signs showing the location of tsunami evacuation points. In my ignorance I'd always thought of tsunamis as an exclusively far eastern phenomenon. I was curious. A little online research soon put me right.

On the morning of Saturday 1st November 1755, some 120 miles (ca. 193 km) southwest of Cape St. Vincent, an earthquake with an estimated magnitude of 8.5-9.0 occurred. It set off a huge tsunami. The wall of water and subsequent fires destroyed the city of Lisbon. On the Algarve, the wave destroyed everything at sea level. We'd walked around the old city walls in Lagos. I'd read that the wave had reached the top of them.

The death toll is thought to have been similar to that of the 2004 Boxing Day tsunami in Indonesia. Something like 200,000.

If there were to be a repeat event today the damage and death toll would be unimaginable.

The town that existed before Vila Real, Santo António de Arenilha, was destroyed by that same tsunami. It had been an important place. Key to trade by sea and land. It needed to be rebuilt quickly.

Amazingly it was done in only two years.

The Marquis of Pombal, who was responsible for its planning, designed the new town in a grid pattern which he also used during the reconstruction of Lisbon. In a pioneering technique, entire buildings were prefabricated in areas outside the town, and then transported to their eventual destination to be assembled. This was key to a fast and methodical construction. Vila Real de Santo António went on to thrive on the growth of the fishing industry, which included the processing of tuna and sardines.

The first building that caught our eye was the appropriately named Grand House Hotel on the main Avenida da Republica running along the waterside.

Built in 1918 it was in the throes of a refurbishment while we were there, but its opulent character was plain to see.

The town was clean, vibrant, and we thoroughly enjoyed our walk around.

After a couple of hours we got our fuel in the dinghy and motored back across to 'Gleda'. I looked up at the International road bridge just upstream. Tomorrow we'd be passing under it and exploring inland. Another adventure awaited.

Just after 08:00 the following morning I pulled the anchor up from the black slimy mud below us. It came up along with an old beach brolly, presumably blown into the water at some point in the past.

With engines, on we motored up past Ayamonte and under the motorway bridge connecting Spain and Portugal. We were heading up on a rising tide. This bridge has a clearance of something like 20 m (ca. 66 ft) underneath it at low tide. Unfortunately, silting means that there are also shallow areas and a mud bar under the bridge. Some larger boats with deep draft and/or tall masts would have a tricky job finding a balance between the two. There was nothing for us to worry about, our masts were only 11 m (ca. 36 ft) high, and we only needed 1.5 m (ca. 5 ft) of water to float. We'd been under the Tamar bridges at Plymouth and the mini Golden Gate Bridge over the Tagus in Lisbon. We were getting used to the optical illusion that the masts must surely hit. That said, this one was far lower, and the masts looked mighty close. It relieved me to clear it for another reason. The bridge didn't look particularly well maintained. On the Portuguese side I could see one strand of the suspension cable had broken and was dangling down towards the river bank!

As we travelled farther up river, the surroundings became more and more spectacular. Nearer the coast, the land was flat.

There was a massive golf resort on the Spanish side with many unfinished apartments seemingly abandoned. Soon though, we saw fewer and fewer houses. The hills closed into the river banks and the country became wilder. The few houses we saw were sizeable villas, some with their own landing stage or floating pontoon. The river is wide and the channel well-marked, although there were a few squeeze points where the river twisted and turned. I had both engines on, and with the tide under us we were moving along at a decent speed. I wanted to reach our chosen anchorage spot before the tide turned back on us again. We enjoyed our little river cruise, although we had one slight scare. Once we were 10 or so kilometres inland we spotted various small marker buoys, seemingly randomly placed out from the river banks. It wasn't until I saw one with a line of floats leading away from it back towards the shore that I realised what they were. They marked the end of fishing nets laid out at 90° from the bank. Some of these nets stretched right out into the marked navigation channel. It's a lazy kind of fishing. The tide does all the work, as the fish get trapped one way or the other as they swim with the current.

We had one close encounter. Gail was at the wheel when we spotted a random buoy right in the middle of the channel. I told her to keep our course and just leave it to port, Suddenly I saw a line of floats just under the water and directly in front of us. It was too late to change course and steer around them. I slammed both engines astern at maximum revs. We stopped just a few feet away. It's the one and only time I've had to do an emergency stop on a boat.

About lunchtime, we rounded a bend in the river to see a wonderful vista open up ahead. The river widened. Rows of boats became visible, tied to mooring buoys, and beyond them, the two towns of Alcoutim on the Portuguese side and Sanlucar on the Spanish side. As we got closer, we spotted our friends Ian and Jackie aboard 'Rivalady' and Pat and Duncan on 'Samji'.

The pilot book suggested anchoring south of the towns, anchoring between them is restricted because some sizeable river cruisers come up this far and need room to turn. Beyond, there are too many permanent moorings. The anchorage was crowded. I motored round looking for a spot I was comfortable with. We'd already decided we would spend a few weeks there, so I figured it was worth trying to anchor somewhere we could stay undisturbed. I spotted what I thought was a nice gap close to the Spanish bank. There wasn't room for us to swing, but I had a plan. I'd use a stern anchor again, just as we had in Alvor. We could lie parallel to the shore, we'd stay put whatever the wind and tides were doing. It was a splendid plan, but my execution of it failed dismally.

I dropped the bow anchor and then motored astern, thinking to drop the stern anchor and then position us between the two. It'd been easy in Alvor. But here it was a different story. The water was far deeper and the current far stronger. I made a right hash of it. Mooring and anchoring is a spectator sport. You can guarantee an audience. The audience is always larger when you get it wrong. There's nothing you can do. All sailors have to accept that sometimes you're the one getting entertained, other times you're the clown providing the laughs. For over an hour I was the clown, and I put on a fine show. Ian and Duncan eventually took pity and came over in the dinghy to help. But by the time I had us safely swinging on a single anchor, in the spot I should have chosen in the first place, I was hot, sweaty, exhausted, embarrassed and angry with myself. The trip upriver had been super relaxing. It took me two days to wind down again.

RIVER LIFE

GUADIANA MAGIC

Truth be told, it didn't take that long to wind down. Alvor had been our ultimate relaxation spot up till then. The Guadiana took things to another level entirely.

Here's a journal entry I made a few weeks after we arrived. It might give you a flavour of how the place affected us.

> *A cockerel crows on one side of the valley, a dog barks in reply from the other. A sheep joins the conversation with a bleat.*
>
> *You open your eyes.*
>
> *Distant mountains shimmer in the haze. Green hills tumble down towards the winding river, clothed with Eucalyptus trees and green grass. Bamboo lines the water's edge.*
>
> *A small boat floats past loaded with a red sofa, soon after, another, this one with a large pot plant sitting in the stern.*
>
> *A windmill, straight out of Don Quixote, sits lazily on a hill above you, its bare wooden arms motionless in the still, warm air.*

A tiny bird with a red head lands close by, it turns to look at you, then warbles as if you understand its musical language.

A man sits, eyes closed, tapping lightly on a Bodhrán whilst another strums a painted guitar and sings quietly of Cornish tin mines.

A ferry goes backwards and forwards in time. Clanging church bells ring different hours in competition. You don't know which is right.

A huge fort floats in the evening sky, the setting sun reflecting orange off its whitewashed walls.

You drift powerless between two countries over and over again. You're a citizen of neither.

The sound of gurgling water and chirping cicadas lull you back towards sleep as you stare at a universe of bright stars and planets floating in the clear inky sky above.

The 'real' world is a fast fading memory.

Is this a dream? No.

The sights and sounds are real. They're a taste of what we're experiencing during our first days here on the Guadiana river.

One year ago today we reached our first port of call after leaving Falmouth. It was Braye Harbour on the island of Alderney.

We're 1000 miles and a world away from there now, we're the same people but different, we're happier, healthier, and more alive.

And we've only just begun our journey.

Dream or reality?

I now have a challenge. Is my writing up to the task? Can I give you any sense of the place? Let's see.

Perhaps a good way to start is to elaborate on what I wrote above.

A cockerel crows on one side of the valley, a dog barks in reply from the other.

Away from the tiny towns of Alcoutim and Sanlucar, the river banks are sparsely populated. Look closely and you'll spot little fincas, wooden shacks and the odd caravan hidden behind thickets of bamboo.

In Spanish, 'finca' means a country estate with a sizeable house. In English usage and certainly along the Guadiana, it's used to describe a small plot of agricultural land or holding with some type of basic living quarters.

Chickens, dogs and sheep are common. Hence the crowing, barking and bleating.

> *Distant mountains shimmer in the haze. Green hills tumble down towards the winding river, clothed with Eucalyptus trees and green grass. Bamboo lines the water's edge.*

The land rises steeply away from the river. The Guadiana is wide, and despite being at water level there were still magnificent views into the countryside all around. The water sustains life. Away from the river the predominant colour is brown. But on the bank's, greenery dominates. One sound I didn't refer to was that of diesel water pumps lifting water from the river into the vegetable plots sloping down to the banks.

The green leaves of giant bamboo lay thick along the water's edge. This bamboo didn't just stay on the river banks. It gets dislodged by water and wind, it floats, it joins together, it forms rafts. These rafts of bamboo became a daily part of our lives. They drifted back and forth with the tide. Some of them were 6 feet (1.83 m) wide and 20 feet (ca. 6 m) long. When going ashore in the dinghy you had to keep a sharp lookout. Day and night we'd occasionally get one of these rafts scraping along the hulls as it drifted slowly past. Now and again one would take aim dead centre between the hulls. It would then foul up on the anchor chain, in effect forming a dam. With a powerful tide this would set the water gurgling and the ends of the raft tapping on the hull. It wasn't unusual for me to have to get up during the night and use the boathook to break the raft up and set chunks free to drift away. Even if these trapped rafts didn't wake us it became a morning routine to clear bamboo away from the anchor chain. Occasionally we'd get something more substantial, like a tree branch or even a chunk of log. As I've mentioned already the Guadiana is a long river. Anything ending up in the water from storms a long way inland would reach us, eventually.

> *A small boat floats past loaded with a red sofa, soon after, another, this one with a large pot plant sitting in the stern.*

Most fincas along the river had no road access. Some didn't even have a footpath. So, everything needed to live there had to be brought in by dinghy. We found out later that the sofa and pot plant were simply someone 'moving in' to their new home.

Despite being over 20 km inland, the tidal range on the river was still nearly 4 m (ca. 13 ft) at springs. A few of these fincas had makeshift floating pontoons tied to the bank. Usually, they comprised oil drums with planks of wood lashed on top. Other places had a wooden landing stage set just above high water level. At low tide there would be a rickety ladder to clamber up. A few places had nothing at all. They just tied their dinghy to a tree and scrambled up the bank.

> *A windmill straight out of Don Quixote, sits lazily on a hill above you, its bare wooden arms motionless in the still, warm air.*

Sitting squat above the village of Sanlucar, on the Spanish side of the river, there was a white-painted windmill (molino). Sadly, its ability to catch the wind had long since gone. Only thin bare poles remained where once there had been sails. But it had been preserved well. Beautifully laid stone paving surrounded it. The views across the river from it stunning. It became a favourite spot to walk to.

> *A tiny bird with a red head lands close by, it turns its head to look at you, then warbles as if you understand its musical language.*

I'm no ornithologist, but the birds on the Guadiana were like none I'd seen before. Brightly coloured Bee-eaters gave themselves away with flashes of vibrant yellow in among the thickets of bamboo. The whooping call of the Golden Oriole became the soundtrack to our time on the river. Herons would fly low past the boat, their huge wings flapping slowly. Azure-winged magpies chattered in the trees. The tiny bird I referred to in my blog turned out to be a Wood-chat Shrike. Occasionally, one would settle on the bows whilst we were sitting on deck. Seemingly fearless, it would cock its head one way or the other to look at you better. As I said, it was as if it wanted to communicate with you.

> *A man sits, eyes closed, tapping lightly on a Bodhrán whilst another strums a painted guitar and sings quietly of Cornish tin mines.*

There was a little bar restaurant in Alcoutim appropriately called The Riverside. Once a week they held a music evening. We'd go early and get a table on the open patio overlooking the river. The place had a simple menu of food cooked by the mother of the owner, Rogario. Whilst we ate, the musicians would start arriving. Most of them were ex-pats living in fincas and boats up and down the river. Some came quite a distance, and it was obvious that these weekly get-togethers were their opportunity to catch up on all the news and gossip. Once everyone had eaten, someone would pick up a guitar and start strumming. Another would start tapping out a beat on the Bodhrán (Irish drum), a harmonica would join in, then a banjo.

It was unrehearsed. Sometimes it went wrong and faded away into laughter, other times it would grow into a beautiful rendition. Either way, it was magical. Sitting with a glass of wine, looking out across the river towards Sanlucar and the mountains beyond, listening to the music.

> *A ferry goes backwards and forwards in time. Clanging church bells ring different hours in competition. You don't know which is right.*

In a hangover from the Spanish Civil War, the clocks in Spain are an hour ahead of Portugal. The dictator Franco changed them in 1942 as a show of solidarity with Hitler. Franco died in 1975. They could have changed them back, they just never got round to it.

There was a little foot passenger ferry that ran back and forth between Alcoutim and Sanlucar, a journey of only a few hundred yards. It may depart at 11:00 and arrive at 12:05. Then again, it may leave at 10:00 and arrive at 09:05. It wasn't the only way to travel through time there either. There was a zip wire running from the hill above Sanlucar to the riverbank just outside Alcoutim. After paying a few Euros you could be strapped into a harness, given a push, and a few adrenaline packed seconds later you'd not only be in another country but you'd also have arrived an hour before you left!

Alcoutim is the compact, tiny town on the Portuguese side. With only a few thousand inhabitants, it is one of the least densely populated towns in Portugal. Its most striking feature is the 14th century Moorish castle built on the riverbank above the town. There were two bar/cafés, a hardware shop, a bank, the obligatory 'China' shop, and one general store. Sleepy would be an accurate description.

Sanlucar is even sleepier. Although it had a bread shop (hard to spot because it just looked like someone's front room), a general store and a beachside bar/café.

We'd planned to stay on the Guadiana for a few weeks, maybe a month. As things turned out we stayed three months.

We passed hot sleepy days sitting on deck under the sunshade just watching the world go by. We got used to the rhythm of the river. The twice a week party boats up from Villa Real. We heard them before we saw them. The deep bass of dance music giving a few minutes warning before the vessel itself appeared round the bend. The upper deck crammed with dancing, cheering day-trippers. Necking drinks, laughing, singing, shouting. The DJ encouraging them.

The boat would stop for an hour or two in Alcoutim before heading back downriver. Peace would be restored.

Another once a week visitor was the river cruise ship. In contrast to the party boat, it would glide past almost silently. Its passengers considerably older and less energetic. At some 110 m (360 foot) in length it was impressive to watch it perform a 180° turn between the two banks of the river.

FLOATING IN TIME

The long, hot days encouraged my mind to wander. It struck me that we were floating in time and history on the Rio Guadiana. Three thousand years of time and history.

Phoenicians from the Eastern Mediterranean had sailed up this river 1000 years before Christ.

Romans, Visigoths and Moors had lived, worked and died here.

On the riverbed, just ahead of us, lay the stones of an old causeway.

No one knows for sure who built it, probably the Romans. It was mostly removed in the mid-1800's so that ships, heavily laden with copper ore, could more easily pass. If you looked closely, you could still see evidence of its existence hidden among the bamboo on each bank. We'd seen yachts struggling to anchor over what remained under the water. Modern anchors and big bits of old stone don't work well together.

On the Portuguese side, the quaintly named 'Village Castle' overlooked us. It had stood there since the 1300s. On the Spanish side another, Castillo San Marcos, a new build in comparison. It'd only been there 370 years or so.

Actually, there have been people populating the area since Neolithic times. It wasn't hard to see why.

Down the centuries, this bit of river had echoed to the sounds of warfare, industry and trade.

When we were there, it was much quieter.

It'd be easy to call the place sleepy, forgotten, hidden. To some extent it was all of those things, but simultaneously it was very much alive.

The river both joined and divided. Boats crossed back and forth constantly. Two countries, two time zones, two languages, but with nationality seemingly irrelevant to everyday life. It was impossible to resist. We frequently shopped in both countries on the same morning.

It hasn't always been so. We're talking of two proud nations here. A few hundred years ago those two castles would have been lobbing cannonballs at each other. Flags still flew prominently to leave the visitor in no doubt as to the sovereignty on each side.

The national and political border was clearly defined, but socially it was blurred. The history of occupation by people from around Europe continues to this day. The area around the Guadiana has long held a reputation for being a place that visitors find hard to leave, and in the brief time we'd been there we'd seen the truth in that reputation.

We'd spoken to more than a few who'd bought land, settled, become part of the place. The locals seemed to embrace them; they knew that without these incomers their towns would be poorer financially and poorer culturally. It seemed this mix of nationalities helped towards the easy-going feel of the place.

On the Spanish side of the river we found a nature trail called the Camino's Naturales, it ran alongside the river right down to the coast at Ayamonte.

One day, we walked part of it.

Chattering azure-winged magpies led the way. We came upon little lizards sun-bathing in the dirt. We caught glimpses of Golden Orioles and Gail spotted an even more colourful Bee Eater.

Flowering cacti lined the path. The air smelled fresh and clean.

It all felt very foreign. It reminded me of what our travels were all about.

As we walked further, we spotted some signs of habitation. Half hidden sheds, the odd white-painted wall glimpsed through the undergrowth. Later we came across some bigger plots with gardens, chickens, orchards. We'd stumbled across some of the Guadiana's fabled 'Fincas'.

I wondered what it would be like to live in one of these places. Completely 'off-grid' with no road access, no near neighbours, totally self-dependant.

Looking at a few of the buildings, I couldn't imagine how they'd even been built, given that all the necessary materials could only have got to the site by means of a small dinghy and a rickety landing stage.

In some respects there was a bit of a 'Deliverance' vibe in the air. It almost felt like we were intruding. If a guy in dungarees pointing a shotgun had appeared out of the bushes, I wouldn't have been surprised.

Time was getting on, we were hungry and thirsty, so we turned around and headed back to the boat for lunch.

As I ate, I had no idea that my old friend serendipity was about to pay a visit.

A few hours later, I spotted a dinghy heading our way. The dinghy belonged to a guy called Christian who we'd met in passing a few days before. His partner Polly had been aboard 'Gleda' to talk to Gail about some possible holiday accommodation for Gail's Mom.

Anyway, it turned out that Christian needed some help. He, Polly and their two girls had plans to be away for a few weeks during July. They'd arranged for a friend to look after their place while gone. But he'd just had an email telling him the friend couldn't come, he was in the lurch.

He came straight to the point, Polly had told him we'd planned to stay around for a while. Would we consider looking after their home for two weeks? A dog, a cat, some chickens and a small flock of sheep, not a lot to do. In return, the place would be ours to enjoy.

He pointed down the river towards his moored boat. I told him that, funnily enough, we'd just come back from a walk down there and that we must have been close. It turned out that we'd stopped right by the corrugated tin roof of his workshop before heading back.

Just two hours before, I'd been trying to imagine what it'd be like to live there, now here I was being offered the chance to find out. If that's not serendipity I don't know what is.

THE FINCA

Before I continue this story, it's worth considering what had just happened.

In 'normal' life, under what circumstances would you stop a stranger in the street, suggest handing them the keys to your home and asking them to look after it for a few weeks?

Christian had never met us before, he'd just seen us around. He'd been living on the Guadiana for over 20 years. He and his wife Polly had raised two daughters on the finca. So, what possessed him to ask such a crazy question?

The answer lies with the Guadiana magic. He'd seen us sitting on the river for weeks, he knew we'd fallen under the rivers spell; he knew he could trust us.

Isn't it wonderful to know that there are still places where that happens? That there are still places where people trust each other, places where people help each other out.

Places floating in time.

So, the following afternoon we found ourselves clambering up a wet muddy ladder and onto a somewhat rickety landing stage jutting out from the side of the river bank. We followed a narrow path through a thicket of bamboo, and emerged into what may as well have been another world. A lost valley if you will. The ground had been cleared either side of a dried-up creek bed running down from the hills behind. It was the height of summer. The grass was brown. But around the creek bed olive, juniper and lemon trees grew, providing shade. Christians little dog Sula ran down to greet us. A few dark brown sheep were foraging under a huge olive tree. Several chickens pecked around on the sparse grass. The path wound up the hill, over several small wooden bridges, and then emerged in front of a quaint little single storey whitewashed house. An old sofa and two easy chairs sat under the bamboo-shaded patio. Christian's wife Polly greeted us. Wine and tapas appeared, and we chatted. Their two young daughters came to say hello. Bubbly and confident, a marked difference from most girls of that age. Christian told us how he'd bought the land and tumbled down finca decades before. The deal done with a handshake and the exchange of a wad of peseta notes. The two girls had been born and raised on the finca and were now going to school in Villa Real on the Portuguese side. Their unique lifestyle beggared belief. Remember they lived in Spain, the finca had no road access; it was a 40-minute walk along the riverbank to Sanlucar.

To get the girls to school they had to be rowed across the river and then walked up the fields to the road. There, in a small lay-by, they kept their car. It was then a 45-minute drive to Villa Real. This trip happened twice on every school-day. And remember, the one-hour time difference between river banks had to be accommodated.

In the grounds of the finca there was a big workshop with a pitched corrugated iron roof constructed Australian style, with an overlapping gap at the eves to let the hot air escape. Also, there was a guest cabin in the grounds. Christian was a good way into building an extra bedroom onto the house for the girls. Every brick, bag of cement and length of timber had been transported by dinghy and hauled up to the house manually.

It didn't take long for us to agree to look after the place for them. Truth be told, we'd decided before we arrived. Our only concern had been the dog. Neither Gail nor I are dog people. But Sula seemed to be the most docile canine on the planet. She never barked, and spent virtually all her time lying on the patio sofa.

So, a few days later we moved 'Gleda' down river and picked up Christian's now vacant mooring just off the landing stage. Over the next fortnight we spent our days ashore and our nights back aboard. It was cooler on the water, and we felt more comfortable in our own bed. We soon got into a routine. I'd row ashore early morning, let the chickens out, feed the dog and the cat, and switch the fridge on. Then head back to the boat for breakfast and to make Gail her cuppa.

When we were both ready, we'd come ashore and spend the day, reading, writing, and trying to stay cool. We'd have our evening meal, put the chickens to bed, then head back to the boat as the sun went down. It was the perfect way to live.

Sula got used to this routine and seemed happy with the arrangement. She even started coming down to the landing stage each morning to greet us.

During the day we'd mostly laze about. Gail read, and I'd write. When I wanted a change, I'd work on stitching a new leather cover around 'Gleda's' wheel, which I'd bought ashore. I also took advantage of Christian's workshop to make a few wooden bits and pieces for the boat. Each evening we'd round up the chickens and shut them in their wire-fenced run. Usually, all it took was a shake of the feed tin, and they'd come running, but there was one hen in particular who started getting stubborn. She gave us the runaround for a few nights then disappeared completely. We never found out where she went. The sheep were far easier. I'd just chop down some bamboo with fresh leaves on it and throw it in the field, they looked after themselves.

The house itself was basic when it came to amenities. Although, unlike many of his neighbours Christian and Polly had mains water.

Some years previously Christian had got together with two of his neighbours and run a water pipe all the way down the river bank from Sanlucar. With the local council's approval it had been connected to the village supply. From the riverbank several hundred metres of black PVC pipe snaked up to the house. For most of the year the sun was powerful enough to heat the water substantially during its journey, so they had hot water.

There was no mains electricity. A couple of dusty solar panels on the roof charged two 12v batteries. These were used mainly to run an ancient Engel fridge box. Christian warned us to turn it off at night though. The batteries weren't up to that job. The other major power drain was the internet router picking up on a 3G mobile signal from Portugal. A few 12v lights completed the electrical conveniences. Talking of conveniences, there was a liquid only loo in the house, but the main toilet lay outside in a wooden shack on stilts built into the hillside. It benefited from a roof, but other than that it was open to the world. There was a spectacular view over the river. This was a long drop composting toilet. We were used to that as we had a composting toilet aboard 'Gleda'. Ours differed in not having spiders running round the toilet bowl. We used our own floating facilities for No2's.

I spent many hours sitting at the old oak dining table inside working on my second book 'Foolish Odyssey'. Gail spent most of her time sitting on the shady porch reading. Sula the dog spent the entire day lying on the old sofa doing nothing.

It was idyllic, and we both began to dream of owning our own little paradise.

It's a strange thing. We both loved living aboard 'Gleda' and we both loved travelling. But at the same time we both liked the idea of having somewhere permanent to call home. Christian and Polly were away nearly three weeks. The time passed quickly. Soon enough it was time to vacate the mooring and drop the hook again. Our shore side adventure was over.

14

OFF THE HOOK

PENHA D'ÁGUIA

It hadn't taken long on the Guadiana to decide that it was a place we wanted to spend time. I'd realised that just because we were travelling, that didn't mean we'd always have to be moving. Almost everyday I'd see boats coming up on the tide from downriver. They'd drop the hook or tie up to one of the pontoons, they'd stay a night and then be away again. Heading for their next destination, with the Guadiana ticked off the list. I knew we were privileged; we were time rich. But so many I spoke too seemed to live their lives afloat in the same way they lived their lives ashore. The clock and the calendar ruling their every decision.

That's what I'd been so desperate to escape, and if ever there was a place to do it, the Guadiana was it.

I've mentioned time already. Clocks didn't matter here. They couldn't agree on the time anyway. Days and months seemed equally irrelevant. It was summer, and summer takes up a sizeable chunk of the year in this part of the world.

Another little blog extract that captures my mood back then.

Shoeless In Sanlucar

    I've done it a few times now.

    On the boat I'm always barefooted. That means that anytime I go ashore I have to remember to throw the flip-flops into the dinghy.

    I keep forgetting.

    I forgot the other day, when I rowed to Spain.

    I wanted to explore Sanlucar a bit more and climb up to Los Molino (The windmill).

    I could have gone back for them but, as Gail keeps telling me, I have Hobbit feet, so I didn't bother.

    I set off, the cobbles were cool in the shade, gravel on the dirt track stuck to my heels, the spiky brown grass felt prickly under my feet, concrete was too hot to walk on.

    I felt more connected with the place.

    The few folks I saw didn't seem to notice my lack of foot apparel. My self-consciousness soon evaporated.

    Shoeless in Sanlucar.......... Felt good.

The weeks passed quickly and, as we were staying put, Gail took the opportunity to make a quick trip back to the UK to see her mom. Despite our remoteness, Faro airport was only just over an hour away by car, and flights to and from Birmingham cheap and frequent. We didn't know when we'd next be somewhere so convenient.

The only problem was getting a car. After asking around someone suggested talking to the outfit in Alcoutim that ran the little river ferry. Called 'Fun River' they had an office near the pontoons where we landed the dinghy. We already knew of them as they ran the little launderette Gail used. They also hired SUP's, kayaks and quad bikes, plus they ran adventure tours on and off the water. We'd seen two their SUV's running about. They were hard to miss as they were all sign written and plastered with graphics advertising all the activities they offered.

Anyway, when we asked about a hire car, the girl in the office said "sim, sim, não tem problema" (yes, yes, no problem). We told her the dates we wanted and got the same response. I asked how much, she said, 40 or 50 Euro. I said fine, she said OK. No booking form, nothing written down, no deposit. This was a few weeks ahead of Gail's flight, and every time we passed by the office subsequently we'd put our heads in the door, stick a thumb up and ask if everything was still OK for the car. The response was always the same, "Sim Sim……". I said to Gail that if worst came to worst and a car never appeared she'd just have to take a taxi. Anyway, the afternoon before her morning flight I went down to the office to get the car. I wasn't exactly brimming with confidence. The office was closed, but after a short wait the owner Jose, came driving down the road in one of the sign written SUV's, he parked up, got out and held out the keys towards me with a smile.

I should have been used to it by now. Why on earth would I think that here on the Guadiana things would be done as they were in the outside world? Jose never asked to see my driving licence, he didn't ask for a copy of my passport; he didn't ask for a deposit. The cautious, sensible side of my brain prompted me to ask him about insurance. He said "yes it's insured" then he handed me his business card and winked as he said "if you have an accident just tell the policeman to ring me".

I probably should have walked away shaking my head. I probably should have got Gail in a taxi. But we'd been on the Guadiana too long, I just smiled, shook his hand and thanked him. I drove Gail to and from the airport; we did a big shop at the supermarket in Villa Real; I put a bit of fuel in the car and gave Jose a €50 note. Everyone was happy. 'Não problema'!

While Gail was in the UK, I spent time thinking, writing, re-thinking, not writing. When she got back, I decided it was time for a change of scene.

So, the next day we lifted the anchor and headed upstream

with the tide, pottering along at a few knots enjoying the views.

As I mentioned earlier, many of the boats that come up the Guadiana never went further than Alcoutim and Sanlucar. They missed a treat.

The signs of human habitation become fewer, the occasional 'Finca' with obligatory pontoon or landing stage, a boat on a mooring and maybe a bit of cultivation. Apart from that, there was just the odd ruined building, missing roof, crumbling white painted stone walls. The countryside on either bank drier and sparser.

Some 8 km on from Alcoutim, after passing the Rio Vascão, we reached the old Spanish mining port of Puerto de Laja. The old ore bunkers above the quay dominated the place. This was where, until the 60s, copper ore had been loaded onto sizeable ships and transported worldwide.

The ore used to come from various mines in Huelva province between the Rio Guadiana and the Rio Tinto some 70 km east. The Rio Tinto gave its name to what is now one of the largest mining companies in the world. It was formed in the late 1800s and dug up a sizeable chunk of Spain to get at the valuable ore and sulphates.

Inevitably though, the industry went into decline. The mouth of the river silted up preventing the ships getting in, the mines became less productive and then, in the late 50s, Rio Tinto pulled all the English staff, families and belongings out. It happened overnight. The first the Spanish workers knew about it was when they turned up to work next morning to find the gates locked. Rio Tinto left the land scarred and the people bitter.

Do some web searches on The Rio Tinto Mining Co and you'll soon see that this shameful behaviour was just the start. Their record of environmental damage and human abuse spans decades and continues to this day. As I write this in June 2020, the company is in the news again for blasting a 46,000-year-old

Aboriginal site in Australia to expand an iron ore mine. I guess they deserve credit for consistency at least.

Another 5 km upriver we arrived at Pomarão, once again the ugly rusting remnants of mining dominated the place. There were some signs of life though, a small pontoon, a few cafés. It didn't appeal enough for us to stop.

Pomarão is notable mainly as a river junction. On the east side lies a huge dam holding back the Chança river and its massive reservoirs beyond. It's here that the Spanish border splits from the Guadiana and heads north. For the first time since entering the river we now had Portugal on both banks as it swung west.

Reaching Pomarão meant that we'd now sailed the entire navigable water border of Portugal, saltwater and fresh. Coincidentally, we did it almost one year to the day since we first entered Portuguese waters north of Viana de Castello.

The river changes character past Pomarão, it's much narrower, the sides become steeper and rockier. Navigation becomes more of a consideration, shallower water, less mud and sand, more rocks. This is where having a shallow draft catamaran reduces stress, and using the excellent Navionics chart and eyeball pilotage we had no trouble.

A few kilometres past Pomarão we found a slightly wider stretch of river between two bends and dropped the hook in 3 m of water close to the bank. It was time to chill out and take in the peace and quiet.

Chilling out is a poor choice of words. We stayed for three nights, and the temperature didn't drop below 25 °C (77 °F) the whole time, and maxed out at 42 °C (107 °F). The breeze was coming directly from the inland area of Iberia known as 'the oven of Spain'. We were right in front of that oven door.

We'd come south for heat, and finally, we'd found it.

Everyone warned us, 'July and August are too hot' they said, 'most people head down to the coast where it's cooler' they said.

OK, fair enough, it was sound advice. But here's the thing. I'd spent years building my boat in a cold, damp, draughty, barn in the UK. The memories of torrential rain, sleet, snow and ice were fresh, the memories of fingers and toes numb with cold were fresh, the memories of biting winds and freezing fog were fresh. I was more than ready for hot and dry, Even now I'll still take dry heat over cold and wet any day of the week.

That's not to say it didn't cause a few problems. The first was with the new Waeco fridge I'd installed in the pod back in Lagos. Up to then it'd been brilliant, but on the first night at anchor we realised there was a problem. The fridge temperature had climbed to 8° despite being set for 2° and, as I watched the display, the low voltage indicator light flashed on, before the entire thing shut down. After a few minutes, it would start up again only to repeat the sequence. This was puzzling as the battery voltage as shown by the charge controller was nearly 13v. At first, I thought it was an overheating problem, I'd put plenty of vent holes in the cockpit seat locker but the unit still felt hot. It was too late to do anything about it that night, so we pulled the whole fridge out on deck and connected it direct to the battery. The compressor kicked in straight away and soon bought the temperature down.

By the next morning I'd figured out the problem was two-pronged. Firstly, there wasn't enough airflow around the fridge. That was easily fixed with the drill and hole cutter, apart from when the cutter came loose in the chuck and dropped through the hole into the Guadiana. The power issue was down to voltage drop. The cable I'd used wasn't beefy enough, so I ran a new heavier cable direct from the battery and checked/re-soldered all the connections. It was a mornings work I hadn't planned on, but well worth it. After that the fridge held at 2 °C day and night no problem. Chilly drinks are not a luxury in this climate.

One issue I couldn't resolve though was keeping the smaller

galley cool box going. It drew a lot of current anyway, and the fan was running non-stop trying (and failing) to cool its contents. Even during the day the solar panels could only just keep the battery charged and after the first night it was flat. There was only one solution, switch it off and suffer the minor inconvenience of having to fetch the milk and butter from the Waeco in the pod.

I made a mental note to replace the wind generator and fit a bigger battery over the coming winter.

Anyway, back to the heat. Yes it was hot, but we coped. The new sunshades over the deck helped, we kept well hydrated, and, three or four times a day, we lowered the stern ramp and got into the cool river water. Even in the upper reaches the tide still runs strong though, and it was only sensible to swim at slack water. Hanging onto the ramp and letting the tide flow round you was bliss. We were far enough away from civilisation to skinny dip as well. In our three days at anchor there we saw one yacht, one motor cruiser, a jet ski and a canoe. For one 24-hour period we didn't see anyone at all.

What we did see were a Kingfisher, Herons, Golden Orioles, Swallows and lots of fish. At night a canopy of stars came out above us. One night we both glimpsed a fireball trailing its fiery tail as it burnt up in the atmosphere. The Milky Way lay across the sky like a star-spangled brush stroke. Our connection with the modern world had faded. We had no internet and no mobile connection. Our world became that little stretch of river, the surrounding hills and the universe above. It was magical.

After a few days of relaxation we picked up the hook early in the morning and gently motored another 8 km or so up to Penha da Águila. This stretch was particularly spectacular. On the north side steep rocky hills ended in sheer cliffs that dropped into the water. There were large rocks in the river to keep me alert and just before Penha, Ilha Maria, passed via a narrow twisting channel.

I'd expected to anchor again, but to my surprise there was just enough space on the small pontoon there for us to squeeze in, so we nosed up to it carefully, avoiding the lump of rock positioned in the approaches, and were soon tied up with the kettle on.

Later that morning we walked up the steep hill to the village.

There wasn't much to it, a dozen houses, three or four of which were up for sale.

We woke up the local dog population, but the cacophony of barks bought no human to investigate.

There's a restaurant overlooking the river, but according to the sign it only opened Sundays.

The place was a one horse town without the horse.

We went another 24 Hours without seeing a soul.

The views were amazing though.

We stayed two nights; it was pleasant being tied to a pontoon again, we'd been anchored every night since we'd left Lagos three months previously, and it can be uncomfortable on the Guadiana when the constant breeze blows against a strong tide.

We were now some 60 km upriver from Vila Real de Santo António and the sea, and just 10 km short of the absolute limit of navigation at Mértola. I toyed with the idea of going the whole way. It's possible, even with deeper draft than ours. But it's tricky. There are two rocky drying fords to pass and many other hazards. It's not recommended without a river guide.

In any case, we'd already visited Mértola by bus the first week we'd arrived, it was amazing. An ancient city dominated by its hilltop Moorish castle. Occupied by Phoenicians, Carthaginians and Romans over the centuries because of its strategic position. Taken over by the Moors in the year 711 it became the centre of Islamic culture in the Alentejo Region for over 400 years. Its huge mosque still stands as a monument to that era.

Fantastic though it had been, I decided a second visit wasn't worth the stress. We'd already come much farther than most visiting boats ever get.

On our last night at Penha I wondered if I'd been too cautious. It was about 22:00 and, with no moon, very dark. Gail spotted some strange lights heading up river towards us. I got the binoculars out. It was a boat. A single red light over a single white glimmering above the dimly lit wheelhouse, and a bow wave that showed she was moving at a rate of knots. I thought she must be heading to the pontoon but no; she ploughed right by. A blue and yellow fishing trawler some 30ft (ca. 9 m) in length.

As she came abeam of us, I could see no other lights but the red and white ones at the masthead, I couldn't imagine how the helmsman could even see where they were going as the boat rounded the narrow turn and disappeared toward Mértola.

I mentioned the incident to Christian at the finca when we came back downriver. After describing the boat he nodded his head. 'Yeah, that sounds like José, he was probably drunk. He's piled the boat onto the rocks more than a few times, he's a superb river pilot when he's sober though'.

The following morning we untied and headed back downstream, happy that we'd had a proper taste of the more remote parts of the Rio.

In total, we spent nearly three months on the Guadiana.

One quarter of a year, it's a long time, but still not enough to say we truly knew the place.

Before we arrived we'd heard tales about the 'Guadiana Glue'. How folks sailed up river and never left. It's no myth, we met many who'd done just that. We heard similar stories about Marina Lagos. 'Port Velcro' some called it. Personally, I couldn't imagine staying there, I couldn't see the attraction. The Guadiana felt very different.

From the start, I'd felt its pull.

Why should that have been? I'd put a lot of effort into becoming a 'sea gypsy'. Why would stopping in one place even have crossed my mind? I'm not sure.

It's true that I'd had occasional feelings of insecurity, they seemed to go with the lifestyle. I think maybe it's easier to roam when you know you have a permanent place to call 'home'. Most cruising couples we'd met had a house somewhere. They may have had no intention of returning there anytime soon, but it was there, waiting for them. Whatever happened, they could always go home.

Gail and I didn't, and still don't, have that luxury. I knew Gail wanted it; I didn't think I did, not till the Guadiana started me thinking.

How cool would it be? A little plot of land by the river, 'Gleda' on a mooring close by. A cosy stone house with a wood burner for those chillier winter nights. Four walls and a floor that didn't move when the wind blew. It was hard travelling all the time. I could never fully relax, I had to stay alert, keep us safe. In a 'castle' of my own I'd be at ease.

It was then, and remains now, a nice little fantasy, an escapist dream floating through like scudding cloud.

Even if I wanted to make it a reality, it'd be impossible. My bank balance is more than a few zeros short of being able to buy into that particular dream.

It was a pleasure to meet those who'd chosen to let the 'Guadiana Glue' hold them though, they seemed happy with their choice and I wish them well.

We took many fond Guadiana memories away with us.
The characters.
The history.
The skies.
The castles.
Mertola.
The wild river.

The sound of the Golden Oriole.
The cheap living.
The river beach.
The authenticity.
Finca life.
Music nights at the Riverside Inn.
But we took a few not so fond ones as well;
The river is a hard place to anchor, at least it was on 'Gleda'. Frequent strong winds blow down the river valley, often against 2 or 3 knots of tide. We had some rough nights and uncomfortable days.

The floating debris was a pain too, tree branches and rafts of bamboo. Scraping down the hull at night, fouled up round the anchor chain in the morning.

None of these things are the rivers fault, it does what it does. If you want to stay, you have to adapt.

Even after 3 months we'd only had a taste. Maybe one day we'll return, get to know it a little better, adapt better, but for now, we'd had enough.

It was time to move on, get back to being proper 'sea gypsies'. We'd been a little over a year in Portugal. Now Spain, Gibraltar and the Mediterranean lay before us.

GUADIANA FOOTNOTE

Before I continue my story, I wanted to reference an event which occurred during our time on the Guadiana. An event which, ultimately, had a significant impact on our lives.

I'm talking about the referendum that took place in the UK on 23rd June 2016. The UK government under the leadership of David Cameron asked the nation a question, namely:

"Should the United Kingdom remain a member of the European Union or leave the European Union".

Time will tell what the true motives were for calling that

referendum, and I don't propose to speculate here. But those that have followed my writing for any length of time will know that I believe a "power elite' exists, and that it cares not a jot for ordinary folk like us. I believe that the 2016 referendum was designed to create massive financial benefits for the few, and with complete disregard for the division, damage and long-term disadvantage caused for the majority.

During the build up to the referendum I'd been disinterested and detached. I'd chosen to leave the country of my birth. And with no fixed address I didn't believe I could vote anyway. I felt more European than British. As Europeans, we had free movement within member countries. We could stay as long as we wanted, get healthcare if we needed it, work if we wanted to. We took that for granted and I never dreamed it could change.

But I was interested enough that I stayed up throughout the night as the results came in. We had a good 4G signal anchored in the river; I watched the BBC hour by hour.

An exit poll had predicted that 52% would vote to remain. By the early hours of the morning, as the results came in, it became apparent that the poll had been wrong.

The result was announced at 07:20 BST on 24th June. Seventy-two percent of the UK population had voted. 51.89% voted to leave. 48.11% voted to stay. Leave had won with a majority of 3.8%. I felt sick.

The day before I'd been to the cash point in Alcoutim. I'd received 1.30 Euro for every one of my British pounds. In the weeks leading up to the referendum it'd already dropped from highs of 1.48.

Over the following days that exchange rate dropped to 1.15 Euro, and by the end of the year it was down to 1.10 Euro.

We were living cheaply, but every cent counted. Thanks to that vote our income was effectively cut by 25%. It wasn't the end of the world, but it made a significant difference to us.

Remember my theory about the power elite? One of the

major players in the Leave campaign was a guy named Nigel Farage. He'd been on TV everyday stirring up hatred and division. Talking about immigrants taking jobs, the poor fishermen being screwed by Brussels, pressing every button he could. He masqueraded as one of the lads. Flat cap, pint in hand, saviour of the working class. Man of the people.

Not long after the exit poll came out he made a surprise announcement on TV. Despite the closeness of the poll he as good as conceded that the Leave campaign had lost. The financial markets responded immediately. Sterling soared.

In the city the hedge fund investors rubbed their hands with glee as they placed their trades; betting that the pound would plummet if Leave won.

Some say that Mr Farage had inside information when he made that concession statement. Some say he knew exactly what he was doing. Some say his mates in the City rewarded him well. Some say that they, and he, knew damn well they'd won.

Perhaps it's coincidental that Mr Farage spent some 20 years working in the City as a commodity's trader. Perhaps his surprise statement was a spontaneous and generous gesture based on what he truly believed.

What's certain is that fortunes were made on the back of that vote. That once again we ordinary folk had been played.

As I write this in June 2020 Coronavirus has killed tens of thousands. Racial tensions are high, the economy has been crippled, and it looks like we're six months away from crashing out of the EU without a deal.

Mr Farage is still in the news. He's just returned from the U.S. after being granted 'special exemption to travel' by the U.S. Department of Homeland Security. His reason for travel? To attend President Trumps rally in Oklahoma.

I'm sure they had a ball together.

The Guadiana days have gone forever.

SO LONG PORTUGAL

We pulled up the anchor at first light on 3rd August and caught the tide down river again. Three hours later we anchored in the same spot near Ayamonte where we'd been the previous May. Our last night on the Guadiana was the worst we'd ever experienced at anchor. The wind gusted over 30 knots, funnelling between the shorelines. Heavy rain showers passed through frequently. When the tide turned against the wind, we had two opposing forces trying to force the boat to its will. 'Gleda' veered about one way and then the other. Every few minutes she would end up lying sideways to the wind and waves with the anchor chain grinding under the hulls. It was horrible. Gail got as frightened as she'd ever been at sea. She felt sure the boat was breaking up under us. I was up on deck all night trying to do what I could, which wasn't much. There were three choices open to us. First, we could leave and head to sea. That didn't appeal given the darkness, sea conditions and falling tide over the bar. Second, we could try to get into the nearby Ayamonte Marina for shelter. But I'd seen how narrow the entrance was. We'd be 90° to the wind and tide trying to get in. It was a recipe for disaster. In any case, both these options depended on me being able to get the anchor up, something I wasn't confident I could do in these conditions. The third and only choice was to ride it out. I knew the wind would ease, I knew the tide would turn, and so it did. It was a shame our last memory of the Guadiana was such a bad one.

We left Ayamonte just after 08:00, a moderate NW wind blowing us out with the tide at 7 knots, a splendid start.

We had 65 miles (ca. 105 km) to track across Huelva Bay to our next destination, Rota.

It was a great sail; the wind stayed W or NW; it died down a little around midday, but just as I was about to crack and lower an engine it came back, and we rode 15-20 knots all the way to Rota.

We averaged nearly 6 knots and maxed out at 10. The seas were moderate. We washed a lot of Guadiana mud off the hulls.

Huelva Bay was busy with fishing vessels and gas tankers, we were sailing fast. I'd forgotten how physically hard it was to sail. My Guadiana laziness got washed away with the mud.

We arrived off Rota Marina in the early evening after 12 hours sailing. A sleepless night on anchor watch and a tough day had left me feeling shattered. I just wanted to get tied up safe.

We'd booked ahead, and our call on VHF was answered promptly with directions to our pontoon. We motored in and found our slot next to a 40ft (ca. 12 m) powerboat. Gail said it looked too narrow, I thought it was tight but OK. Gail was right.

I got 'Gleda' in, but the fenders were squashed near flat on both sides, we couldn't stay there. After another call on the VHF and a short wait, we were allocated another berth, C68. It was in the next row down.

We motored round for a bit but couldn't find it. I called on the VHF for directions, no one answered. The wind was picking up a bit, and I aborted an attempt to get alongside a hammerhead pontoon. I was getting more and more wound up, but eventually the VHF was answered, and they sent a 'marinero' down to guide us in. A few folks had seen us driving around and came down to take lines. Berth C68 didn't exist, the girl on the radio had said C6 and 8, it was two berths side by side.

It'd been a long day.

We'd planned to stay in Rota for a few days at least. We wanted to explore the town, visit Cadiz, maybe take a trip to Seville.

As things turned out, time wasn't a problem.

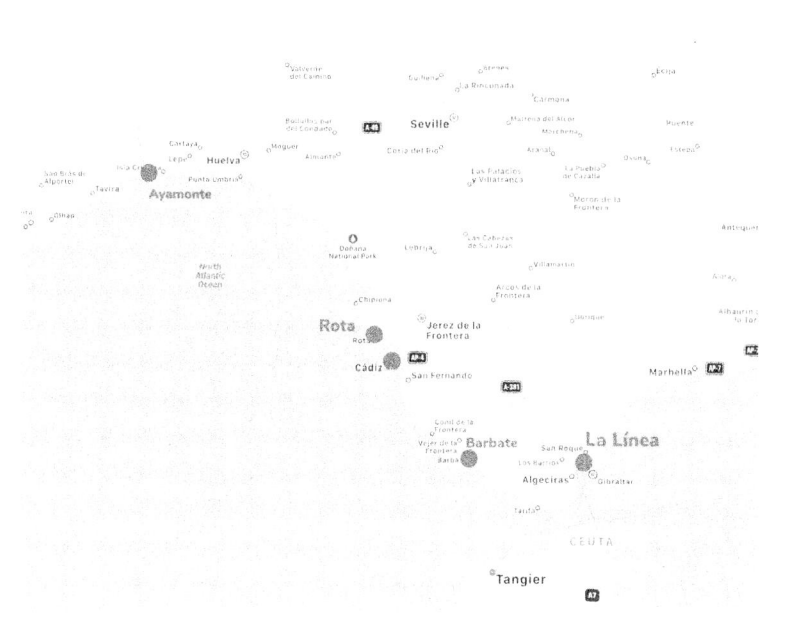

ROTA & GIBRALTAR

OUR QUOTA OF ROTA

A week later we were still there, and it looked as if we'd be staying put for another four or five days at least.

It seemed the weather gods didn't want us to see the Mediterranean just yet. They'd sent the 'Levanter' wind to keep us out.

Some explanation is needed I think.

The Straits of Gibraltar are one of the worlds best known maritime passages.

At the narrowest point, Tarifa, you're as far south as it's possible to get on the European mainland. It's just 8 miles (ca. 13 km) away from North Africa.

The stretch of coast we were on, near Cadiz, is well into what is known to sailors as 'windy alley'. The lie of the land plus the mix of Atlantic and Mediterranean weather systems mean that it's nearly always blowing. Tarifa is a wind and kite surfing mecca with good reason, it's reputed to blow around 30 knots there for more than 300 days of the year.

When it's blowing it either blows from the east, The Levanter, or from the west, The Poniente.

It wasn't a complete surprise to me. This weather is well documented, and I fully expected that when we got to Rota we'd have to wait 3,4, maybe 5 days for the right conditions to get to Gibraltar. What I hadn't expected was for our arrival to coincide with an exceptionally long and strong spell of Levanter. It'd already blown for 11 days, and even in the marina it'd rarely dropped below 15 knots. Out in the Straits, it'd been up to 40.

The marina had been quiet, a few local boats had braved the choppy bay for an exciting couple of hours, but the only other movement had been a French 30 footer towed in by the lifeboat. I strolled up to see what was happening. The boat's mainsail was shredded and wrapped around the mast. The skipper looking like he was mighty glad to be in. His pregnant wife even more so.

It would have been easy to get depressed being stuck in Rota. Twelve nights in an expensive marina knocked an unwelcome hole in our meagre budget. It came as more of a shock after our months of cheap living on the Guadiana. The money we'd set aside for a trip to Seville had to go towards filling the hole. The marina was OK, but because of its fairly exposed position in Cadiz Bay, high stone breakwaters surrounded it. They kept us safe, but they felt like prison walls. Listening to wind howling through rigging, accompanied by manically tapping halyards 24/7, amounts to psychological warfare. It was getting to me. Seeing that French skipper being bought to safety reminded me to get things in perspective.

There were far worse places to be stuck. Rota was a nice little town. A holiday resort for the Spanish, the few foreigners around came from the marina and the nearby U.S. Naval base.

There was a gorgeous beach and a long wide promenade. We walked that prom daily to escape our marina prison.

In the town itself the streets were narrow, shady, and full of character. It was hard to find your way around. There were some beautiful old buildings, and the wonderfully named 'Castle of the Moon'. On our second night, we accidentally stumbled across a small town square near to the castle. They had set up a stage and seating for a Flamenco competition. We stood under the castle walls and watched for a while. This felt like real travel.

In the afternoons the town was deserted, the tradition of siesta still strong in this part of Spain. But by the late evening the place was buzzing with families eating at the many restaurants, Even at 11:30pm it was hard to walk down some of the little streets. Crowded tables, hurrying waiters and waitresses, plates of steaming seafood, a babble of voices and laughter. Amazing.

It was authentic, traditional Andalusian. It was authentic, traditional Spain.

On one of the few days that the ferry was running, we took a trip across the bay to Cadiz.

Apparently, Lord Byron called it the most beautiful city in the world. It's certainly spectacular.

It had the same narrow streets as Rota, but scaled up hugely. Big open plazas, an impressive Cathedral, and a fascinating collection of buildings mixing hundreds of years of history and North African influences. It made for an interesting skyline. As we wandered around, I thought about the histories of my country of birth and Spain. My middle name is Francis, and being a sailor I've always felt a link to Sir Francis Drake. Forever associated with Plymouth, we still consider him a national hero. Most know the story of his playing a game of bowls on Plymouth Hoe when news that the Spanish Armada had been sighted came through. He famously finished his game before reacting. Landlubbers interpreted that as a sign of coolness. Sailors know the real reason he didn't panic. There was half a gale blowing straight into Plymouth Sound and the tide was in flood. There's no way he could have got his ships out of harbour anyway.

Before that he'd been skipper of the Golden Hind, the first British vessel to complete a circumnavigation of the globe.

We had launched 'Gleda' 10 minutes down the road from Buckland Abbey, Drake's home for 15 years. Plymouth Sound had been the starting point for that, and many other of his voyages. It had been our starting point too. Now here we were in Cadiz, the site of perhaps Drakes most audacious action. In 1587, he attacked the Spanish Fleet assembled the port. He occupied the place for 3 days and destroyed 31 ships. This event became known in England as 'The Singeing of the King of Spain's Beard'.

Drake wasn't the only one to wreak havoc on the city. Nine years later, the English returned with their Dutch allies. Another 32 ships were destroyed, and the city was captured, looted and occupied for almost a month. When the Spanish King refused to pay a ransom for the safe return of the city, they burnt it to the ground before leaving.

I was thankful that 500 years had healed the wounds. That said, even today, the Spanish refer to Drake as the pirate 'El Draque'. It's a fair description.

We had lunch at a simple-looking street café and ordered tapas. Pork in pepper sauce, spicy chicken strips, a potato salad flavoured with onion and garlic. Delicious and not expensive. Our taste for tapas had continued since Coruña.

Cadiz was fun, but after our months in the Guadiana, the sights and sounds of a big city were somewhat overwhelming. It was great to experience, but I was ready to escape after a few hours of exploring.

The fast ferry whisked us back across the bay to Rota, and soon we were back aboard enjoying a cuppa and planning our departure.

The Levanter was finally easing. There looked to be a

window of opportunity. It'd been an interesting time, but we'd had more than our quota of Rota. Gibraltar called.

We had a challenging coastal passage to look forward to. Some 75 miles (ca. 121 km) of natural hazards such as off-lying shoals and tidal overfalls. There were man-made hazards too, huge tunny nets, fish farms and lobster pots. There are large fishing fleets along this stretch of coast. They'd undoubtably be at sea after such a lengthy stretch of poor weather. I'd plotted our passage to keep us well clear of the main shipping transiting the Straits, at least until Gibraltar Bay. Once there, I'd read that the fast ferries to and from Africa needed watching.

I'd planned as much as I could. The marina in Barbate wasn't well thought of but remained a place to shelter if needed. There was a possible anchorage near Tarifa. A good passage might see us keep going for La Línea. It all depended on what we got and how we felt once we got out there.

I was excited to get started.

NEW DAWNS

We finally got away from Rota an hour before dawn on Tuesday 16th August. The forecast was less than perfect. The winds were still coming from the east, but easing through the day to fall light and variable by evening. I knew we'd be motoring, but at least we could make some progress.

All went well to start with, Actually there was little wind at all. Sunrise was spectacular.

As we progressed towards Cabo Trafalgar, our first waypoint, the wind picked up, as did the seas. Nothing to worry about, just uncomfortable and wearing. The Sahara dust being blown up by the Levanter made visibility hazy.

I'd been looking forward to seeing Trafalgar. On the boat I had a small box made from oak and copper taken from Admiral Lord Nelson's flagship H.M.S. Victory, a gift from my daughter.

We'd be sailing close by the scene of the historic battle with which the ship and the man are forever linked. It was cool to think I'd be bringing part of that iconic ship back to the place that made her famous. I keep a dry ship at sea. But once we'd arrived safely in our next harbour, I planned to place my hand on that box, raise a glass of Nelson's Blood, and toast the men of the Royal Navy who sailed and fought on those waters all those years ago. 'Hearts of Oak' every one of them.

In the event we could only just make out the Cabo through the haze, nonetheless it was special.

The tidal stream and overfalls around Trafalgar kicked up the seas even more. The wind had strengthened to F4/5, and we had both right on the nose.

We stuck with it for a while but soon I decided it was time for Plan B. We were being slowed close to 3 knots each time 'Gleda' pitched into a wave trough, I'd had to open the throttles more and so fuel consumption had gone up. We were looking at another four hours of the same to get near Tarifa. It was a no-brainer, I turned north, and we headed to Barbate.

We got in at 14:30 having taken 8.5 hours to cover 43 nmi, all under power and using 30 litres of petrol.

Barbate town looked bleak as we approached, the marina was, as everyone had told us, soulless. We moored to the reception pontoon until the office opened after lunch, then after checking in, motored to the fuel dock on the other side of the harbour to replenish our tanks, then back to our allocated berth.

It was a good job we got in early. Not long afterwards there was a steady stream of arrivals as boats that had left Cadiz Bay behind us decided, as we had, that they weren't up to slogging into the wind and waves.

Barbate may have been soulless, but it did the job. We slept safely, and the next morning we were on our way again. This time the dawn was even more spectacular. We motored through a glassy calm under hazy skies and with zero wind.

The wind stayed light as we approached Tarifa. We were fighting a foul tide, but kept the speed up to 4 knots without too much effort. Before long, out of the haze, distant mountains appeared. The Atlas Mountains of Morocco, Africa.

Then Tarifa, the most southerly point in mainland Europe, the most southerly point in our voyage so far.

Now we were in The Straits of Gibraltar, things got exciting.

This is one of the world's busiest shipping lanes. They posed no problems for us though as we were sailing in the inshore traffic zone well away from them. I altered course once though to keep clear of a fast ferry inbound from Rabat. According to the AIS she was doing 26 knots, The VHF radio buzzed with traffic. We got a reminder of the troubled world we live in when Tarifa Radio broadcasted a Pan Pan message. It was asking all ships to keep a lookout for 10-12 persons in a rubber dinghy reported as being adrift somewhere near the Straits. I can't imagine how desperate you'd need to be to try crossing that stretch of water in a small dinghy.

By now, as per forecast, the wind was picking up from the west rapidly. I could haul the engines up and get us sailing; it felt great.

We had a super downwind sail along the coast, and before long Gibraltar loomed into view.

It disappointed Gail; it didn't look like the iconic rock she'd seen in all the pictures. As it turned out, we just needed to be patient.

As Gibraltar Bay opened up to port, the wind was up to F6. I got the jib and foresail down as we came onto a reach and headed towards La Línea right up at the head of the bay. The next 30 minutes were exciting to say the least.

Anticipating the high traffic levels in the bay, I'd set up the laptop plotter in the cockpit, so I could keep a close eye on the AIS info.

As I studied the screen, I felt like a fighter pilot tracking missiles locked on and aiming to wipe us out. But I'm not a fighter pilot. I couldn't cope. Information overload is just as dangerous as no information at all. I switched it off and used my eyes instead. That I could deal with.

Although we only had the mainsail up, we were still doing eight knots plus, so things changed quickly.

In the end I managed to avoid everything. Although we had too close an encounter with yet another fast ferry. He was approaching our bows from the port side at well over 20 knots; it looked as if he was turning astern of us, but I wasn't happy. I turned to port so he would pass ahead of us, and so he did, but only at about ¼ mile distance.

The wash off these fast cats is scary. I immediately turned bows on, and we just had time to shut the main hatches before crashing into at least 3 waves, each about 2 metres from trough to crest and close together. Gail was hanging on below, I was hanging on to the wheel. The bows pointed skywards, then fell into the trough, sending green water over the foredecks before rising again for the next. It was a real fairground ride for a few seconds. No damage done, 'Gleda' just shrugged the water off and kept going.

We moored up to the reception pontoon at Alcaidesa Marina, La Línea de La Concepción, just after 15:00. Another 8 hour passage, another 40 nmi covered.

Two marineros helped us into our berth. It was tricky. Despite their help I still managed to put some white paint from our stern on to an adjacent boat, I could have blamed the crosswind, or that the engine didn't go into gear when I selected it. But I was the skipper, and I was responsible. I felt bad about it, but the paint polished out OK, no damage done. The following day the owner of the other boat appeared on the pontoon. The marina had obviously told them about the accident. I came clean and described what had happened, showed them I'd repaired the damage. Everything was fine.

Remember I mentioned that our first sight of Gibraltar had disappointed Gail? Well not any more. Our berth could not have had a better view of The Rock. We sat on deck that evening looking directly at that iconic view as the sun shone its last rays onto the towering cliffs.

The rum bottle was opened. I bought the Victory box up on deck. We made the toast. "To Nelson, To Hearts Of Oak, To Us".

All the pilot books say it's far easier going east into the Straits than west out of them. It'd taken us nearly two-and-a-half weeks to get here from Ayamonte, and it hadn't been easy. But we'd made it. I wasn't planning to go in the other direction any time soon.

The gateway to the Mediterranean was now open, and a new dawn for our adventures awaited.

GIBRALTAR

Gibraltar is a unique place. An iconic lump of rock sticking out from Europe, geographically and culturally.

As with much of Spain, it was occupied for centuries by distinct cultures and empires. The Phoenicians, the Romans, the Visigoths, and of course the Moors.

For three or four hundred years it was a permanent Islamic territory called Jabal Tariq (The Mount of Tariq). From our deck we could see the tower of the Moorish Castle still standing strong, 900 years after they built it.

Once the Moors had been dislodged in the early 15th century, it became Spanish and stayed that way until 1713. Then, to end the War of Spanish Succession, the Treaty of Utrecht was signed. It ceded control of Gibraltar to Britain, and it has remained a British Overseas Territory ever since.

But the fighting didn't stop. Military sieges and diplomatic disputes have continued. Spain continues to assert a strong claim to the territory. Minor skirmishes between the Spanish and Royal Navies are an almost daily occurrence in the waters of Gibraltar Bay. Spain will undoubtably use Gibraltar as a bargaining chip in the upcoming Brexit negotiations. In some respects, Gibraltar continues to be fought over.

Our berth in Alcaidesa Marina was in Spain, just. As the crow flew, we were only a few hundred yards from the border. We had a plane spotters dream view of the Gibraltar airport runway.

Gibraltar may be separate from Spain, yet it's reliant on Spain. Many in Spain are reliant on Gibraltar. Gibraltar is rich, the adjacent part of Andalusia is poor. It's estimated that about 15,000 Spaniards commute daily back and forth across the border to work. It's hardly surprising. The unemployment rate in Spain is well over 30%. In Gibraltar, it's near zero.

There's a lot of money there. Shipping, offshore banking, gaming and tourism. The economy is one hundred percent services. No industry, no agriculture. How could there be? The entire place occupies only 2.5 square miles and a 1400-foot-high lump of rock takes up most of that.

It's crowded as well. A population of 29,500; those 15,000 workers and something like 10 million tourists a year. Yes, you read that right. The official figure for 2017, the year we were there, was 10.54 million. Like I said, crowded.

Cadiz had seemed overwhelming after our time in the Guadiana. Nothing could have prepared us for Gibraltar. After a couple of days just relaxing, we set out early one morning for a day exploring.

As we walked towards the major road leading to the border crossing, we saw two lanes of traffic stretching as far as the eye could see. It was barely moving. Horns blared, arms gesticulated out of windows, drivers shouted abuse at each other. We walked alongside this queue of madness until joining our own pedestrian queue leading into the border customs point. With our British passports in hand we had an easy passage through and soon popped out the other side into little Britain. A red phone box, policemen in their 'Bobbies' helmets, roadsigns in English.

We carried on walking towards the town along Winston Churchill Avenue until we joined the back of another queue. I mentioned the airport runway earlier. It runs parallel to the border and forms another barrier to access. The traffic lights were on red as a plane was just taxiing to takeoff. We all stood and waited. The engines throttled up; the brakes came off, and a few seconds later the Easy Jet flight screamed past us and lifted off into the clear blue sky.

Then the traffic lights went green, the barrier lifted, and we were free to continue our increasingly strange trip. Now we were walking across an airport, literally. Acres of baking tarmac stretched either side of us as we followed the white-painted lines, across the runway with its layers of tyre rubber, more tarmac and finally, under another barrier and into Gibraltar proper.

I can sum up my feelings about Gibraltar in a sentence. I loved the Rock; I hated the town.

The town was dirty, noisy, crowded and money-centric. Duty-free booze, perfume, jewellery, watches, tourist tat. Expensive cafés and bars, fast food.

All the things I'd hated about my old life back in the UK were laid out in front of me again. Actually, not so much laid out, as compressed and amplified.

The old part of town is set back from the sea now. With space at a premium, land has been reclaimed from and developed. Apartment buildings, offices and the cruise ship terminal occupy that space. A historic waterfront has been destroyed and, as far as I could see, the soul of the place had gone with it.

Having highlighted the bad, it's fair to say that there were high points. I walked up to the Trafalgar cemetery, right on the edge of the town. It's a peaceful little oasis of calm. A small sunken plot right up against the old city wall. It's been there since 1798 and, despite the name, contains only two internments from the battle itself. The others are mariners who died in other sea battles or of disease. There is however a Trafalgar memorial to commemorate the 1500 British seaman who died during the battle.

As I stood quietly in front of those moss covered stones, I thought back a few days to our own passage through the site of that carnage. I tried to visualise those same waters crowded with some 60 gigantic sailing ships fighting at close quarters. Cannon and musket fire, death and destruction unleashed. Unimaginable.

Perhaps Gibraltar isn't the best place to seek peace and calm anyway.

As I hinted at earlier, it's one of the most densely fortified and fought-over places in Europe. War features prominently in its two thousand five hundred-year history. One sight we visited was the great siege tunnels on the northern side of the rock. Between June 1779 and February 1783 Gibraltar was totally besieged on sea and land by the French and Spanish. It was one of the longest continuous sieges in history. Mind you, they knew all about sieges in Gib. The Great Siege was the fourteenth in its history.

The tunnels dug during that siege run directly behind the sheer side of Gibraltar Rock, looking northeast towards Spain. The tunnels connect galleries in which they placed guns. Over 4000 feet (1.22 km) of tunnels blasted and dug in appalling conditions.

It's thought that over the centuries the British Army has dug some 34 miles (ca. 55 km) of tunnels through the rock. There are water reservoirs, storage areas, living accommodation and more. No one really knows what secrets are kept within that enormous lump of limestone. It's believed that by the Second

World War there was space for some 16,000 men along with all the supplies, ammunition and equipment they'd need for a prolonged stay.

We did some tourist stuff; we rode the cable car to the top, soaked up the views, took photos with the apes. A day was enough. It was a blessed relief to get back to 'Gleda' and relax.

Gib was weird in many ways, not least in its weather.

Remember the Levanter that kept us in Rota? Well, it returned with a vengeance not long after we arrived in Gib. A stay of a few days had been all I'd planned. Again the weather scuppered us.

Eleven days it blew. It turned out that the day we sailed from Barbate to Gib was the only day the Levanter didn't blow strongly for over three weeks.

We got used to seeing the Levanter cloud sitting on top of the Rock. We'd been lucky the day we went up in the cable car, it'd been clear and the views spectacular. But for much of the time we were in Alcaidesa cloud shrouded the top. It sat there like a blob with a clear blue sky all around it. We could see mist and fog drifting down into the town, even while we sat in hot sunshine less than a mile away.

At 1400 feet (0.43 km) high, the Rock completely shelters the town from the east. The calm produces high humidity, heat and stagnant air. Add in the pollution from road traffic and it can become unbearable.

I read that the Gib population that lives in town has higher than normal rates of asthma and arthritis, partly because of the poor climate.

All in all, I was disappointed with Gibraltar. I'm glad we saw it, but it's not somewhere I'd go out of my way to return to. But I did buy a souvenir. A bottle of scarce Pussers 'Gunpowder Proof' Rum. It's the only original, authentic rum of the Royal Navy. Sailors used to be issued with a daily ration whilst aboard ship. It was known as the 'tot'.

Given its importance, sailors took their daily rum rations seriously. When rumours spread on board ship that the 'Pusser' (Pusser is Royal Navy slang for a purser) was watering down the rum, the sailors weren't happy. To 'prove' the rum's strength (along with his character), the Pusser would douse a few grains of gunpowder in the rum and attempt to light it with a magnifying glass. If the mixture ignited, the rum was 'at proof'. If not, they could toss the Pusser into the sea!

At duty-free prices I couldn't resist the opportunity to restock.

La Carolina

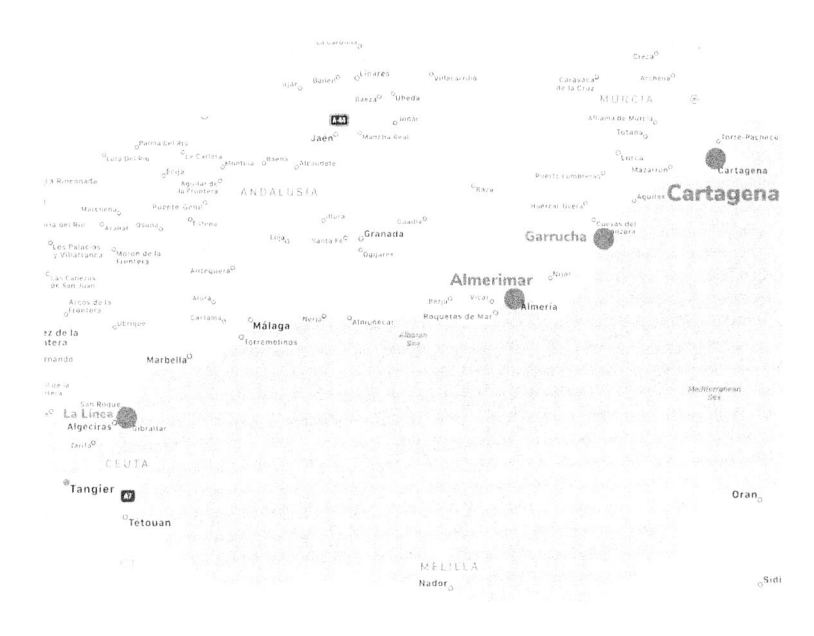

Úbeda
Linares Villacarrillo
Bailén Cieza
Jaén Archena
Baeza Caravaca de la Cruz
MURCIA
Jódar Alhama de Murcia
Mancha Real Totana
Palma del Rio Torre-Pacheco
Lora del Rio La Carlota Lorca
Écija Montoro Bujalance Alcaudete Mazarrón **Cartagena**
La Rinconada Aguilar de la Frontera Baza Águilas
ANDALUSIA Puerto Lumbreras
Marchena Puente Genil Huércal-Overa
Osuna Huéscar Cuevas del Almanzora
Arahal Lucena Guadix **Garrucha**
Les Palacios y Villafranca Loja Granada
Morón de la Frontera Santa Fe Órgiva
Las Cabezas Antequera **Almerimar**
de San Juan Berja Níjar
Arcos de la Frontera Álora Vícar **Almería**
Utrera Roquetas de Mar
ez de la Cártama Nerja
atera **Málaga** Almuñécar Albor
nando Torremolinos Sea
Marbella
uerte Mediterranean
na Sea
San Roque
La Línea
Algeciras Gibraltar
Tarifa
CEUTA
Tangier A7 Oran
Tetouan
MELILLA
Nador Sidi

THE MEDITERRANEAN

INTO THE MED

I'd been looking at the charts, trying to decide where we should head to next after leaving Gib.

Whilst there, we'd made an important decision. We'd found and booked our next winter berth. It was to be the yacht port in Cartagena, right on the southeast corner of Spain. I'd done my research. The marina looked safe; the city looked interesting, and there were places to explore nearby. It would also be the perfect stepping off point for our next season, with the Balearic Islands, Sardinia and Corsica all within easy reach.

It was now the end of August, and we wanted to be in Cartagena by the middle of September for the famous Romans and Carthaginians Festival.

By my calculations, Cartagena lay some 280 nmi away. With fair winds that'd be about a week of day sailing. But since leaving the Guadiana fair winds had been in short supply. We needed to head east, and that's exactly the direction the wind had been coming from for weeks. On the rare days it didn't, there was no wind at all.

Looking back at the log, I realised that we'd taken the best part of a month to travel the 150 nmi from the Guadiana. I didn't want a repeat of that.

I knew that once we'd rounded Europa Point, the southernmost tip of Gib, we'd got two choices.

First, we could do what we'd done since crossing Biscay; sail along the coast in short easy hops, seeing places as we went. I wasn't keen on that for two reasons. First, the stretch of Spanish coast heading east from Gib is the famous, or infamous, Costa Del Sol. Home to the resorts of Estepona, Marbella, Fuengirola, Torremolinos and Malaga. Some worthy of a visit I'm sure, but they just didn't appeal to us. Anchorages were few along this stretch and the marinas expensive and crowded. Getting weather-bound in any of these places would be a problem.

As an aside, I was reading a history of Spain some months later and stumbled across an interesting fact about this stretch of coast. For centuries, it was called the 'Costa del Viento' (Windy Coast). There was good reason for this. To the north lie the mountains of the Sierra Nevada. To the south, the Atlas Mountains of North Africa. In between, the relatively narrow Alboran Sea leading into the Straits of Gibraltar. It's a perfect funnel for the easterly Levanter blowing right along the length of the Mediterranean, and the westerly Poniente blowing from right across the Atlantic.

When, in the 1960s, this area became the epicentre of Spain's new tourist industry, the marketing boys rightly thought advertising holidays on the windy coast might not be the best idea. It must have taken hours of brainstorming to come up with their alternative. The 'Costa del Sol' (The sunny coast)! Anyway, it stuck, and given that some 13 million tourists now spend their holidays there every year, it obviously worked. That said, ask anyone of those 13 million how they enjoyed their holiday, and they'll likely reply, "Yeah, it was great. The sun shone every day. It was windy though!"

So, I opted for Plan B.

I decided that we'd skip that part of the coast entirely and head directly for the province of Almería. Specifically, the port of Almerimar, some 140 nmi to the northeast.

TWENTY-FOUR HOURS TO ALMERIMAR

I'd dreamt about sailing my own boat into the Med for decades. In those dreams I envisioned flat seas, bright sunshine and a pleasant sailing breeze on the beam.

Well, I guess two out of three ain't bad.

Ask any experienced yachtie about sailing in the Med, and they'll probably say the same thing. It's hard. It's either blowing a gale or there's no wind at all. We were to learn the truth of that over the coming years.

For the first hour of our departure from Gib, we had no wind at all. I'd expected that. The Levanter had finally eased; the forecast talked of light easterly dying out, then veering west. As we motored out of Alcaidesa and down towards Europa Point, we were still in the Rock's lee. We left just after 09:30 to catch a fair tide round the point. I hoped that by mid-morning we'd at least have a gentle breeze helping us on our way.

It didn't happen.

We ended up motoring for the next 24 hours. To save fuel, I alternated the port and starboard engines to keep us moving at an average of about 5 knots.

Our course took us ENE roughly parallel to the coast and some 20 miles (ca. 32 km) out.

Once clear of the anchored ships to the east of Gib we saw little else.

About lunchtime, the breeze shifted slightly. It was still too light to sail, but I got the foresail up to help the engine along a little.

There were a few minutes of excitement when a large pod of

dolphins crossed our bows. But they were a way off and seemed intent on a destination. I'd hoped they might come and play. We'd not seen many since Biscay, and we missed them.

As darkness fell, we could just see the bright lights of the Coast del Sol off to port. It was a cloudy night, with no moon. Before long we were motoring into pitch-black nothingness. Only our navigation lights glowing in the damp and dark.

I'd been on the wheel pretty much since we'd left and needed some sleep. Gail stepped up to take a watch. The first night watch she'd done. I showed her our heading and what to look out for on the AIS, and got my head down in the deckpod berth. I gave her two unbreakable rules to follow. One, under no circumstances to leave the deck pod while I was asleep. Two, to wake me if she was unsure about anything. She did brilliantly. With no visual references and no autopilot, it's hard keeping a boat on course. The plotter and the compass can become hypnotic and it's easy for concentration to lapse.

I needn't have worried; she did a splendid job. I got a much-needed hour of shut-eye.

In the early hours though, she woke me. She'd seen ship's lights suddenly appear out of nowhere, not too far ahead of us. It wasn't showing on the AIS, and she couldn't decide if it posed a danger to us.

It took me a few seconds to clear my head and get my eyes focused, by which time I could see she would cross our bows well ahead of us. At about the same time her AIS signal suddenly appeared on the screen. Strange. By this time we were crossing the point where cruise ships and other vessels transit between Malaga and Cabo De Gata to the east.

There was plenty to keep me awake till dawn.

As the sun rose higher, we were closing on the Almería coast. It was easy to see because it looked white against the blue sky. Almost as if covered in snow.

But I knew what we were looking at, I'd read about it in the pilot books. It was polythene.

The province of Almería is one of the poorest in Spain. Well, it was until it became Europes largest greenhouse.

It's estimated that polythene now covers some 165 square miles of its coastal area.

A shimmering sea of plastic under which a variety of fruit and veg is grown to stock supermarket shelves all over Europe.

The pilot book mentioned it not only as a visual reference but also as a hazard.

Remember the winds I mentioned earlier? According to the pilot book, those same winds regularly ripped up enormous sheets of this plastic and blew them out to sea, there to wreak havoc on marine life, but also to wrap itself around the propellors of boats.

It struck me once more how much damage we humans do to the planet in the name of progress.

We'd just avoided a hundred miles of Spanish coast full of concrete high-rises, and now we were heading for a sea of plastic.

If I hadn't been so tired I might have felt a tad depressed. Twenty-four hours of hand steering and constant engine noise had taken its toll.

Those engines eventually got switched off 26 hours and 36 minutes after leaving Alcaidesa, as we pulled alongside the reception berth in Almerimar Marina.

First impressions were good. A straightforward approach, a nice-looking reception office with a four-storey brick built watch tower adjacent. The staff friendly.

Gail did the paperwork with them whilst I sat on the sofa and fell instantly asleep.

She woke me when it was done, ready for our next challenge and a first for us: Mediterranean mooring.

I'd read a lot about it, and there was no avoiding it. More

than likely we'd be doing it for the foreseeable future, so I wanted to start well.

So, what is Med mooring?

Well, most of the world's marinas are in tidal waters, they're usually constructed using floating pontoons. Boats tie up to the pontoons and everything rises and falls with the tides.

In the Med there is no tide. OK, that's not strictly true. The western end gets some rise and fall, but it decreases the farther east you go. Atmospheric pressure also influences the water level. But remember what I wrote about the tides in Brittany? That the tidal range there is 7-8 metres (23-26 feet) normally, and as much as 15 metres (49 feet) at spring tides?

Well the largest tidal range in the Med is about 1 m (3ft). To all intents and purposes the sea stays at the same level.

This means that boats can moor up tightly to dry land and/or blocks on the seabed without problem. It also means marinas can pack more boats into a compact space by parking them at 90° to the shore or pontoon instead of parallel to them.

Here in Almerimar we'd be picking up a buoyed bow line, then backing into a space to tie our stern to the concrete quay.

In the event, and despite our fatigue and lack of experience, we did OK. It helped that they put us into a gap between two other boats. Once into the space we couldn't drift anywhere.

Now here we were. Our first proper Mediterranean harbour and two days to explore it. But first sleep.

ALMERIMAR

We found Almerimar to be a strange place. The marina had been purpose built in the eighties. It had a very Mediterranean feel with the boats moored stern to against quaysides lined with shops, bars and restaurants. Problem was, as with so many places in Spain built around the same time, they had built all of this in a boom and a bust inevitably followed.

Spain, perhaps more than any other European country, has been locked into this cycle for decades. Even before the most damaging recession of 2008, Spain's building industry epitomised that cycle.

Almerimar's marina waterfront was a microcosm of that.

They had laid the marina out in a series of basins surrounded on three sides by 3 or 4 storey concrete buildings. Many of them were empty when we were there. Graffiti covered the walls, litter blew through passages like tumbleweed. It was depressing.

Only one basin seemed to have kept some life. We'd heard from a few folks that Almerimar was an enjoyable place to winter. It was cheap, there were enough facilities and a friendly community. As we walked around the quays exploring we soon found where more than a few of that community hung out. They were sitting outside 'The Stumble Inn', drinking pints and eating chips. It wasn't hard to see that for many, the idea of tying your boat up just a few steps away from the pub would hold great appeal. Fair play, if that's what they wanted. But it wasn't for us.

Whilst in Gibraltar, we'd considered Almerimar when looking for our own wintering spot. We'd chosen Cartagena instead, despite the extra cost, and before we arrived in Almerimar, I'd wondered if I'd made the right decision. A few hours in the place was enough to dispel any of those doubts.

To be fair, it was OK. Away from the marina there were decent beaches on either side. Above the town, the bright-green grass of the golf course contrasted vividly with the acres of plastic in the fields beyond. The staff in the marina office were efficient and friendly. They told us that in the winter there were more motorhomes than boats in the place. Like I said, it wasn't for us.

ALMERIMAR TO GARRUCHA

Almerimar had served its purpose. We'd rested, filled the boat with fuel and water. It was time for the next leg.

I knew it would be a tough one. The forecast was OK, but there was a problem.

For the first part of the trip we'd be sailing east along the coast and past Almería. Our first waypoint was off Cabo De Gata, some 30 nmi away. Once there, we'd be turning the corner and heading NNE towards Cartagena. I knew we wouldn't have a favourable wind for the entire trip. Not only that, but despite the lack of tide there is still a significant tidal current around the Cabo, and its high cliffs can play havoc with any forecasted wind. We'd just have to see what we had when we got there.

For the first few hours we had a decent sail with the wind on the beam. I interrupted our progress twice though to investigate objects we saw floating in the water. They were both easy to spot. The first was bright rescue orange. It turned out to be a lifejacket. It'd obviously been in the water for some time. Seabirds had been using it as a roost, and a few molluscs clung to the straps dangling underwater. The boathook soon had it on deck where I could inspect it. Written in black marker pen the words CH/Engineer Singh, MT Marie Celeste. OK, I made the names up because I forget what they were. But I know that it was MT (Motor Tanker) something, and I remember that I looked her up on the AIS to make sure she was still afloat. She was, and had just transited the Straits heading west to the USA. Hopefully, Chief Engineer Singh hadn't been attached to his life jacket when it went overboard.

The second object that caught my eye flashed like a signal mirror in the water. That turned out to be a child's balloon in the form of a metallic unicorn. We saw more than a few of these things on our travels. Yet more of man's disgraceful efforts to clog the sea with plastic.

By midday we were closing on Cabo de Gata. It's an unusual place in several ways. It's part of the largest coastal protected park in Andalusia. The coast is wild and isolated. Volcanic rocks tumble down into the sea. The sand is black. Strange coloured mineral deposits stain the cliffs. We sailed close into shore near the Cabo itself. There's no mistaking it. A large patch of bright white agate has been exposed close to the waterline. It stands out starkly against the black surrounding rock. It's this agate that gives the Cabo its name.

Inland from the Cabo lies Europe's only desert, the Desierto de Tabernas. It's unique. Temperatures can reach 118 °F (48 °C) and rain is rare. The film director Sergio Leone discovered the area during the 1960s. He decided it would be the perfect place to film his spaghetti westerns.

The Good, the Bad and the Ugly, A Fistful of Dollars and For a Few Dollars More were all filmed there.

The place is still a filming location today, standing in for the real Wild West. Scenes from Game of Thrones and Dr Who have also been shot there in recent years.

We could have been sailing along the coastline of another planet. Alien, deserted and fascinating.

The strangeness was compounded a little farther up the coast when a huge concrete building loomed into view. It would have been incongruous enough, but had been made even more so by the large black letters daubed onto its frontage spelling out the words 'HOTEL ILEGAL'. We could see no signs of life anywhere near it. Given its location, it seemed most likely that aliens had abducted the residents and staff.

I was intrigued enough to do a little research later.

Apparently, in the early 90s a building developer had a vision. A grand 3,000 room hotel right on the sea. It would have an 18-hole golf course and 1500 holiday homes in landscaped grounds. In 2003, the local council gave permission. They started work.

Protests started immediately. The site was in a protected area, part of a national park and nature reserve. How had it been allowed?

A few years later the Government ruled that laws had been broken and ordered its demolition.

The lawyers got involved, but work continued. By late 2006, the building was 95% complete.

But protests and legal cases continued. Greenpeace took an interest. Court rulings swung one way, then the other.

In 2015, the year before we sailed past, Spains Supreme Court ruled that it was indeed illegal and ordered it be demolished. My guess is that it's still there. A monument to stupidity.

I used the words 'sailed past' just then. That's not strictly accurate. The mainsail was up but sheeted in hard amidships. As I'd expected the wind had swung round onto the nose, and we were making heavy going of it.

The seas were short and sharp, progress was slow even with both engines on. I'd had it in mind that if things were looking good once we rounded De Gata, then I'd set a course directly for Cartagena. It would have meant another overnight, but I was prepared for that. Anyway, it wasn't going to happen. Instead, I paralleled the coast up to Garrucha. With a night's rest there and a refuel, we'd be a day sail away.

It was a slog even to reach Garrucha. We'd left Almerimar just after 07:30. We pulled alongside the pontoons in Garrucha marina just after 20:30 that evening. We'd had a couple of hours with the sails driving us along. The rest of the time we'd been under engines. 13 hours to cover 66 nmi.

Once again I wondered whether I'd made the right call. It seemed we'd been fighting the wind and weather ever since leaving the Guadiana. Was I just bad at passage planning or was I just a poor sailor? I guess it didn't matter. We'd arrived at each port safe and sound, and that's what counts.

Garrucha hadn't been a place I'd intended to visit, and on first impressions it wasn't a place I'd have wanted to stay.

As we entered between the breakwaters we passed a large aggregate carrier being loaded with Gypsum. There was a lengthy line of lorries stretching back along the quayside waiting to unload. A huge crane with a mechanical grab was scooping up tons of Gypsum at a time and dumping it into the gaping hold of the ship. Each time it did that, clouds of dust drifted across the marina pontoons. If I hadn't been so tired the sound of roaring diesel engines and reversing beepers would have kept me awake all night.

We initially tied up to the visitor pontoon astern of two other yachts. Most of the marina seemed deserted. As we were only staying one night, I hoped we could just stay where we were, but no. Two marineros's appeared a few pontoons down, whistling and shouting at us to move towards them in among acres of empty pontoons. To be fair, they were helpful in tying us up. I asked Gail if she'd go with them and book us in for the night. I just wanted to get the boat sorted, eat something, then crash out.

When she came back, she wasn't happy. One night here would cost us the same as three nights in Almerimar. No wonder the place was empty.

But we'd had no choice, and I'd already decided that whatever the weather we were getting to Cartagena the next day.

JOURNEY'S END

We were both more than ready to get to our new home in Cartagena.

It was still early in the season; I knew there'd be plenty of opportunity for more sailing if we wanted it. But for now, we just wanted to stop somewhere for a while. Somewhere safe, interesting, and where we didn't get ripped off with berthing costs.

I was sure Yacht Port Cartagena was the place we'd get those things.

But first we had to get there.

It was only 50 nmi in a straight line, pretty much northeast to pass close to Cabo Tiñoso.

The wind had been blowing all night, and although it had eased it was still blowing, and, of course, from exactly the direction we wanted to go.

I didn't care. I warned Gail we were in for an 8-hour slog. It wouldn't be pleasant, but we'd be there tonight. We both wanted it.

We untied early and snuck round to the fuel pontoon half an hour before it opened at 08:00. As we approached, I spotted a big motor cruiser heading for the same berth. I didn't let up, my intentions clear, I would not wait for an hour while he filled his massive tanks with diesel.

The plan worked, and surprisingly for Spain, the fuel guy arrived on time. We were heading out of the harbour by 08:15.

The aggregate carrier was still loading as we passed. Much lower in the water, but still with some way to go. As we cleared her and turned to port around the end of the breakwater I realised how much she'd been sheltering us from the wind. The waves were rolling in across a relatively shallow spit running off the end of the quay. We pitched nicely as we ploughed through it. We weren't alone. A tiny fishing boat followed us out. We waved our goodbyes at each other. All of us grinning with the fun of it all.

That was pretty much all the excitement we got for the bulk of the day. I stayed at the wheel to ward off my sea sickness. Gail read, made tea and kept us fed. The coast was too far off to provide any interest. Just hazy brown outlines way off to port.

By late afternoon we were passing the imposing Cabo

Tiñoso. Its cliffs rising 1000 feet (0.3 km) above the Mediterranean. Once past it, the wind and swells started building rapidly and thing got more interesting.

We hadn't had a ride like it since coming through the Chenal de Fort and Raz du Sein.

'Gleda' rode the rolling swells as beautifully as before. With the wind picking up and coming over the port quarter, all the sails filled and powered her along. As each swell approached, her bows would point upwards towards the clear blue sky before dipping down again and racing down the backside of each wave, sending glistening crystals of water flying into the air on each side as the sharp bows cut through the water.

Looking astern I saw each swell as a rolling unstoppable barrel of green water coming up behind at twice our speed. Each advanced inexorably until it seemed inevitable it would overwhelm the boat, dumping tons of water onto the stern deck and pushing us down into the deep. Then, just as it seemed inevitable, our twin hulls rose like an express lift, smooth, fast and silently. The unstoppable force of water disappeared beneath the boat as the bows dived, and we sped up again. I paid close attention to the wheel as I kept us pointing straight downhill. Then, at the bottom, we'd slow as we hit the dip and the bows lifted again. I'd look behind and watch the next one barrelling towards us before repeating the entire sequence. I never got bored. Each wave was unique. Each slightly different, each demanding full attention, each pushing us towards our destination. I was happy for the diversion; it eased my queasiness. It was nice to get a decent sail at last.

Several large tankers and general carriers were anchored in the bay. Half a dozen fishing boats zigged zagged back and forth in front of us.

I'd expected to see Cartagena ahead, but all I could see was the huge industrial complex of Escombreras.

Oil and gas tanks, chimneys belching strange coloured smoke. Bright yellow piles of something I took to be sulphur.

I worried I'd made another mistake. This didn't look like the sort of place to spend any time.

As we got closer I spotted a huge, seemingly lifeless chimney on a hill just inland of the port.

What I couldn't see was Cartagena. But I'd learned by now that not being able to see a port when approaching from seaward is the best thing. It means the place is shielded, encircled by land or breakwaters, protected from the sea. Cartagena had been a safe harbour for thousands of years, it's one of the most protected in the Mediterranean. I'd find out a lot more about that later.

The plotter soon showed us to be almost abeam of the harbour, and yet it seemed we were headed directly for the cliffs in front of us. I could now see that not only was Cartagena well protected from the natural dangers of the sea, but that it had also been protected from another enemy. Concrete and stone gun emplacements and walls lined the cliffs.

But we kept plugging away, getting closer and closer to Escombreras until gradually, everything opened up to us. Two inviting breakwaters, and behind it the city with a backdrop of hills, one of which contained a castle. It looked much better.

I could see from the chart that there was a sizeable area inside the breakwater where we could get the mainsail down in sheltered water, so that's what we did. There are two marinas in Cartagena. The Club Nautico, on the west side, and the Yacht Port to the east. YPC is by far the larger of the two. I called them up on VHF and was answered immediately by a friendly voice. They gave us clear directions and confirmed that they had given us an 'alongside' berth as requested. As we swung around the end of the cruise ship dock and into the marina proper, I could see two marineros on a golf cart waving at us and pointing us in the right direction. They watched us all the way and gave confirmation over the radio. By the time we approached the pontoon they were already there, poised to take our lines. Once tied up they welcomed us, said how great it was to see us, told us where the office, showers and laundry were. Then they shook us by the hand and left us smiling.

It was the best marina welcome we'd had since Lisbon the previous year. Any concerns I'd had fell away instantly as I hugged Gail. This place felt right, and we couldn't have been happier to be there.

Here's a summary of what it took to make it.

It was the 4th August when we finally pulled the anchor free from the thick Rio Guadiana mud and headed back to the open sea.

It was 1st September when we at last tied up to our winter berth in Cartagena.

It took us nearly a month to cover the 398 nmi (458 land miles) in between.

77 hours at sea, including a 26-hour passage. That's an average speed of 5 knots.

Of those 77 hours we managed only 15 under sail.

Sea conditions varied from flat to choppy, with 3 m swells.

Winds varied from calm to F6 (25-31knots).

Our ports of call were:

Rota (13 nights)

Barbate (1 night)

La Línea — Gibraltar (11 nights)

Almerimar (2 nights)

Garrucha (1 night)

The Easterly 'Levanter' fought us all the way. It kept us an additional couple of weeks in Rota and La Línea combined while we waited for a lull. The only decent sailing breeze we had was from Tarifa to Gibraltar and the approaches to Cartagena. For the rest of the time it was calm or blowing against us.

The highlights had been:
Passing Cabo Trafalgar (even though we could hardly see it).
Clearing Tarifa and seeing Africa on the horizon.
Gibraltar and rounding Europa Point into the Mediterranean proper.
Sailing close to the wild, volcanic coastline around Cabo de Gata (Agate Cape).
Seeing some big pods of Striped Dolphins, a pod of Common Dolphins and flashing blue Flying Fish.

Cartagena

Paseo de Alfonso XIII

Yacht Port

Cala Cortina

Escombreras Port

Mar Mediterrània

17

THE ANCIENT CITY

QART HADASHT

It didn't take long to feel at home in Cartagena. It felt right from the first day we arrived; the place had a lot going for it from the get go.

The location of the marina was near perfect, close to town yet safe and quiet. The port reminded me of Falmouth in many ways, always something happening on the water. Super-yachts, Containerships, Cruise Ships, Warships, Pleasure Craft, even Dragon Boats and Outrigger Canoes. The city had so much to see, Roman ruins, museums, architecture.

Oh, and being a Brit, I have to mention the weather. Cartagena lies on the Costa Cálida (Warm Coast) of Spain. It is recorded as being the warmest city in continental Europe with a 'hot, semi-arid climate'. Average annual temperature is >20 °C. That sounded great to us.

After spending winters in Falmouth and Lagos, I had more than a few pre-conceptions about being in a marina for so long. I considered the entire process a necessary evil, something to avoid unless essential. Yet here we were, in a marina weeks before we needed to be, and yet I wasn't regretting it. We'd made a deliberate choice. Back in Gibraltar, when I'd started my research, I'd discovered that Cartagena was host to one of the most spectacular events in Spain. The Romans and Carthaginians Festival. I wanted to find out what that was all about, so sit back, here's a brief history lesson.

Cartagena, in common with many natural harbours around the Mediterranean, has a lengthy history. The Phoenicians had been using its sheltered waters for hundreds of years before the city itself was founded in 223BC, by a Carthaginian named Hamilcar Barca. At that time the Carthaginian Empire extended over much of the coast of North Africa, its capital, Carthage, was nearly 600 years old. Hamilcar gave this new port on the Iberian coast the same name as their capital; Qart Hadasht (New City).

The Roman Empire was also expanding, they wanted Qart Hadasht for themselves, but lacked the strength to take it. They even feared that the Carthaginians might take their trading port of Sagunto further north. They made a treaty with Hamilcar that they'd keep away from Qart Hadasht as long as the Carthaginians kept clear of Sagunto. But the treaty and peace didn't last long.

Hamilcar died, and his son-in-law Hasdrubal assumed command. Among his generals was a guy called Hannibal.

You've probably heard of General Hannibal and his elephants crossing the Alps. I had, but I did not understand why or when he did it. I hadn't known that he'd started that journey 2,233 years ago, and less than a mile from where we had 'Gleda' berthed in the marina.

Hasdrubal and Hannibal weren't interested in treaties, they wanted to fight. Hannibal first went north and took Sagunto, then decided he'd strike right at the heart of the Roman Empire and attack Rome. That's where the march over the Alps came in.

100,000 infantry, 12,000 horsemen and, they reckon, about 40 elephants.

Many consider Hannibal to be one of the greatest military commanders and strategists in history. But this campaign was a disaster. Thousands of men died, his army fell apart, he never attacked Rome. Worse, his departure left Qart Hadasht vulnerable. The Romans grabbed the opportunity and in 209 BC the city fell to them. It was the end of the Carthaginians in Iberia; they lost everything.

Renamed Carthage Nova, the city then prospered for hundreds of years. The Romans did what the Romans did; they built roads, temples, theatres, villas. An amazing amount of that construction still exists, we'd already seen it during our early explorations.

Ultimately though, the Roman Empire weakened and lost control. The Vandals devastated the city around AD 425.

Between them the Carthaginians and the Romans had ruled Cartagena for nearly 600 years, but in the end both Empires collapsed.

All this happened some two millennia ago, but every September in Cartagena the events of that period of history are remembered and re-enacted.

It was something we just had to see for ourselves.

We didn't know what to expect. It didn't matter. Nothing could have prepared us for the sheer scale and spectacle of it.

For a start, it goes on for 10 days and it takes over the entire city.

The Festival has a base camp set up in the grounds of the football stadium just outside the city centre. Some 5,500 participants split into 50 distinct groups. The groups take on the identity of Roman Legions, Carthaginians and Mercenary armies. And when I say 'take on the identity' I mean it. They wear their costumes for the duration. And what costumes. We're not talking cobbled together fancy dress here. We're talking theatrical standard. Highly polished and decorated helmets and breastplates. Downright dangerous swords, catapults and lances. Leather, animal fur, the lot.

And the encampment itself was amazing. I'd expected a few tents and marquees. But oh no. Here were enormous sculptures, pillars, and archways. OK, they'd made them from polystyrene and glass-fibre rather than marble, but they were impressive nonetheless. They decorated each unique area with colourful banners, insignia and hangings. Each provided food and drink. Huge barbecues blazed away, there was singing, dancing, laughter and drinking, lots of drinking. Just behind the encampment lay an artisan fair selling all manner of trinkets, food and sweets. It was all impressive.

They had set a giant stage up on the promenade just down from the marina. There was another in front of the town hall. Every evening there was a play telling the original stories from that era. The founding of the city, the destruction of Sagunto, the wedding of Hannibal and Himilce. We couldn't understand a word of it, but still the drama and spectacle were enthralling.

On several evenings there were grand parades through the principal streets of the old town. Once again the scale defied belief. The biggest one took nearly three hours to pass and included horses, oxen and even a flock of geese. These squeezed through narrow streets lined with spectators seated on plastic chairs and standing with backs against shop windows. No barriers, no crowd control. Just folks being sensible and dragging their kids out of the way before they got trampled.

The culmination of the festival is a re-enactment of the fall of the city to the Romans. Hannibal is away with his army, the city is vulnerable and the Romans take advantage. After the battle they march into the city triumphant and Qart Hadasht becomes Carthago Nova for the next several hundred years.

They hold the battle on a big open space of grass outside the city walls called 'Cuesta del Batel' (Battle Slope). There are hundreds of participants. Swords clash, spears and arrows fly. There's smoke and fire, galloping horses, battle cries and cheering. It's a fitting end for such an amazing ten days.

Should you ever get the chance to visit Spain in September, take it. Go to Cartagena and see what we saw, you'll not regret it.

Even when the festival isn't on its impossible to walk around the city without seeing evidence of its Roman and Carthaginian past. The biggest draw is the Roman Theatre, right in the centre of town. It was only discovered in 1988. They had built over the site and it had been forgotten. Over the next decade or so more and more of it was uncovered, and then in 2003 they opened it to the public. Now some quarter of a million people visit every year, many of them from cruise ships.

There's another Roman Theatre in Cartagena. This one was an amphitheatre, one of the largest in the whole Roman Empire. Unfortunately, they demolished it in the 18th century and used the stone to build the city's defensive walls. Then in the mid-1800's they built a bullring on the site. That's now derelict. Ironically, it collapsed because they had built it over the underground vaults of the amphitheatre. The Romans had the last laugh.

I could go on. The Forum area, the Temple, the Merchant's house, the Necropolis, The Punic Wall. Walk through Cartagena and you feel that you're walking through ancient history.

SURPRISING CARTAGENA

After the festival we continued to settle in, enjoying the weather, enjoying the city, enjoying life.

By October there was still no sign of any rain. We'd not seen any since mid-May.

We had only one day of showers, which was a bit of a shame,

as they came on the last day of the holiday for some surprise visitors.

Our wonderful friend and third crew member Jake came over for a quick break with his girlfriend Lucie.

We hadn't seen Jake since he'd left us in Camariñas in June the previous year. That was after he'd spent 3 weeks crewing for us from Alderney and across Biscay. It was great to have them both aboard and to see their shared enthusiasm for adventure. I just knew that they'd be following in our wake before long. I wasn't wrong. A few years later they did exactly that, aboard Jake's grandads boat 'Ragtime'.

Of course, it didn't rain for weeks after they left, the weather stayed glorious. It may have been October, but for us, it was still summer. So, to make the most of it we, and some other liveaboards in the marina had an afternoon at the nearest beach, Cala Cortina.

A decent walk of about 45 minutes took us out past the fishing port and container terminal in Santa Lucia, and on towards the Escombreras commercial docks that had been so prominent when we'd first sailed in.

It was the working end of town and, as expected, not particularly scenic. But even here Cartagena continued to surprise. Beautiful themed street art brightened our path. We passed a statue of St Peter guarding the fishing boats. I later found out that this statue marks the start of one of the 'Camino's' leading to Santiago de Compostela.

It's called the Camino de Levante and it runs north to Valencia, then cuts right through the high central plains of Spain and onto Santiago. Now that's a hard route. Brutally hot in summer, brutally cold in winter. The best part of 1000 km that'll take you a month, even if you walk 20 miles (ca. 32 km) a day.

I'm sure those hardy devotees will consider the walk worth the reward. I thought back to our visit to Santiago. We'd got there by hire car. A twinge of guilt passed through my mind, but only briefly.

The beach at Cala Cortina was made up of fine shingle and the shallow bay surrounded by rocks made for excellent snorkelling. It was the first time I'd ever snorkelled in such clear water with so many fishes. It was something I'd do many more times in the months ahead.

That said, it was a shame to see some plastic and litter in among the rocks. I guessed the lack of tide and proximity of the city and docks had much to do with it, and we'd seen much worse. But it was another sad reminder that we're slowly but surely ruining our environment with seemingly unstoppable momentum.

¡VIVA LA NIEVE!

I've talked a lot about Cartagena history, and early in 2017 we were lucky enough to witness some in the making. I'm back to the weather again.

They classified the year 2016 in the Region of Murcia as 'very warm' overall. January 2016 in Cartagena had been the warmest for half a century.

When we'd arrived in September of that year it hadn't rained for months. Farmers were protesting in the capital Murcia because their crops were dying from lack of water. It was the warmest and driest September many could remember.

Then the week before Christmas, Cartagena had 221 mm (8¾ inches) of rain in 48 hours. That was more than the usual total average rainfall for an entire year. It turned out to be the wettest December in 75 years of records.

The farmers that had protested a few months before, had their crops washed away.

January 2017 followed on by breaking records for being the coldest in decades.

Earlier I mentioned that Cartagena is one of the warmest cities in Europe. It had been one reason we came. But in January, we were feeling a little short-changed.

One particular January week springs to mind. Here is my blog post:

Yesterday (Wednesday) the highest daytime temperature was below 3°C, making it the lowest daytime temperature recorded here in 33 years.

But it wasn't the temperature that made it so historic.

It was the fact that it snowed for an hour.

I had been huddled below at the nav desk, writing and trying to keep warm. I glanced out of the portlight above the desk and blinked, not believing my eyes. Because it was snowing, big wet flakes of it floating down past the window. I called Gail, and we went up on deck just to stand in it.

Big deal you might say.

Well, consider this. The last recorded snowfall in the centre of Cartagena had been 78 years previously in 1939. The Spanish Civil War was in its last months.

So for many in Cartagena, it was a big deal.

Along the promenade we could see folks just standing and staring upwards. Little kids ran around screaming and shouting with amazement. Arms outstretched as they tried to catch these mysterious fluffy white objects floating down from the sky.

Apparently, the deputy mayor of Cartagena was giving a press conference in the old town hall. As she was speaking, an aide approached and whispered something in her ear. She turned to the assembled audience and said, "I am informed that it is snowing in the city". At which point, they adjourned and went outside to see.

That evening there was a snow feature on the Cartagena News TV station. Reporters out in the street interviewed people. They showed pictures of it falling along with atmospheric shots of the snow-covered hills around the city.

> They interviewed some old folks who'd obviously got childhood memories of that last recorded snowfall all those years ago.
> As one of them said with a big toothless grin and a chuckle, ¡Viva La Nieve!

SEMANA SANTA

Semana Santa (Faith and Passion Week) in Cartagena ran from 7th to the 16th April in 2017.

It's one of the biggest Easter events in Spain, and designated as being of International interest. Semana Santa in Cartagena is unique, and in very few ways resembles processions in other parts of the region, despite having the same core elements. The city's military background and long naval history have resulted in regimented processions, silent lines of synchronised penitents, staffs tapping in unison, smooth satin shining in the glow of polished lamps.

As with the Romans and Carthaginians Festival back in September, it was a non-stop period of parades and events. The earliest started at 3.30am and the latest finished at 2am. The longest procession on Easter Wednesday had 13 of the huge 'Tronos' decorated sculptures taking part, and took over four hours to pass by.

These 'Tronos' (Thrones) are perhaps the most impressive element of these parades. These huge platforms can weigh several tons and feature ornate sculptures, enormous flower displays, gold leaf and chandeliers. Each moves along on the shoulders of over 100 men or women. Watching these gigantic works of art sway down the street and manoeuvre around tight corners is truly amazing. The effort involved is huge, as the beads of sweat on the foreheads of the carriers testify. On the front of each platform is a small bell. Every few minutes it rings once. The bearers stop walking. Once steady the bell rings twice more, and they lower the throne gently to the ground. After a brief rest they take their positions once more and, as the bell chimes, shoulder the weight and begin again.

The organisational and logistical challenges involved in running these events is staggering. It was exhausting just keeping up with what was happening.

There are four 'Brotherhoods' (Cofradías) in Cartagena that share this burden.

The Marrajas (Founded mid 1500s)
Literally translated this means 'The Sharks'. According to tradition, the name originates because the fishermen who founded the brotherhood used money from the sale of a Mako Shark to get things started.

Its full name is The Royal and Illustrious Brotherhood of Our Father Jesús Nazareno, and it is the oldest in Cartagena. The colour purple dominates their costumes and emblems.

The Californians (Founded 1747).
Definitely a more tongue friendly name than their official title of; 'The Pontifical, Royal and Illustrious Brotherhood of Our Father Jesus in the Sorrowful Step of Apprehension and Hope for the Salvation of Souls'.

They are known colloquially in Cartagena as the 'Californios'. The story goes that in 1768 sailors returned from the recently discovered New California (Las Californias) and compared the lavishness of the processions with the riches of the California mines. These links continued into the 18th century when Californian miners came to the area to work in the nearby Sierra Minera.

They wear predominantly red velvet and their gold insignia carries the emblem of a miner's lamp and two anchors.

. . .

The Socorros (Founded 1691)
'The Illustrious Brotherhood of the most Holy and Royal Christ of the Succour' was founded as an aristocratic brotherhood by the Duke of Veragua, to give thanks for the miraculous cure of his son. He also built a spectacular chapel in the old cathedral of Cartagena, but sadly this was gutted during the Civil War. They also dress in red.

The Risen Ones (Founded 1943)
'The Royal and Illustrious brotherhood of Our Lord Jesus Resurrected'. The youngest of the four. Dress in pure white.

Regardless of brotherhood, all these 'Nazareno's' wear tall, pointy hats and matching robes with their faces completely covered, apart from their eyes.

Inevitably these costumes get compared to those of the Ku Klux Klan, but there is no connection whatsoever between the two. The 'Nazareno's' were wearing them before they even discovered the Americas.

Also known as 'Penitentes' (penitent ones), it's believed they hide their faces as a sign of shame for the sins they have committed throughout the year.

All the parades were memorable, but perhaps the most striking happened on Holy (Maundy) Thursday. On this night the streets go dark and the penitents walk in silence and by candlelight. It's an atmospheric, moving procession, with the silence pierced only by the sound of a Saeta, sung from a balcony above the street.

I wrote this description of the parade shortly after watching it. Remember that this all took place in a large city centre with thousands of people crowded together. It was an incredible experience.

> *A lone drum beat carries on the warm still evening air. Its slow cadence echoing between the tall buildings. Suddenly, the brightly lit street plunges into darkness. The crowd falls silent and waits, heads turned in anticipation.*
>
> *The drummer appears, silhouetted in soft flickering yellow light. He marches slowly towards us, followed by strange apparitions. Two rows of shadowy figures stretching back into the gloom. Tall conical hats swaying back and forth. Faces masked by cloth draped beneath. Two small black holes where eyes should be. Long gowns and cloaks sweeping the floor.*
>
> *The drummer passes, the beat softens and slowly fades into the distance.*
>
> *The 'Nazareno's' continue slowly past. Gloved hands grasping wooden staffs topped with ornate candle lanterns. The glass teardrop crystals hanging below, swing and tinkle as wood taps against marble. The only other sound, the soft footfall of their flat leather sandals on marble paving.*

This was one of two occasions we heard the 'Saeta'. This is an evocative song sung 'a cappella'(without musical accompaniment). The raw emotion and passion of these unique sounds will live long in our memories.

Being agnostic, I guess I found the whole Semana Santa week a little strange. Whilst there were many participants with a strong religious faith, I got the impression that for most it was more about the tradition than the meaning.

The week before Easter I found out that Alberto the head marinero at Yacht Port was a member of a brotherhood. I asked him politely if that meant he and the city in general were staunchly religious. He said "si si, we are, for one week every year".

Another thing that struck us was how inclusive these parades were. The tiniest babies and the smallest child had costumes. The older children in the parade delighted in handing out sweets to other kids in the crowd, At the other end of the scale the elderly. Some in wheelchairs, some being helped along. It was a theme carried through to every single event we saw in Cartagena. Over the decades these parades have, in many respects, remained the same. Yet they've also adapted, and I guess that's what's allowed them to survive. In Spain, the survival of these old traditions seems certain.

My words will never do justice to all we saw of this memorable Easter.

HYPNOTIC CARTAGENA

Time flew for us in Cartagena. Neither Gail nor I had ever experienced a place like it. Neither of us, me in particular, liked cities. And yet Cartagena felt different. It felt relaxed yet vibrant, peaceful yet buzzing.

We joked that it was impossible to go into town without seeing something new. Apart from the major festivals, there was a seemingly unending stream of smaller events. Temporary staging and seating looked like a lucrative business to be in around here. Every week stages would appear in front of the town hall or in Plaza San Francisco. Craft fairs, farmer's markets, music, dancing, exhibitions.

The constant comings and goings of cruise ships, naval and merchant vessels, super yachts and every type of cruising yacht imaginable kept me fascinated.

The marina staff were the friendliest we'd ever come across. The liveaboard community an easygoing and varied bunch. Sunday barbecues were the focal point of the week. Fifty or so folks chatting, eating and drinking. An impromptu music session often followed.

As March and April arrived, the weather started improving. Many around us began talking about their summer plans. Most were heading north and east to the Balearic Islands, some heading farther east with Italy and Greece on their radar.

Over the winter Gail and I had been thinking of doing the same, but now another idea took seed and grew.

Money was the driving force behind it. Everyone said the Balearic's were expensive, that free anchorages were in short supply, with pricey moorings the only other option. Neither of us felt ready to go farther afield. We'd pretty much decided that we'd come back to Cartagena for another winter anyway.

I guess one thing led to another, and in April I decided we'd stay. That didn't mean we wouldn't sail. We could still explore the Mar Menor and maybe spend a few weeks exploring up and down the coast. But keeping our berth would give us some security. We'd not been able to have any summer visitors from back home since we'd left. If we stayed put, they'd know where we were, they could make plans.

Staying put also meant I could relax and get some work done. Finish writing my second book, explore some extra ways of putting money in the bank. Also, 'Gleda' needed some work. Improvements to the rigging, a new autopilot, a haul out. A year in one place would make all these things so much easier, and we could think of no better place to stay than Cartagena.

We both felt happy about the decision, relieved even. It passed me by at the time, but looking back now I can see a big clue there. A clue that goes a long way towards explaining what happened later.

A SUMMER OF MUSIC

Once we'd let people know we were staying in Cartagena it didn't take long for them to take advantage.

In early May, Gails mom and stepdad came over for a week.

They stayed in an apartment just a few minutes from the marina. We showed them the sights, and we took them out sailing.

Gail hadn't seen them since her visit from the Guadiana. It was a great week.

The weather got hot. Gail spent days making a custom awning to cover the centre deck. We'd chased the sun for the longest time and now we had to get out of it.

In July, there was another big festival. Mar de Musicas (Sea of Music). Every night for two weeks there were free concerts in the city. A huge variety of music from all around the world. It was magical wandering around listening to the different sounds or standing in a plaza watching a band.

There were some standout moments.

One particular evening we stood in front of the old town hall and listened to Aurelio Martínez, from Honduras. Aurelio is the worlds foremost 'Garifuna' artist. His music a heady mix of guitars and 'bongo' drums with a distinctly African vibe.

We leant against the wall of the Roman Theatre museum to watch and soak up the sights and sounds.

This was feel good music. Aurelio soon had the crowd clapping and singing along. Even passers-by couldn't resist dancing to the rhythm.

Aurelio has apparently served in the Honduras National Congress representing his community. The Garifuna (or Garinagu) are descendants of African slaves who intermarried with the Carib Indians when shipwrecked there in the 1600s.

Today they mostly live in a series of villages and towns along the Caribbean coastline of Belize, Guatemala, Honduras, and Nicaragua.

He's done some serious work as a politician. If only some of our own politicians could make people as happy. Maybe being able to play the bongos should be a qualification for public office.

The highlight of the festival for us was walking up to Parque Torres behind the marina to see the reggae band UB40, (or as they were announced on stage "ooooo beyyyy quarenta"!) It was surreal. Watching a band from my birth city of Birmingham outdoors singing 'Red Red Wine' in the warm Mediterranean air, perched high above a Roman theatre in an ancient Spanish City.

A real highlight and one we'll never forget.

In July, we had more visitors. Gails best friend Maria, her husband Ian and one of their daughters Laurel.

Again we showed them the sights, took them sailing, enjoyed each other's company.

MERCHANTS & SLAVES

MAGNATES & MIGRANTS

I did a lot of thinking in Cartagena. Having time to do that had been one of the foremost reasons to stay. I had no regrets about that choice.

But for a while, during the summer, I started feeling uneasy. I couldn't pin down the reason. It just felt as if I was missing something.

I've mentioned before that I don't like cities. And yet here I was, living in the middle of one that never seemed to sleep, but with no urge to escape.

I realised the last time I'd been as happy had been on the Guadiana, and there could not have been a greater contrast between that peaceful river and our berth in Yacht Port.

On the Guadiana, we forgot the world outside. Reminders of its existence were rare. We'd truly escaped.

But in Cartagena, the world beat a path to our door every single day, almost hour by hour. Yet still we remained detached from it somehow. Sitting on deck in the heart of it all, yet observers only. Watching a world that wasn't ours.

Cartagena was the world in microcosm, a modern city looking to the future yet deeply rooted in the past. And now I realised why. It's people that make places what they are, and people haven't changed.

In Roman times, the city had merchants and slaves. Today it has billionaires and migrants, and both sat right on our doorstep.

Here's a post I wrote during our first winter.

Our Neighbour Larry

Larry's place is just down the dock from us. It's nice.

He's got a few nice places has Larry.

We hear tell he's got a couple of dozen houses in Malibu and a historic villa in Kyoto, Japan.

Then there's Beechwood House in Newport, Rhode Island, where he keeps his art collection.

There's also his estate in California. Apparently modelled after a 16th century Japanese emperor's palace.

Oh, and I mustn't forget the Hawaiian island of Lanai, all 140 square miles of it. That's his as well. A bargain at $300 million.

He's quite well-off is Larry.

As at November last year, his net worth was estimated to be $48.7 billion. He's one of the richest people in the world.

He must be a busy guy. I guess that's why he hasn't had time to visit since his yacht 'Musashi' got here in November. Shame though. 130 million dollars worth of boat sitting here, waiting.

The crew are looking after her though. I'm sure she'll be ready whenever he gets a chance.

I hope he makes it here, I'd like to say hi. We have a few things in common.

He's a sailor and loves the sea.

He was an academic disaster.

He was self-employed for a while.

He said, "I believe people have to follow their dreams, I did." — I could have said that.

Yep, it'd be cool to sit down and chat with Mr Larry Ellison. He's come a long way. He must have some marvellous stories.

Here's a quick bio.

Lawrence Joseph Ellison was born in the Bronx on August 17, 1944, the son of a Russian immigrant.

When he was 9 months old, he came down with pneumonia and his mom sent him to Chicago to live with his aunt and uncle.

He dropped out of college twice then moved to California where he flitted from job to job for a while.

In 1977, he founded a software company for $2000.

The company developed something called a relational database.

That company became Oracle in 1982.

Steve Jobs invited him onto the board of Apple in 1997. He quit after a short while; he didn't have the time for it.

Last year he received $3.48 billion in cash from just one deal.

He's done well for himself.

I like some of the things he's said:

"I had all the disadvantages needed for success,"

"Each of you has a chance to discover who you are and not who you are supposed to be."

"Don't let the experts discourage you when you challenge the status quo. Like Mark Twain says, what's an expert anyway? Just some guy from out of town."

He's got a reputation for enjoying himself. Why shouldn't he?

Sailing is more than a hobby. His Team Oracle USA won the America's cup in 2013 and are preparing to defend the cup this year.

He's worked hard to get where he's at, and he's not afraid to boast.

"At some point, it's not about the money. At some point, you can't spend all of it. Trust me, I've tried."

Many say it's obscene that individuals have as much money as he does. Recently, Oxfam published research claiming that the top eight richest men in the world had a combined wealth greater than that of half the world's population put together. Larry is one of those eight.

But there's another side to that coin.

A good few on that list created that wealth from zero and use a lot of it to benefit others.

Mr Ellison is one of them.

He has reportedly given away at least $808 million in his lifetime.

The Ellison Medical Foundation provided more than $300 million in funding for biomedical research on age-related disease.

The Lawrence Ellison Foundation supports wildlife conservation, particularly that of mountain gorillas.

Oracle gave $1 million to the National Geographic Initiative to fund the education component of a project to stop ocean degradation.

And that Hawaiian island is being used for a huge experiment in sustainability.

Who knows what else he'll do before he's through.

I'd say he deserves a break.

So Mr Ellison, if you're reading this and you make it over to Cartagena, scoot up the quay and look us up. It's catamaran 'Gleda' on A pontoon. We'll get the kettle on. That's what good neighbours are for.

When I wrote that I was feeling magnanimous and even a little in awe. I guess it's not surprising. Surely deep down we all want to be Larry.

But as I saw more and more of these floating palaces come and go, my thoughts started changing.

There was one in particular that did the job.

Another blog post snippet;

Astounding. Amazing. Awe-Inspiring. Astonishing. Alien. Abomination.

All words that could describe Sailing Yacht 'A'.

Others might include Obscene and Ugly.

One thing's for sure though. Every single person who gets to see SY A in the flesh will have a reaction and an opinion.

No one will ever say "Meh" because they'll never have seen anything like her in their lives.

She arrived in Cartagena last week after a much publicised extended stay in Gibraltar. She was temporarily impounded there because of a dispute about money. The yard who built her claimed they were owed millions.

Who knows what that was about. It seems unlikely that the owner Mr Melnichenko had run out of rubles. He's supposedly worth some $13 billion with assets that include the world's largest coal mining company and one of the world's largest producers of fertilisers. I guess he knows the truth in the old saying 'where there's muck there's money'.

Anyway, whatever the dispute, it was resolved and now SY A is here at the Navantia shipyard for some more work to be done.

I'm not going to discuss the ethics and morality of excessive wealth such as Mr Melnichenko's. For all I know, he's a good human being who's worked hard for his money and shares it to the benefit of others. Just because he's a Russian oligarch friendly with Putin doesn't mean he's evil, does it? That said, his boat would make the perfect vehicle for a Bond film villain.

At this point I'd encourage you to stop reading and go Google some images of Sailing Yacht A, and while you're at it, look at Motor Yacht A as well. That was the one Mr Melnichenko had built before deciding he wanted to go sailing instead. She came to Cartagena as well. We saw them both together. I think that's when I started wondering when enough is enough.

In Roman times it was silver and spices, olive oil and slaves. Today it's weapons and technology, crude oil and stocks. In

Roman times it was opulent palaces, today it's super-yachts. The world changes, the merchants and billionaires remain.

And what of the slaves? Surely they don't exist any more? Perhaps not. Yet huge inequality remains, and nowhere was it more visible than the harbour-side in Cartagena.

100 miles (ca. 161 km) south of Cartagena lies the African coast. Algeria, to be precise. With the eastern end of the Mediterranean and Libya becoming more and more difficult to cross, migrants from sub-saharan Africa had moved west and looked to that 100 mile passage as their last leap to the promised land. We saw them arriving almost every day. Sometimes numbering ten or twenty, sometimes in their hundreds. The rescue boats of the Salvamento Maritimo and the Guardia Civil would bring them in. Pulled from crude inflatable boats or rotten wooden hulks sinking under them.

I tried to imagine what must have been going through their minds as they huddled together on the deck of a rescue vessel entering the harbour. 'I'm alive' must have been the first thought. What stories must they have heard about this Shangri-la? How desperate would you have to be to risk everything on such a journey? However far-fetched the stories, they would have been eclipsed by what they saw as they entered the harbour.

If sailing yacht 'A' seemed incredible to us, what would they make of this alien spaceship right here on earth? Would anyone tell them it was but a rich man's toy? Would they have believed it anyway?

Migrants were in the news for a lot of that summer. I wrote about them on my blog. It was the hardest post I'd ever written. Here it is:

This post is a bit late. Sorry.
　I had it all but written, then I changed my mind about it.

It was another about our life in Cartagena. How I'd been up the mast again. How we'd been to a fantastic concert in the town square. But then I saw the news.

Dwight D. Eisenhower once said;

"There is no tragedy in life like the death of a child. Things never get back to the way they were."

Last week children died.

Children died in a terrorist bomb explosion in Manchester UK. Western leaders spoke of their outrage and expressed solidarity.

U.S. President Donald Trump used these words speaking in Bethlehem.

"And the innocent life must be protected, all innocent lives. All civilised nations must join together to protect human life and the sacred right of our citizens to live in safety and peace."

The U.K. Prime Minister Theresa May put troops on the streets and declared that the British people would never be defeated by evil.

The deaths of those children in Manchester struck a nerve. It reminded many of us that our first duty as parents is to keep our children safe.

A few days later, more children died. But this time there was no outrage, no speeches, no action.

These children drowned in the Mediterranean Sea, some of them locked below decks in a rotten wooden boat.

They died a stone's throw from where those same Western leaders who'd been so sickened less than 48 hours previously were meeting for the G7 summit in Sicily.

The rescue boat carrying 34 corpses and 593 survivors had to steam another 48 hours north to disembark their sad cargo because they weren't allowed to land in Sicily for 'security reasons'. Their trauma was extended whilst the politicians wined and dined.

Over the past 10 days alone, almost 10,000 people have been rescued off the coast of Libya. Dozens have died, including many children.

This year so far 69,574 migrants have arrived in Europe by sea.

Most of these into Italy and Greece. At least 1,569 have died. Many were children. Who knows how many more lie entombed in shipwrecks beneath the waves.

The Italian government proposed a pre-summit initiative to draft a stand-alone G7 statement aimed at addressing the problem. The United States and U.K. opposed and blocked it.

The charity Oxfam said that as a result "the summit produced no concrete steps to protect vulnerable migrants or to address the root causes of displacement and migration,"

Robert Barbieri, Executive Director of Oxfam Italy also said: "The G7 leaders have been absent without leave on some of the biggest issues of our age. Their focus on security is understandable in light of recent cruel attacks, but this should not be at the expense of tackling famine or the challenges of migration. President Trump, more than anyone else, has assumed the role of spoiler-in-chief — blocking agreement on many of these key concerns that affect millions of the world's poorest people,".

Trump and May talk endlessly about immigration. Both talk about stopping people coming, building walls and fences, arrest and deportation.

They dance around with bullshit answers and deceitful words, but their message is clear.

"Immigrants are stealing your job, making you poorer and ruining your country. Never mind the facts, just feel angry at foreigners. Particularly if they have a different skin colour and religion."

May has been doing it for years. As Home Secretary, she oversaw a billboard campaign telling illegal immigrants to "Go home or face arrest".

Their actions this week have shown their true colours. They believe that the only lives that matter are those of the people who vote for them.

They are stirring hatred and division.
They want to create a 'them and us' world.
They know exactly what they're doing.

But there is no them and us. We are all human; we are all equal. What's the old saying? "There but for the grace of God go I". Have we forgotten what that means? It's got nothing to do with God or religion. It's simply an acknowledgement of truth. None of us got to choose our parents or the place of our birth. We didn't get to choose if we'd be brought up in a peaceful country with a loving family, a roof over our heads, food on the table. The children who drowned this week didn't choose to be born into war torn poverty-stricken countries. They didn't choose to live in fear of being bombed and shelled every day. They didn't choose to be starving and sick. Their parents didn't choose that for them either. Their parents had long since run out of choices.

That's why they were in an overcrowded leaky boat miles offshore. Their parents put them there. They did it trying to keep their children safe, trying to give them a chance in life. They deserved more.

What did Trump say? "All civilised nations must join together to protect human life". Yeah, right. Talk is cheap. Our 'leaders' have mastered the art of saying the right thing at the right time. It's actions that prove what they really mean.

I'm just a simple guy with a bit of common sense. If it's obvious to me, then it must be obvious to those in power.

First: Thousands of men, women and children are risking their lives in the Mediterranean Sea every single day. Hundreds are dying.

For now, we cannot stop them. They are desperate. We have no concept of how bad their lives must be for them to even contemplate this journey.

We cannot allow them to drown like rats. ACTION: Adequate government funded Search and Rescue resources to save their lives.

Second: Building walls and fences won't change anything. Telling voters that you'll limit immigration won't change anything. Pretending it's someone else's problem won't change anything.

These people want a little of what we have, and why shouldn't they? We use water to wash our cars; they have none to drink. We throw food away because it's past its sell by date, they're starving.

Which of us could look any of these fellow humans in the eye and say 'No'.

Many of those who drowned this week were from Nigeria. There are 160 million people living in that country. It's one of the world's largest oil producers. Of that 160 million population, nearly 120 million live in extreme poverty. Many have no access to fresh water, are close to starving, and have no prospects for employment. The country's infrastructure is falling apart. Twenty of the twenty-four billionaires in Africa come from Nigeria. The immense wealth of that minority comes at the expense of the masses. Nigeria overtook South Africa to become Africa's largest economy in 2014.

Look at the list of U.S. and UK Companies operating in Nigeria and you'll see many of the biggest names in Banking and Oil.

And there it is. The problem that will never be solved because those in power don't want it to be solved.

Banking and Oil. The largest, most corrupt businesses in the world. All powerful, global, above the law. Both with enough money to lobby, payroll and corrupt any politician they choose. Both with enough money and influence to destroy anyone who tries to change the status quo.

The Acting President of Nigeria, Prof. Yemi Osinbajo was invited to that G7 summit in Sicily. He had his picture taken with Trump. Both of them grinning and giving the thumbs up. Just offshore a ship was sailing past with those 34 bodies on deck. Sick.

It's all very depressing. I fear for the future. I feel ashamed of my own country. If Trump and May hold on to power, things will only get worse.

I'm glad we're in another country. Spain is more welcoming, more open than our own. We know that because we're migrants too.

I guess I was naïve about putting those thoughts out into the world. I paid a high price for doing it.

Within hours the nasty comments started arriving. I was told I had no idea what I was talking about. I was told that people like me were a danger to civilised Western society. I was asked if I was a Muslim lover.

Before publishing that post I'd felt detached. I was simply an observer. Literally floating between different worlds but part of neither. I felt free to say what I thought without danger. My post about migrants destroyed that illusion, and my response was cowardly. I shut up.

I'm not strong enough to shoulder responsibility for others, I can barely support myself. I decided that from then on I'd shield myself, play it safe, keep my head down.

The following morning I took an early stroll down the quay to clear my head. As I walked, I heard police sirens and looked around. It was a little convoy of vehicles coming round from the Muelle. Boxed in by police cars and motorcycles, there were two minivans full of people. The previous night's batch of migrants plucked from the sea as their boat sank under them. I saw black faces pressed against the glass, all grinning and laughing. Arms pushed out through the bars of the open side windows and waving excitedly. For them, joyous optimism had replaced despair and hopelessness.

I'd thought to compare migrants to slaves, but I was wrong.

I'd overlooked one monumental difference. Two thousand years ago, a galley slave might have been just as awed by what he saw as he arrived in Cartagena. But it wouldn't have changed his feelings of despair and hopelessness one jot. A slave he was, and a slave he'd remain until he breathed his last.

But those smiling faces belonged to people who'd been free to gamble their lives to find something better. Who knew what lay ahead for them? Most would probably spend long days picking vegetables destined for supermarket shelves in the UK. Some would sell souvenirs on the beaches, or leather bags in the streets. Maybe one or two dared to dream bigger, after all, they'd seen the impossible made real as they'd entered the harbour.

But who could blame them for being happy, and what right have any of us to deny them?

As for me, I continued feeling unsettled. I was feeling lost and maybe even a little ashamed. I was doing nothing, achieving nothing and wanting nothing. Was that a good thing? Was that a bad thing? I just didn't know, so I went quiet and tried to get my head together.

19

CHALLENGES

ESCAPE ARTIST

It took a while. Another blog post:

If you are reading these words, thanks for sticking around.

It's been nearly two months since I wrote anything new. My apologies for that.

You deserve an explanation.

I'll try to give one.

It's eleven years almost to the day since I cut the first piece of plywood in 'Gleda's' construction.

Tonight will be my 1304th consecutive night sleeping aboard her. Three years, six months and twenty-three days to be precise.

Eleven years ago I revived a dream.

The Universe knows how hard I worked to bring that dream back.

My goals were clear. To build a boat. To make her a home. To escape.

I have achieved The first two.

'Gleda' is afloat and functioning as a sailboat.

After that, it was a given she'd be a home for me.

What's more amazing is that she's a home for Gail too. She's back in the UK at the moment. She told me on Skype last night that she's looking forward to coming home.

There was a time when neither of us could imagine those words being said. Certainly not in relation to pieces of plywood glued together in a damp, cold barn.

That leaves the third goal; To escape. What about that?

1982 – Dire Straits, Telegraph Road (Love Over Gold Album)

"Just stay with me baby and I'll take you away. From out of this darkness and into the day. From these rivers of headlights, these rivers of rain. From the anger that lives on these streets with these names,".

Well, she stayed, and we did it.

We've escaped many things. The weather. The cold, the rain, the gloom. That's huge for me.

As is escaping TV and CCTV. Tabloid newspapers. Health & Safety. Shopping centres. Crowds. Traffic jams and other varieties of bullshit.

Don't get me wrong. There are a few things I miss about the old country.

The green fields, the trees, the history, the pubs, the sound of leather on willow on a summer's afternoon.

But those picture postcard memories are fading with each passing year.

The Brexit vote came as another axe blow to the last few roots of my Britishness.

Maybe it's for the best. 'Make Britain Great Again' is right up there with 'Make America Great Again' in my book.

If this is the 'new normal' then I want no part of it.

Yes, we've broken free of a lot. But some things can't be escaped.

I fear the world has gone past the tipping point. Global warming, migration, plastic in the oceans, over-population. An ever-increasing list of planetary problems that our so-called 'leaders' continue to ignore.

Even if that changed tomorrow, it's probably too late.

Earlier in the year, I wrote about the migrant crisis.

It was hard to do. It had repercussions. It caused me hurt. It impacted on me personally but made not a jot of difference to the subject in hand.

It left me wondering.

Why do that to myself?

Just a few weeks ago another load of desperate Algerians arrived here in Cartagena.

They'd been rescued from a fleet of barely afloat rubber boats just offshore.

The authorities set up a temporary tented reception camp. It was on the Naval dock just across the harbour from 'Gleda'.

Convoys of Guardia Civil vans and Cruz Roja ambulances passed by just behind us. Sirens wailing.

Plenty of folks around here know about the migrant crisis. So do many farther afield.

I don't need to tell them.

From time to time unpleasant things cross our paths.

You'd think we'd try to avoid them as much as possible.

But no. We've all been conditioned to read/watch/listen to the 'news'. This 'news' is never good.

This 'news' is always about suffering and hate. Lives lost, families destroyed, financial ruin, natural disasters.

All the evils of the world brought straight to your living room.

Elements of the print media are worse. The world is burning, and they're pumping petrol onto the flames. Laughing as they do it.

1989 — Chris Rea, You Must Be Evil (Road To Hell Album)

"I come home from work. I see my little girl. She's crying on the floor. She's been watching that TV. This ain't late no, this ain't even dinner time. To show them things on that screen. What's wrong with you? You must be evil."

I used the word 'conditioned' just now.

Maybe I should have used 'brainwashed'.

Millions of deep down decent people in the USA voting for an ignorant narcissist with the attention span of a fruit fly to be their President.

Millions of intelligent people in the UK voted to start a potentially catastrophic 'let's leave Europe' process. That decision made despite a complete lack of meaningful information and with no guarantee that any benefit would be gained.

In both cases, it seems obvious that fear and frustration played a huge part.

The roots of that fear and frustration? News media.

Does 'brainwashed' seem too strong a word now?

Democracy is dangerous when a large percentage of the population makes choices driven by media fuelled fear and outright lies.

So, what has all this got to do with my blogging?

It's relevant because I've come to a decision.

It's a decision that some might think selfish and uncaring. They may be right.

-But it's a decision I have to make.

The world is going to hell in a handcart and there's not a damn thing I can do about it.

I could watch rolling news 24/7. I could blog daily about what's wrong with the world. I could fight.

But it wouldn't change a thing.

The only world I can have any influence on is my own.

I talked about escape earlier. But I know it's impossible.

Maybe at some point before I die I'll live on a desert island somewhere, completely self-sufficient, completely isolated.

But I'd still be on the planet. Trump and Kim Jong could start lobbing nuclear missiles at each other anytime. There'll always be a Trump and a Kim Jong.

No, I can't opt-out completely.

What I can do is to be selective.

I can take what I need and ignore the rest.

I can focus my time and attention on what's good and ignore what's bad.

My time on this planet is running out. If the Universe is kind, I've got perhaps 20 years left to roam, and another 10 to do what I can.

That's not long for what I've got in mind.

I can't afford to waste it on things that don't make me happy.

It doesn't make me happy to write about what's wrong with the world.

Nor does it make me happy to write about day-to-day life when not a lot happens.

Almost a year ago I made the decision that we'd stay put in Cartagena until April 2018.

I had three primary goals:

MONEY: I wanted to find a way to make the cash I need to live the life I want to lead, and to do the things I want to do.

GLEDA: I wanted to tackle an extensive list of maintenance tasks and desirable improvements.

HEALTH: I wanted to pay more attention to my physical and mental health.

Looking back over these past 12 months I'm pleased to say that regarding points 2 & 3 I've made excellent progress.

'Gleda' will be better equipped and ready to sail again by 1st March 2018. More on that in a later post.

I'm certainly healthier. I now run 10 or 12 miles a week, regularly. My head is in a better place thanks to some wide-ranging reading.

Is it a coincidence that I've improved things in two areas that make me happy? I don't think so.

Number one on the list though was money.

Progress here has been pretty much non-existent.

The reservoirs here in Spain are at record lows, and for years now there's not been enough rain to top them up. There's talk of them drying out. A better metaphor for my finances I can't think of.

It's taken a lifetime to realise that chasing money will never work for me.

It just doesn't matter enough.

What matters to me is doing meaningful work. Work that stimulates. Work that contributes something.

That work is writing.

I knew it, yet I let myself get distracted.

I'd wanted 'A Foolish Odyssey' published before Christmas; It isn't going to happen.

I haven't done the work. Resistance has kicked my arse.

But I've finally realised something.

My entire life I've disliked being told what to do.

My resistance to it has grown over the years.

-Only now has it dawned on me that this resistance extended to myself.

When I told myself I needed to do something, I resisted. The harder the work, the more often I'd say "screw you" and walk away.

I was trying to pull off the most incredible escape ever; I was trying to escape myself.

It can't be done.

Recognising that means I can stay and fight.

It means I can choose to knuckle down.

The first draft is nearly finished. 100,000 words covering nearly thirty years of my life. It's proved to be a far greater challenge than I expected.

That's another reason I've not blogged so often. My writing energy is limited.

The book will be finished before 1st March 2018.

Then I'll start on the next one.

I will do the work.

The money will follow.

Living the dream is all well and good. Chasing new experiences and exploring new places are what this life is about. No-one ever got sick of new. But there's an important proviso.

You can't keep doing that without a break. You need time out in between to ground yourself, take stock, re-charge.

> *That's the gift Cartagena has given.*
> *I'll write more about 'Gleda' soon.*
> *-In spring we'll be resuming our sailing adventures.*
> *There'll be plenty of interest to write about then.*
> *Until next time.*

I was full of optimism when I wrote that post and I talked about making the most of the time we had left.

Christmas came, and we celebrated as before. A BBQ in the marina, food and drink, time spent with friends.

I had no way of knowing that before the new year arrived, my life would be turned upside down.

THE STORM BEGINS

I can't write this part of the story any better than these blog posts I wrote at the time.

> DECEMBER 31, 2017: *It's New Year Eve 6:30am. I'm writing this sitting on a sofa, in a lounge, in a centrally heated house, in the UK.*
> *Twenty hours ago I had no thought I'd be here.*
> *Yesterday morning I jogged to Cala Cortina. I swam in the Mediterranean. Floating with my back to the shore, the chilly water prickling my skin. I closed my eyes and turned my face towards the warm sun. I lay still for a minute, my body weightless. At one with the ocean that makes life on this planet possible. It felt good.*
> *After a slow jog back to Yacht Port, I showered, chatted with a few folks on the pontoon, made some tea, then sat at the nav station to check my email. There was one from Dad. Two words in capital letters - 'CALL ME'.*
> *I got through straight away. At the first sound of his voice, I knew. My Mom had passed away a few hours before. Right around the time I'd been floating in the ocean.*
> *Salt water stung my eyes again.*

Within hours a flight and car were booked, and a bag packed. Dad needed me.

I needed to be with him.

Six hours after the aeroplane took off, I was there.

My brother is on his way from the wilds of Ontario, Canada. His journey will be far longer.

It's been dark since I arrived back. Dark, wet and windy. I hadn't set foot on UK soil in two-and-a-half years. I hadn't slept off the boat in three-and-a-half. I was going to say how lost I was feeling.

I have no right to.

At the beginning of this month Mom and Dad celebrated their 66th year of marriage. Dad is the one who's truly lost.

Tonight will bring a new year. Gail and I will be 1000 miles apart. Dad and I will hopefully be sleeping.

Yesterday I thought I knew what the New Year would bring. Now I've been reminded that none of us have any idea.

Wherever you are and whatever you're doing, I wish you a very Happy New Year. Don't waste it. Don't settle. Make it your best year ever.

In the words of that old classic by Guy Lombardo:
"Enjoy yourself, it's later than you think
Enjoy yourself, while you're still in the pink"
No Choice?

JANUARY 5, 2018: Firstly my deepest gratitude goes to those of you that left messages and condolences after my last blog post. It means a lot to me. I hope you'll forgive me for not replying to each of you personally.

It's now 5 days since I put my life on hold and returned to the UK.

My Dad has lost someone who was in his life for 7 decades. Someone who was a lover, a wife and a friend. Most of those twenty-five thousand days would have been spent together.

I was going to say I'm here to help him deal with that loss. But I can't. Nobody can. All we can do is stay close and wait for time's tranquilliser to slowly ease the pain.

I know I've been blessed more than most. I've reached later life without once having to deal with the death of a close family member. Only now am I finding out just how much needs doing in the aftermath.

It's a good thing I've got some project management skills in my armoury. I've needed all of them to keep track of everything. I've used my mobile phone more in the last few days than I have in the last 3 years.

My brother is doing what he can. But his life is as different from mine as it's possible to be. It makes demands that can't be disregarded. His time and his energy are extremely limited. Much as he wants to give more, he just can't.

That's OK. We can only work with what we have.

I've written many times about freedom. It's been my goal for a long, long time. Perhaps the most important goal in life.

The freedom I'm talking about is the freedom to choose. Freedom to choose what you do, where you go and when you go. Freedom to choose how you use your limited time on this planet.

I worked long and hard to achieve that goal and I'm grateful for it, always. But this week that gratitude is stronger. Because most people, my brother included, don't have it. They can't do what I can do.

How many times have you heard someone say 'I have no choice'? They're the default words to use when life dumps on us aren't they? I could have said 'I had no choice but to drop everything and get on a plane'. I could say 'I have no choice but to stay and help Dad'.

But to do that would be a copout. It would be a spineless attempt to shift responsibility for my actions onto others. Others who could be blamed. Others who could become targets for resentment and anger.

I have a choice, and I choose not to do that.

I know it's not as straightforward as that for everybody. Physical, mental and financial issues are but three that could make some choices impossible. But we're all programmed to focus on the negatives aren't we? Our blinkers leave us staring down the no-choice road like a rabbit in the headlights. But take the blinkers off and look around. There are loads more choices all around you. There are always other choices. Sometimes just knowing that is enough.

So today I chose to make and take calls. I chose to be patient; I chose to listen.

This afternoon I was able to snatch an hour to myself during a lull in the rain. I drove down to Castle Beach in Falmouth, parked the car, then walked around Pendennis Point.

The air was tinged with the smell of kelp and sea spray. I breathed it deep. It restored me. I thank the Universe that I'm close to the sea during these dark days. I need it.

I'm not a machine. I've lost my Mom, and it hurts. There were some tears on my walk today, but I'll get my chance to grieve properly somewhere down the track. For now, just like my life, it has to wait.

Until then I'll be a mule for the loads, a sponge for the tears and an ear for the words.

2018 — REBOOT

Gail and I got back to 'Gleda' on Saturday evening, the last day of January.

It'd been a hell of a way to start a new year

Our friends Garry and June picked us up from Murcia airport and ran us to Lidl, so we could get some provisions, then soon enough we were back through the marina gates.

All was well aboard. Everything just as Gail had left it. If ever you need to leave your boat safe and snug in this part of Spain, you won't do better than Yacht Port Cartagena.

I'd wondered if it would feel strange being back afloat after nearly a month. It didn't. It felt right.

I don't say that lightly. Circumstances aside, my time spent in the UK had reinforced a few things. The place was no longer home, and I had no desire to return there.

The UK weather tried to follow us south.

It poured with rain Saturday night, and there was some wind. But it was nice to feel the boat pulling on her lines, to hear rain pattering on the cabin tops.

We spent Sunday unpacking and bringing the boat back to life. The sun came out. I sat on deck with a coffee, feeling its warmth on my face.

Gradually I realised how much the last month had taken out of me. Physically and mentally, I felt washed out. Gail had picked up a cold in the UK. She always shared them with me. A sore throat, aching muscles and thick head added to my lethargy. Sleeping 12 hours through wasn't normal for me. I did it for two nights before the cold kicked in, and now I wanted to sleep in the daytime too.

I knew it would take a while for any kind of normal to resume.

After a few days, I took a gentle jog towards Cala Cortina. I made it as far as the viewpoint up above the bay. Sitting on a bench, I soaked up the view, listening to the water surging against the rocks. I knew more of that would see me right.

I walked most of the way back, thinking it would take some work to get back to my old jog/swim/jog routine.

So, there we were. A day away from February and pressing reset on the year.

I hoped it ran a little smoother this time.

Whatever. I'd decided something. I'd decided to take the year one month at a time.

I had only two goals for February.

Number 1: Finish and publish 'A Foolish Odyssey'.

Number 2: Get myself fit, healthy and happy again.

It felt good to be home.

20

BACK TO THE SEA

By the end of March, I had achieved those goals. 'A Foolish Odyssey' came out on 15th February. I'd ordered a few copies in advance, and just after publication day a package arrived in the marina office. I tried to stay calm as I ripped open the box, but barely contained my excitement.

My first book had been a slim volume, less than 200 pages. This one was over 350. It looked like a proper book; it felt like a proper book; it smelt like a proper book. And I'd written it. It felt like a real landmark.

With the book out of the way, my mind turned back to the sea. Gail and I had talked it through. Winter had been tough, we'd stayed still long enough, we were both ready to sail again. That said, we'd made another decision. We'd come back to Yacht Port for another winter. We needed that security, and we'd still have six months to explore the Balearic Islands. That was the plan.

I'd bought the charts and pilots, I'd spent hours talking to others who'd been there, and I'd made a big purchase over the winter that would transform our passage making. It was an electronic autopilot. Now 'Gleda' could steer herself on any compass course I chose. We'd tested it in the bay, I couldn't wait to test it for real.

There was another sizeable expense coming up. We'd booked a haul out at the Ascar boatyard next door. 'Gleda' had been afloat for years now. I'd been over the side and scrubbed the hulls frequently, but now the anti-foul paint was thin and just wasn't working. Sitting motionless in the warm Mediterranean water hadn't helped. There was a whole marine ecosystem living on our hulls.

Truth be told, we'd been trying to get 'Gleda' out of the water for a while. We'd originally booked for early December, but a crazy wind storm kept us pinned to our berth. We'd re-booked for January, then January happened, so now here we were at the back end of March only now getting the job done.

All went well. It's always nerve-wracking watching a boat hanging in the air. But the guys at Ascar knew what they were doing. Their travel lift regularly lifted far bigger boats. I asked the operator if he could tell me what 'Gleda' weighed, as I'd always been curious if my estimated 4 tons was accurate. He tapped the gauge on his control panel and said "less than 10 tons", so I ended up none the wiser.

Apart from the clean and anti-foul, I had two other jobs to do that I'd not had the opportunity to do before.

First up were the keel strips. Way back in December 2007, as I finished building the lower hulls, I'd had the bright idea of fitting ultra-high-molecular-weight polythene (UHMW) strips to the keels. I'd thought they'd provide some extra protection if we grounded. Turned out I was wrong.

To be fair, the idea might have worked if I'd used a different fixing method. I used bronze screws thinking they'd be most resistant to corrosion. But bronze isn't strong. The first time we'd grounded, several of the screw heads had sheared, allowing the UHMW to come away from the bedding compound.

The first I knew about that was a few nights later as we sat anchored in the river Fal. A persistent light tapping on the hull had been driving me mad. I eventually tracked it down to a loose piece of the keel strip being moved by the fast flowing tide. After nearly an hour in the water, I'd finally managed to cut away the offending section with a hacksaw.

When we'd dried out in Alvor I'd wanted to check them again. But the hulls had sunk into the sand, making it impossible.

Now, with the hulls clean and lifted high, it was easy to see the problems. Apart from the missing sections, the strips had distorted in other places. The travel lift strap had pulled another piece off. There were some now redundant bronze screw heads sticking out below the keel. The solution was obvious; they had to go.

It took about 30 minutes with a hacksaw. The soft bronze screws were easily cut, what remained of the bedding compound soon scraped off. Job done.

Next up were the rudder lashings.

Again, we need to roll the clock back. This time to June 2014, just after the boatyard had craned 'Gleda' into the basin at Weir Quay.

I'd had to dig holes in the mud to get the bottom rudder lashings in place. It's hardly surprising I didn't get them tight enough. Neither had I been able to glue them in place to prevent slippage. So in our first heavy cross-sea, they shifted sideways a few inches.

It's funny. I'd lost count of how many folks had frowned, gasped and laughed when they spotted that bits of rope were all that held our rudders on.

Yet despite my poor first effort, these rope hinges had kept the rudders in place and allowed them to steer us safely over some 1500 nmi of ocean. Another testament to the simplicity and reliability of Wharram catamarans methinks.

After we had done all the painting, I lifted them back into position and Gail popped some temporary zip ties through the lashing holes to keep them in place.

It then took a good few hours to redo the lashings, glue them, and then paint over. This time I could do the job right.

We were in the yard less than 48 hours. To save money, we opted to stay aboard the boat. It's unfortunate that those two nights were the coldest we'd had all year (4.5°C / 40°F). To save more money, we'd opted not to connect to mains electricity. So, we couldn't even use our little fan heater. Extra bed blankets kept us snug though.

The yard is right next door to the Santa Lucia fish-market. The first catch gets auctioned before dawn. Add in the general noise of a busy commercial repair yard, the dust and dirt, and a persistent cold north wind. Then, for good measure, sprinkle in some hard physical work and a little mental stress. After 48 hours we were both more than ready to get back 'home' to our berth in Yacht Port.

It was well worth a bit of hardship though, just to see 'Gleda' looking shipshape again.

By the end of May she was ready and so were we. It was time to get back to the sea.

On 31st May we untied the lines and headed out of the harbour, clearing Escombreras island before turning east towards Cabo de Palos.

We sailed in company with our German neighbours for a while. Martin and his wife Ingrid had been berthed next to us over the winter. They were also headed for the islands but Martin had decided to go there directly, making a 24-hour passage. I wanted to ease us back gently so had set a more modest target.

We'd been told of a free and safe anchorage just outside the entrance to the Mar Menor near the swing bridge. The location was a strange one, an enormous marina project from the 90s that they never finished. They'd driven in all the pilings and put up some protective steel walls, then run out of money. We'd been told that with some careful navigation, it was possible to follow the channel into a shallow sheltered lagoon with good holding.

Our destination lay about 25 nmi from Cartagena, we had decent sailing most of the way following the scenic coastline. Past the Calblanque regional park and around the unmistakable lighthouse at Cabo de Palos. It was a novel experience being free of having to steer. The new autopilot worked perfectly, and I had plenty of time to relax.

By 17:30 we'd anchored and were sitting on deck with a drink. It felt great.

The following morning, after a good night's sleep, we carefully worked our way back out to sea and set course northwards towards Alicante. I'd found a good-looking anchorage called Ensenada de la Albufereta just to the north of the main port. It lay tucked in close to a nice beach and well sheltered from the northerly winds forecast for that night.

There were a few passage challenges along the way, the first a huge fish farm just past Isla Grosa to the east of the Mar Menor. Covering an area of 5 square miles, they marked it on the charts with navigational buoys at each corner and was obviously something to avoid for larger shipping. Going around it would have added at least an hour to our passage, but I'd been told it was OK for yachts to pass through. The farm comprising individual 'pods' well spaced out and with nothing between them. As we approached, we could see work boats using large cranes to lift baskets in and out of the circular nets. We passed close by a few apparently unnoticed by the hard-working crews. Before long we were in clear water. We got some more entertainment a short while later watching one of the Spanish Airforce jets from San Javier practicing aerobatics right over us. Gail was sure the pilot waved at us during one low pass.

After that we saw nothing. We were a good few miles offshore and the coast flat and uninteresting. Our next navigational waypoint lay just off Santa Pola when we would pass between the headland and the off-lying island of Tabarca.

As we approached things got busier. Alicante is a large port and cruise ship destination. It's a ferry terminal to and from North Africa. It's a big tourist destination and Alicante airport is one of the busiest in Spain. There was plenty to see.

By late afternoon we were anchored as planned, just a few hundred yards off the beach. The anchorage had been crowded when we'd arrived, mainly with local boats out for a day on the water. As we ate our evening meal they started disappearing and before long it was just us and two other yachts. I took the opportunity to anchor a bit closer in, and then went below to check the weather.

The forecast had changed. It had predicted wind from the north and east. That's why I'd chosen this anchorage. Now they said that in the early hours there'd be a 180° shift and the wind would strengthen. That'd put us on a lee shore with miles of open sea to the south of us. I knew straight away we couldn't stay.

I looked for a Plan B. There seemed to be only two options. First was to go into Alicante itself. It was only a few miles away and there was a marina. But I wasn't keen on that idea. It would be dark by the time we got there. We'd have to navigate into a busy port, and the marina had a reputation for being one of the most expensive along this stretch of coast. I wasn't going to take that choice.

The other option was to continue north to Calpe. It had been on my passage plan anyway, as our stepping off point for the leg across to Ibiza. There was an anchorage outside the harbour and a small Club Nautico marina inside.

With winds from the south, I figured we should cover the 30 miles (ca. 48 km) or so in 5 or 6 hours. OK, it meant an overnight passage, but I'd take that in preference to sitting on anchor watch all night. The wind had caused us to change plans, why not take advantage of it?

Gail agreed, so we got sorted and were underway again within the hour.

We motored a few miles east and cleared Cap de'Horta before turning northeast on a direct course for Calpe.

Navigation was straightforward. We'd head past Benidorm Island and the headland beyond, then straight to Calpe.

For the first few hours we motored into light headwinds then, as predicted, the wind veered and I could get the sails up, and we started moving along nicely.

Just after midnight the lights of Benidorm appeared off the port bow, partially hidden behind the inky shadow of the uninhabited Benidorm Island.

It was a dark, moonless night. The wind had picked up and the swell with it. Black clouds scudded overhead, and I put on my jacket to ward off the night chill. As we drew abeam of Benidorm, it hurt my eyes to look at it. Ablaze with lights of all colours. The occasional laser beam slashing across the sky, probably from some nightclub advertising its presence. It struck me that despite being only a few miles away, Gail and I might as well have been on a different planet. No other boats around us, not a soul in sight. Just us and the sea. Yet almost within sight, thousands were drinking, dancing and making merry. To me, that looked like a more alien environment than the one we were in.

By the early hours of the morning we had the entrance lights of Calpe harbour on the bow. The anchorage was a no-go with the wind as it was, so I got on the VHF and called up the Club Nautico. I wasn't sure if we'd get an answer, but on the third attempt a voice came back. I pressed the button on the mic to reply and just as I did, the radio display went dark, as did the tablet screen showing the Navionics charts.

I cursed, it must be a fuse. But as we were closing the entrance I'd got no time to go in the pod and sort it. We'd just have to go in blind.

It wasn't difficult. The harbour entrance was well lit and easy to see. We were soon safely inside. It would have been nice to get some directions to a berth, but I figured the guy who'd answered the radio would know we were close, that he'd see our lights and would come down the pontoon to guide us in. And that's what he did, eventually. But not before we'd gone round in circles a fair few times. The marina was small and there was only one berth that seemed viable on the end of a hammerhead pontoon. I decided that's where we were going. Just then the security guy appeared and waved us in to the same spot. He was friendly enough; he took our passports and told us to report to the office in the morning. Gail made a drink while I made the boat secure and before long we were sound asleep.

EVERYTHING CHANGES

HARD DECISIONS

We woke late the following morning, then went up to the office to check in. The lady at reception was friendly and helpful, the facilities nice, and although pricey, we opted to stay for two nights. I needed to sort out the power issue that had killed the radio and nav screen, and besides, Calpe looked like an agreeable place to explore.

The huge limestone outcrop known as Penyal d'Ifac dominated the marina. Sheer on one side and rising to 332 metres (1000 feet) above the sea, it's unmissable. The Phoenicians knew it as the 'Northern Rock' to distinguish it from its southern counterpart, the Rock of Gibraltar. It has the unique distinction of being the smallest National Park in Spain, being less than half a square kilometre in total.

Like the Rock of Gibraltar, this rock creates its own climate. As we discovered, Calpe gets more rain than the surrounding areas as the rock triggers the clouds to dump it.

The rock and marina lie to the north of the main town.

Calpe is a big tourist destination with a wide promenade full of shops and restaurants, good beaches, a busy town centre and just inland, the large 'Las Salinas' salt water lagoon complete with a colony of pink flamingoes.

Before we went exploring, I got the tools out and set to investigating our electrical problem. The radio was easy, as I suspected it was just a blown fuse. The navigation tablet proved more of a problem. I'd been running the Navionics software on a cheap Android tablet we'd picked up when we were in Portugal. We kept it solely for navigation and connected it to a standalone Bluetooth GPS receiver. A quick investigation established that the problem wasn't the power supply. The tablet screen wouldn't stay on, even on mains power. It would flicker and die almost immediately I switched it on. It was dead.

I figured there was only one solution. Get into town and buy a new Android tablet, swop over the software, and that'd be that.

It was now Saturday, the shops would be shut the next day, and we wanted to be leaving on Monday. That meant we had one day to get things sorted. The office gave us good directions to a couple of electronics places in town and off we set.

The first two were a waste of time, but the third had a selection of tablets to choose from and an English-speaking assistant. We left 30 minutes later some €75 lighter, but with a new tablet. I'd been stressed, but now I could relax.

We spent the rest of the afternoon exploring the town and did some food shopping on the way back. That evening I started getting the Navionics installed onto the new tablet.

I couldn't get it to work. I tried to download the software repeatedly, but without success. By late in the evening I'd discovered why. My Navionics software wasn't compatible with the updated Android version on the newer tablet. We were back to square one.

I'd got paper charts, and I'd got the main chart plotter, but the Navionics charts contained far more information, and it was detail we needed to navigate around the countless bays, inlets and anchorages of the Balearic's. I had to find a solution.

After some research online, I found it. I could get the Navionics running on our iPads but neither of them had in-built GPS and neither would they talk to the old Bluetooth GPS unit I'd been using. The quickest, easiest solution seemed to be a GPS upgrade. I found a Garmin unit on Amazon for €100 and ordered it for express delivery with an arrival date of Monday. All we could do was wait.

On Saturday night there was a big windstorm with heavy rain. I was up most of the night moving fenders and trying to stop 'Gleda' being slammed into the wooden piles at the end of the hammerhead. Some Belgian friends from Cartagena had arrived during the day and anchored their catamaran just outside the harbour entrance. At the height of the storm I could just make out their masthead light gyrating crazily above the harbour wall. We weren't getting much sleep, but I knew they'd be getting none. In the morning, both they and the storm had gone.

We spent Sunday exploring the park and the rock. The views were spectacular. Calpe had impressed both of us.

On Monday, I went into town early and returned the new tablet to the shop. Pleasingly they didn't haggle, and I got my money back. That was a relief, funds were already tight. Unexpected marina fees and the outlay on this new GPS unit had been unwelcome.

I spent the rest of the day looking out for our delivery. I went up to the office every hour to check; they said they'd call me on the radio when it arrived. The afternoon came and went; the office closed. It didn't appear.

There was nothing we could do about it. We couldn't leave until it arrived, we'd just have to bite the bullet, pay for another night and pray it arrived the next day.

It took me a while to drop off to sleep that night. My brain was running through our options. The forecast looked settled for the next few days. That meant that once the GPS unit arrived, we could be away within the hour and anchored in Ibiza 12 hours later. I had plotted the courses, we'd topped up with fuel and water, a big supermarket shop had filled the lockers. We were ready and excited.

Then, just before midnight, my mobile phone jolted me awake. It was Dad. I knew something must be wrong.

I will not go into the details. It was a family problem involving my brother in Canada and not something to share. I talked to Dad for some time, reassured him as much as I could, then spent most of the night on the phone trying to get to the bottom of things and do what I could. Dawn found me awake, stressed and tired. Gail and I sat on deck with a coffee to talk. The bottom line was this. The situation as it now stood was that I couldn't rule out having to travel to the UK or Canada at short notice. That, and sailing to the Balearic's weren't compatible. Once in the Balearic's there'd be nowhere safe to leave the boat, and I couldn't leave Gail on her own with the boat on anchor. Staying in mobile phone range added another problem.

Neither of us wanted to make the decision, but it seemed unavoidable. For the next few weeks at least I needed to be ready to get to an airport, and Gail and the boat needed to be somewhere safe. There was only one thing left to do, go back to Cartagena.

An Email to Yacht Port confirmed our berth was waiting for us. By mid-afternoon the GPS unit had arrived and I'd got it working. An hour later we untied the lines and motored across the bay back towards Benidorm. I'd found a lovely little bay tucked under Ponta Bombara. It had half a dozen mooring buoys and was deserted. By late afternoon we were tied up safely and enjoying the peace and quiet. I was still stressed, and there were more phone calls late that night and early the next morning that did nothing to change that. As I lay awake that night I realised that since returning to 'Gleda' after Mom's funeral I'd gradually disconnected myself again, I'd effortlessly slipped back into the life I'd grown used to, I'd thought I could just pick up the pieces and carry on the same as before. As I lay there listening to the gentle slap of the waves against the hullsides and feeling the movement of my boat beneath me, I realised I'd been wrong. I'd been foolish yet again. My escape had been an illusion, and I was no longer free to do as I pleased, I already knew what that meant but I wasn't yet ready to accept it.

My sole focus now was to get us back to Cartagena as quickly as possible, so I'd be able to do anything required of me. We dropped the mooring in La Mina right after an early breakfast and set course directly for Cabo de Palos. The wind was against us again. The irony wasn't lost on us. It was now perfect for sailing to the Balearic's and here we were, going in the opposite direction. I didn't care; the engines were on; we had enough fuel, I just wanted to get there even if we motored all night.

Seven hours later we were over halfway there, but now, after a hot and sunny day, the skies were darkening and the wind picking up, still on the nose. I didn't like the look of it, but kept my fears to myself. Yes, I was keen to get back to Cartagena, but not at the expense of throwing all caution to the wind, literally. The sea around Cabo de Palos has a reputation for nasty swells and erratic wave behaviour. It would be dark by the time we got there. There were two possible refuges. The harbour of Torrevieja a few miles to the northwest, or the abandoned marina anchorage we'd stopped in on the way up. I opted for Torrevieja as now it was obvious a storm was coming. The wind and waves got decidedly lively as we rounded the breakwaters and entered the outer harbour. Gail took the wheel, and I scrambled on deck to get the sails down. As I did so I noticed a

Guardia Civil patrol boat coming up alongside. They followed us closely, and I wondered if they wanted to board us. I shouted down to an officer stood outside the wheelhouse. "Buenos Señor, todos bien?" (Everything OK?)

He nodded and waved, then the boat turned away. I guess I'd forgotten what an unusual sight 'Gleda' was to folks used to seeing white plastic yachts day after day.

With the sails down, I took back control and turned inshore towards an anchorage I'd read about in the pilot book. I had no desire to go into the large marina for just one night, and it was more expense we could well do without. There were a few other boats on anchor in the same place but there was plenty of space, particularly as once again I made use of 'Gleda's' shallow draft to anchor much closer in than most boats could.

The water was clear and only two or three metres deep, so I could see the anchor on the bottom as it dug into the sand. With lots of swinging room and a storm coming I was generous with the chain. I let out about 20 metres and gunned both engines astern until the chain was bar taut, and we stopped moving.

It was a sound decision. Within hours, we had gale force winds, torrential rain and one of the most spectacular thunderstorms we'd ever seen. Tremendous claps of thunder, sheet and forked lightning, the works.

It was another disturbed night, but I was grateful to be where we were and not somewhere off Cabo de Palos.

In the morning all signs of the storm had disappeared. We had a little less than 40 nmi to cover, and all day to do it. The forecast showed we'd have very little wind in the morning but, once around Cabo de Palos, it'd be on the nose again. The forecast proved accurate. The last few hours of the trip were bumpy and uncomfortable. I just wanted it to be over. All I could think about was that by now we'd have been on the hook anchored off San Antonio in Ibiza. We'd have met up with friends, we'd be chilling out and soaking up the sun. Instead, we were gunning the engines into a sloppy sea and headwinds under cloudy skies, and I had no idea what the next few weeks and months would bring.

They welcomed us with open arms back in Cartagena. Everyone wanted to know why we were back, what had gone wrong, what was happening.

I couldn't tell them. I wasn't sure myself. But I knew deep down that the events of the last week had changed everything.

NEW PLANS

The immediate cause of our return to Cartagena resolved itself within a few weeks. In theory that meant we were free to roam again. But theory and practice are two different things. I'd had time to do a lot of thinking in the meanwhile.

I'm not proud to say that I did a lot of that without sharing with Gail. She knew what the problem was, but I felt the solution was down to me.

A few things had become crystal clear during my pondering. For decades, I'd had a deep-seated burning desire to escape from the life I was living, and for me, a boat had seemed the perfect vehicle. Given my history that's not surprising, or maybe it is. Either way, for me, the sea represented escape from the rules, freedom from everything. It happened by default. I never gave much (if any) thought to how I was going to do it. It was simply the path of least resistance for me personally.

It's strange then that it took over a year of sailing and living aboard before I even began to think about how successful I'd been in my escape. Sure, there was no doubting that I'd changed my geographic location. Equally, there was no doubt that I'd escaped from many of the chains that bind the majority. It would have been a stretch to call myself financially independent, but I was paying for what needed to be paid for. I never went hungry or thirsty, and many would have said I was living the dream, on a permanent holiday.

For that first winter in Falmouth my thoughts had been so occupied with preparations for the following year that I'd never once considered how I was feeling. It was only that second winter in Lagos that the real questions started popping into my mind. At that stage I'd achieved the goal which had dominated my life for over a decade. I'd built my boat, I'd crossed Biscay, I'd sailed her south to the sun. Only then did it dawn on me to ask what came next. In truth, looking back, I never properly answered that question. I never again had a clear goal, and maybe that's where the 'foolish' part of my escape comes in. Because it's not enough to just escape. Whatever level of 'the grass is always greener' applies, the facts don't change.

The human condition is to want more, to explore new places.

I'd made a few discoveries about myself as well. I'd discovered that I wasn't a particularly good sailor. The evidence for that had been easy to see from my previous voyages.

Gails trust in me made me stronger when we were at sea. The sense of responsibility I felt for her guided every decision I made. In many cases, it made me too cautious, and yet it also stopped me pushing myself too far. Again, I had a poor track record as far as that was concerned.

I found taking sole responsibility incredibly stressful. I had no one to bounce my thinking off. It was all down to me. I could never fully relax at sea. I was always thinking about the fact that if anything happened to me, Gail would be in serious trouble. She simply wasn't capable of handling 'Gleda' on her own. That meant that every time we went to sea we were taking a risk. I always had to do everything in my power to minimise it.

There were some occasions when I got concerned. Fog on the horizon, the skies darkening, the wind picking up. Each time I had to hide my emotions, play it cool and avoid getting Gail stressed.

All of this may read as if Gail was simply a passenger, and a demanding one at that. Nothing could be farther from the truth. With absolutely zero sailing experience she'd pushed herself way outside her comfort zone just agreeing to come with me. Had I hoped she'd take to sailing like a duck to water? Yes, of course. But equally I knew how unlikely that was. My worst-case scenario had always been that she'd hate it and walk. What happened was neither. She didn't suffer from sea-sickness, she rarely got scared or worried, in some respects she was the perfect crew. Always ready to make a hot drink, always ready to fix a meal, always willing to do what she could. But she had zero interest in sailing or navigation. During our coastal passages she'd sit in the corner of the pod reading happily. It frustrated me sometimes. I was always alert scanning sea and shoreline, enjoying the constantly changing vistas. Gail looked up from her book rarely, and often only when I pointed out something I thought interesting.

It was only when we were safely tied up that we shared our pleasures. We both loved the new experiences, the new friends, the new places.

Gail always told people she wasn't a sailor and didn't enjoy sailing. People always assumed I was, and I did. But now, looking back I could see the balance of enjoyable and stressful sailing was firmly tipped towards the stressful side. It had become a means to and end.

For years, when people asked what my dream was, I'd said "To sail 'Gleda' into the Pacific, to take her to Polynesia". I knew now that simply wasn't going to happen. I wasn't capable of it.

So, where did that leave us? I built 'Gleda' to sail, not to languish in a marina for years. The sea first, people second was how James Wharram described his design philosophy. 'Gleda' could never be a houseboat.

Sure, we could carry on as we'd been doing, day sailing our way along. But that limited our choices, particularly from where we were now. The Canaries and Azores were beyond our capabilities. Maybe we could stay in the Med and work our way east, but it wouldn't be easy.

I think the desire had ebbed as well. We'd joked about how perfect Cartagena had been. Sure, we'd had some weather over winter but nothing compared to farther east. Friends in Sicily and Greece had been battered. Even during the summer months there'd been storms in the Balearics that had caused boats to be lost.

Cartagena boasted the best climate in the Med, we knew we'd probably never find anywhere as nice. Truth be told we didn't want to leave.

Circumstances had changed too. Dad had coped with Moms passing better than anyone could have expected, he was amazingly fit and active for his age. But the fact remained, he was now alone. If he needed help and support at anytime it'd be down to me to provide it. OK, I could do that remotely to some extent, but what if I was needed back in the UK? How would I feel if that situation arose and I couldn't get there? It was a responsibility I'd been able to ignore, but no longer.

The conclusion was unavoidable.

A sea gypsy life-style was no longer possible. The time for change had arrived.

LONG STORY SHORT

There's been a theme running throughout my books. It's one of being helped by serendipity, or as I prefer to call it, the 'Universe'.

Time and time again it's happened. I make a choice; I take some action and what do you know, some bizarre coincidence comes along to encourage me and confirm I'm going in the right direction.

So it was again.

Having reached my conclusion that our sailing days were over, I started exploring our options.

'Gleda' was our home, we had nowhere else to go, buying/renting some bricks and mortar wasn't an option.

We both felt like we wanted to carry on travelling, and the obvious way to do that on land seemed to be by motorhome. We had friends who'd already transitioned from sea to land this way, and it held some appeal for both of us.

I started browsing eBay and specialist websites, looking for options.

One thing became apparent quickly. Any decent motorhome big enough for us to live in full-time was stupidly expensive. Far beyond our means. That was a let-down, but I carried on browsing. Then on eBay, I saw a 5th wheel caravan for sale. I didn't know what it was. It looked like something you'd see in the U.S. Not a conventional tow behind a car type caravan. This was like a mini articulated lorry trailer hitched to the flatbed of a pickup truck.

The main body of the caravan had a slide-out section that widened the living space. The photos showed a separate bedroom, a lounge with leather settees, a dining table, a kitchen with full-size fridge/freezer and a microwave. It had loads of storage, a separate shower and toilet compartment, central heating, running hot water. I didn't need to ask Gail if she liked it.

The price was for the caravan and the pickup truck to tow it. There were some added bonuses. The truck was a left-hand drive, and both were sitting on a site in Cornwall. There was just a day to run on the auction. I didn't hesitate, I picked up the phone and dialled the number. To this day, I don't know why I did that. I hadn't even shown the ad to Gail, on paper we were in no position to buy, I just did it.

There was no point being anything other than honest with the guy that answered the phone. I told him it was a spur-of-the-moment call and explained our situation. It turned out he was a sailor too. He and his wife had lived on a catamaran for a while, now they had a motor cruiser in Greece. They'd visited Cartagena on their travels. I asked whereabouts in Cornwall they were. I couldn't believe it when he told me. The caravan was parked on a permanent pitch, on the same site as my dad's park home and almost within sight of it.

The Universe had done it again.

That happened during the second week in June. By the end of the month, 'Gleda' was up for sale. In July, we travelled to the UK and sealed the deal on the 5th wheeler. We then drove the truck back to Cartagena through France and Spain, leaving the caravan where it was, so we had a base in the UK if we needed it.

In September, my dad came out to Cartagena for a fortnight. We showed him the sights; we took him sailing; he swam in the Med. It was special.

By the end of October, 'Gleda' still hadn't sold. We'd had some serious enquiries, we'd shown folks around the boat, we'd had some time wasters. I was getting stressed again and winter was coming. We decided she wasn't likely to sell until the following year, and that we'd clear out back to the UK. On the last day of October I drove a heavily laden truck onto the ferry at Santander and crossed Biscay again. It was a horrible stormy overnight passage, but the sun was shining as we disembarked at Plymouth. It should have felt good to be back… it didn't.

'Gleda' had been my life for 14 years. From a set of paper plans to a home on the sea. She'd taken me from the depths of despair to the heights of happiness. Letting her go was never going to be easy.

The Universe had already helped me move on, but must still have felt guilty for sending those headwinds. She eased my pain a little.

She sent the perfect person to keep the 'Gleda' dream alive.

He appeared in the form of a tall, handsome German named Michael.

He'd followed the project from day one. His blog comments and emails had sustained and encouraged me right through the build. We'd never met, but we shared the dream.

Michael wanted to buy 'Gleda', and I wanted him to have her. We'd exchanged emails as soon as I'd put her on the market, but it looked impossible. Timing and bureaucracy tried to intervene. But the Universe was on our side. It cleared the way. We agreed on a sale in November.

The following Easter Gail and I flew back to Cartagena for two days to meet with Michael and his wife Andrea and to do a proper hand-over. We went sailing in the bay. They couldn't have been happier.

Michael said he felt privileged to be the new owner.

I knew he'd look after 'Gleda'.

I knew 'Gleda' would look after him.

I knew time would heal my loss.

EPILOGUE

I called this last book 'A Foolish Escape' for a reason. Because ultimately, it was exactly that. I was a fool to think I could escape. I fooled myself into believing that sailing over the horizon would take me to somewhere else, somewhere new, somewhere better. In a physical sense, it did.

Ralph Waldo Emerson once wrote this:

> "I pack my trunk, embrace my friends, embark on the sea and at last wake up in Naples, and there beside me is the stern fact, the sad self, unrelenting, identical, that I fled from."

His words echo the truth I discovered for myself.

I'd thought to escape myself, and that's impossible.

It came as a shock to discover that despite 'living the dream' I could still feel down. That discovery came with an added burden; that of guilt. What right had I got to feel down and depressed sitting on a boat in the sun drinking a cold beer, when others would be sat on a motorway somewhere in the pouring rain trying to get home after another day of boredom doing a job they hated?

It's ironic that the thing that took longest to sink in was the fact that whatever my circumstances, I was entirely responsible for them. In the 'normal' world, it's easy to delegate that responsibility. There's always someone else to blame for whatever isn't right in your world. It's a circle of deceit reinforced every minute of every day by those around you. A shared falsehood perfectly tailored to ease the pain. To help you believe there's nothing you can do about it.

From day one of this entire journey, I knew that. I knew that whatever was going on, I was always free to CHOOSE differently. That's so important, and it's the first step to true freedom. The majority believe they don't have a choice in some of the most important areas of their lives. That's tragic. They spend their days 'HAVING'. I HAVE to do this. I HAVE to do that. I HAVE to do so much. They charge around from pillar to post, blinkered to all the other choices available to them. I know because that's exactly what I did for years. It's hard to break that circle of deceit. Actually, it's impossible. It's a merry-go-round full of people that will never stop. All you can do is jump off into the unknown.

That's what we did when we made 'Gleda' our home in May 2014.

Neither Gail nor I had any idea what was to come. We trusted each other, and we trusted the Universe.

It rewarded our trust more than we could ever imagine.

Four and a half years living a magical life. Four and a half years of memories.

But for me, that life and those memories go back much farther. To the first blog post I wrote on 'The Gleda Project' site in October 2006.

'Gleda' and I had been together for 14 years. Her birth was my rebirth. I grew as she grew. Pride in her became pride in myself.

Nothing lasts forever, life is change, and we must embrace it.

I'll leave you with these words.

They come from the preface pages of 'A Sea Vagabond's World' by Bernard Moitessier. They were written by his friend the Belgian singer-songwriter and poet Jacques Brel.

> I wish you an endless flood of dreams and the intense desire to make some of them come true.
>
> I wish you love for what should be loved and forgetting for what should be forgotten.
>
> I wish you passions.
>
> I wish you silences.
>
> I wish you bird song on awakening and the laughter of children.
>
> I wish you resistance to being swallowed up, to indifference, to the negative virtues of our age.
>
> Above all, I wish you to be yourself.

POSTSCRIPT

September 2020

Michael and Andrea have now sailed 'Gleda' across the Mediterranean via The Balearics, Sardinia, Sicily and Corfu to their new home port near Venice, Italy.

Neil & Gail are still living in the 5th wheeler in Cornwall,UK and planning new post-pandemic adventures.

A GIFT FOR YOU

Thanks for escaping with me!
If you loved the book and have a moment to spare, I would really appreciate a short review. Your help in spreading the word is gratefully received.

As a small token of my appreciation I'd like to send you a gift. It's a small collection of anecdotes about my time in the Royal Navy.

Just visit www.neilhawkesford.com. click on the 'Free Book Offer' and you can download it completely free.
I hope you enjoy it.

ABOUT THE AUTHOR

Neil Hawkesford is a Brit born in 1957.

He's currently a writer and a blogger but given his track record that could change.

In 1785 the English poet William Cowper said:
"Variety is the very spice of life, That gives it all its flavour."

As an academic failure with a long career of disparate occupations behind him, it's safe to say Neil's life has been flavoursome.

Follow along to see more of his foolishness.

Author Website: www.neilhawkesford.com
Blogging Website: neilh.substack.com

Printed in Great Britain
by Amazon